Changing Ireland

Changing Ireland

Strategies in Contemporary Women's Fiction

Christine St. Peter

palgrave

Published by
PALGRAVE
Houndmills, Basingstoke, Hampshire RG21 6XS and
175 Fifth Avenue, New York, N. Y. 10010
Companies and representatives throughout the world

PALGRAVE is the new global academic imprint of
St. Martin's Press LLC Scholarly and Reference Division and
Palgrave Publishers Ltd (formerly Macmillan Press Ltd).

Outside North America
ISBN 0–333–74934–0

Inside North America
ISBN 0–312–22710–8

This book is printed on paper suitable for recycling and
made from fully managed and sustained forest sources.

A catalogue record for this book is available
from the British Library.

Library of Congress Cataloging-in-Publication Data
St. Peter, Christine.
Changing Ireland : strategies in contemporary women's fiction /
Christine St. Peter.
    p. cm
    Includes bibliographical references and index.
    ISBN 0–312–22710–8
1. English fiction—Irish authors—History and criticism.
2. English fiction—Women authors—History and criticism.
3. English fiction—20th century—History and criticism. 4. Women
and literature—Ireland—History—20th century. 5. Ireland—In
literature. I. Title
PR8807.W6S7   1999
823'.914099287'09417—dc21   99–33345
                                                              CIP

10   9   8   7   6   5   4   3   2
09 08 07 06 05 04 03 02 01

Printed and bound in Great Britain by
Antony Rowe Ltd, Chippenham, Wiltshire

To Jane Glavin and George M. St. Peter

Contents

Acknowledgements

It's a long way from Vancouver Island to Ireland. Only the generosity of local hosts and interpreters during my frequent trips to Ireland has enabled me to bridge the distance. The most indispensable of my guides has been the first I approached, Ailbhe Smyth, who has read and commented extensively on this book.

Several scholars or artists have been willing to critique individual chapters. These include Jim Acheson, Ruth (Hooley) Carr, Jennifer Fitzgerald, Sneja Gunew, Michael Kenneally, John Lavery, Ron Marken, Lawrence MacDonald and Christina Strobel. Beyond these, numerous others have helped me on my journeys: Paul Bew, Gráinne Blair, Róisín Conroy, Deborah Cottreau, Ethel Crowley, Carrie Davis, Anne Davis-McPeake, Frances Gardiner, Rosemary Gibney, Kathy Glavinis, Dana Hearne, Toni O'Brien Johnson, Jessie Lendennie, Ronit Lentin, Robert Mahony, Daphne Marlatt, Kathy Mezei, Mary Montaut, Christine Morissette, Jo Murphy-Lawless, Grace Neville, Pat O'Connor, Rianna O'Dwyer, Eimear O'Neill, Sister Veronica O'Reilly, Michael Parker, Marie Quiery, Antoinette Quinn, Bairbre Smith, Jennifer Waelti-Walters, Caroline Walsh, Leah Watson, Bernadette Whelan, Barbara Whittington, Valerie Wyatt, Debby Yaffe and, for inspiration and help that goes back 20 years, Ann Saddlemyer.

I have interviewed some of the artists whose work I discuss, and my hours with them have been the most enjoyable part of my project. Their words are quoted throughout where they have informed my readings or can illuminate my discussions, but my interpretations of their fiction remain my own responsibility. I hope they will feel that the work has been honoured even where I ventured differing explanations. My thanks to Linda Anderson, Leland Bardwell, Mary Beckett, Maeve Binchy, Clare Boylan, Ruth Carr, Evelyn Conlon, Emma Cooke, Mary Dorcey, Breige Duffaud, Anne Le Marquand Hartigan, Maeve Kelly, Mary Leland, Joan Lingard, Dorothy Nelson, Jo Slade and Eithne Strong.

The Macmillan editors Charmian Hearne and Julian Honer have been wonderfully efficient and encouraging, as has copy-editor Janey Fisher. I wish to thank my University of Victoria colleagues Cheryl Lumley, Don White, Chris Petter, Helen Rezanowich, and Jennifer Taylor, as well as research assistants Lara Riecken, Shelagh Plunkett, Jacquie Best and Robyn Smith.

I wish to acknowledge financial support in the form of research and travel grants from the Social Sciences and Humanities Research Council of Canada and the University of Victoria.

Finally, the deepest debt, as always, is to those closest to me: my two sister-travellers, Mary Schmitz and Therese St. Peter; my children, Matthew Breech and Katie Tucker, who accepted my comings and goings with steadfast good cheer; and John Tucker who facilitated all aspects of this work even though, this time, he did not have to type the manuscript. I owe much to his unerring editorial skills and generous presence.

1
Introduction

> Now there are reasons
> for the unleashing of words
> torrents of speech fall into
> the pool – all in a moment
> we change we have found
> our own tongues we can
> explore faces and hands.
>
> Jo Slade, 'Reasons' in *Waterfall*[1]

In the past generation, Irish women have unleashed a torrent of published words – a social development of profound importance in a country where expressive words and their creators count as national monuments. With their newly crafted literature, and the rediscovery of lost works by their foremothers, Irish women today are creating different possibilities for themselves and, by this means, for the whole 'pool' of Irish society.

Literary creation is always a triumph, no matter what one's position in a society. But it is especially so if the speaker or writer emerges from a group that has traditionally been barred from swimming in a particular pool, the situation of all but the most privileged of Irish women in the past. Finding one's tongue demands courage, skill and luck. It might also be an act of transgression, which can have the effect of dis-ordering the inherited culture. The discovery will be exhilarating ('we can / explore faces and hands'), but may be dangerous. The international women's voices gathered in *Waterfall* by the Irish painter and poet, Jo Slade, speak of the joy of finding their 'own tongues', but express, just as eloquently, the pain of strong action and challenging speech: 'everywhere there are soldiers / who

1

want to crush our hands / and sew our lips like seams / to close this century' (p. 32).

Jo Slade's images evoke the subject of this book: the extraordinary production of fiction by Irish women, about Ireland, in the last generation. While it has become almost a commonplace among commentators to remark that few societies have changed as much as Ireland in this period, relatively little attention has been paid beyond the island to the ways women's writing, in its many different forms, has functioned as an important agent in effecting these changes.[2] In the following chapters I focus primarily, but not exclusively, on literary texts, analyzing some of the different strategies fiction writers are crafting to create public tongues. Because my focus is Ireland, I do not include some remarkable works set in other cultures by such Irish authors as Julia O'Faolain and Dolores Walshe.[3] Moreover, when I refer to Ireland, I intend the Republic of Ireland (the South), and the bulk of my study is devoted to texts from the Republic.[4] I specify Northern Ireland (the North) when that part of the island is intended. While any such division has been highly contentious in historical and political terms – and for at least some of the northern women I interviewed, in emotional terms as well – the differences in subject matter and focus in the fiction are generally so distinct at this time that any erasure of the border seems even more contentious.

The unleashing of literary creativity is not limited to the publication of fiction; Irish women, from the North and the South, have also been publishing a good deal of excellent poetry, and every chapter here offers some evidence of this richness.[5] Moreover, many of the writers whose fiction I examine are also poets, dramatists, artists, journalists or academic writers. But the focus of my study is fiction because it is particularly here that we discover elaborated narratives that refashion inherited histories, reimagine the present, and enable different futures. In other words, I am interested in the ways that 'making story' can function to remake 'reality' in the human imagination and, consequently, in the material conditions of human life.

While the 'Troubles' in the North have presented painfully obvious changes since their revival in 1968, the Republic of Ireland, too, has undergone revolutionary shifts. What we discover in the North is how difficult it has been for Northern women to insert their 'voices' into the extravagantly militarized 'masculine' discourses that still predominate, even in the present peace process that affects all Northerners. What we find in the Republic is a far greater presence of women's political and literary agency, but a continuing need as well to challenge some of those changes, or conversely, some of the persisting traditions. In North and South, however, we find striking evidence of the entry of Irish women into hitherto forbidden public sites including – but certainly not limited to – multiple sites of publication and representation.

The term 'representation' in these pages is not meant to suggest a mirror that fiction is holding up to reflect what already exists. Rather I am intending that form of representation within which, and by means of which, women are being constituted as new kinds of subjects: artistic work that enables women to discover or to create places from which to speak. This is the achievement of contemporary Irish women's fiction, yet the magnitude of these changes is largely unknown outside Ireland, often unacknowledged even within. This struggle for the 'authority' of authorship is the subject of Chapter 2 which attends first to theoretical discussions among women writers and cultural critics, then offers close readings of three novels of an idiosyncratic genre, the self-begetting novel, which fictionalizes Irish women's struggle to write and publish.

Very few critical studies of Irish women's fiction have been produced, and this dearth of interpretation was the impetus for this study. The Irish critic Ann Owen Weekes has published the only single-authored monograph on Irish women's fiction at the time of writing. In *Irish Women Writers: an Uncharted Tradition* she uses the 'Objects Relations Theory' of the American psychologist Nancy Chodorow to chart what she argues is a cross-cultural tradition shared by Anglo- and Gaelic-Irish women novelists from the eighteenth century to the twentieth.[6] Under this lens, she discovers a commonalty of the 'purposes the women share, the map of Irish female experience their words may reveal' (p. 9). One of the important contributions of this pioneering work is the assertion of a history where 'despite centuries of oppressive conditions, Irish women have written, initially in Gaelic and English and latterly chiefly in English and judging by what remains of their writing, they have written well' (p. 2). But Weekes includes only three contemporary writers, Jennifer Johnston, Julia O'Faolain and Molly Keane, all born in the 1930s or earlier. Her study does not attempt to include within her interpretive grid the wildly prolific and very diverse contributions of the last generation.

Because I am so often the first public critic of the fictional works examined in the following chapters, or, where preceded in print by others, often have only an occasional book review as possible guide or barrier, I attempt no overarching interpretation, no iron-clad critical 'judgments', nor any claims to be discovering a 'women's tradition' within contemporary fiction. I think such efforts would be premature and reductionist in any case, but particularly from a foreign critic like myself. The more useful task at this point is map-drawing: examining the landmarks, exploring the uncharted spaces, discovering lines of connection or significant discontinuities. In this task I use various theories and critical commentaries to see what is discernible under different kinds of lenses. In each chapter, I hazard some interpretive routes among the few internationally known works of fiction while also introducing several other works worthy of larger audiences, if only to give a better idea of the lie of the land. Most of the authors who appear in these pages are still writing, with some at the beginning of a literary career. Although I have worked with the criterion of inclusivity in so far as space and focus allow, some fine writers make only a fleeting appearance as parts of lists offered in several of the chapters.

While I quote some non-Irish scholars in my critical analyses, I primarily use the voices, either published or from interviews I have conducted, of dozens of Irish women fiction writers, poets, historians, sociologists, journalists, literary critics, feminist theorists, political scientists and women's movement activists. This kind of interdisciplinary approach brings new social and cultural issues into focus, and helps to locate writers and texts in their time and place. In all of this, I am indebted to the generosity of many extremely articulate Irish women, including those literary artists who granted me interviews, for helping me understand the revolution they are creating.

The following essays can be read as a collection of discrete interpretive studies, with each chapter considering a different kind of fiction, social issue, life experience, artistic experiment. Despite the differences, however, readers will discover certain preoccupations recurring throughout. Two of the most prominent are difficult to disentangle: the importance of women's sexuality, sexual orientation and reproductive lives as sites of conflict and resistance within Irish society, North and South, and a ubiquitous sense of the contradictoriness of forces that together are reshaping life on the island. While the latter may be the inevitable experience of any deeply traditional culture undergoing rapid change, the works examined here inscribe an almost dizzying sense of the simultaneous interplay of the forces of liberation and repression, of cosmopolitanism and parochialism, of valued traditions and radical challenges.

An illuminating example from the Republic of this lived contradiction can be found in Mary O'Donnell's 1996 satire *Virgin and the Boy*. Here a bold combination of outrageous (hetero)sexual transgression in the life and performance of the female rock star, Virgin, is at war with arch-conservative defenders of traditional Catholic Ireland. Virgin (Ginnie Maloney at home) takes the youth of Ireland by storm with the sexual rhythms of her concerts ('fuck me, fuck me'), which climax with the gesture of oiling her protruding nipples as 'hundreds of inflated condoms tumble from the darkness high above the lights'.[7] While the whole audience goes berserk and 'the boy' of the title, 19-year-old Luke, struggles to 'control the insistent hardening within his jeans' as he reflects that Virgin 'reminded him of a saint, a picture in his mother's bedroom of a young woman with a crucifix resting on her arm the way other women held babies (p. 15). While all these ructions are taking place in the assembly hall of a provincial town, the 'Guardians of Christian Destiny' arrive to shut down the concert, resorting to ever more pathological attacks on the star and her audience as the novel proceeds.

What is particularly strategic about this representation of outrageous sexual transgression and its antithesis is not some simple opposition of the forces of extreme libertarianism and warped traditionalism. The more original insight is the way the moral weight of the novel rests on the ethical dilemmas faced by Luke and Virgin after they break with family, social, and religious codes. The conjuncture of religious ecstasy and sexual energy – saint/rock star as icon – traces more than just a residuum of traditional practice; it reveals the ways in which Catholicism lives on in the Republic in the most intimate personal experiences as well as the most public of 'post' Catholic displays.

O'Donnell's fictional characters inhabit what Irish writer Mary Dorcey calls in another context 'this second Ireland'.[8] While mention of a second implies a dominant 'first', it also points to a tension between the two that needs exploring. Mary Dorcey's inspired phrase in a 1990 interview suggests both these possibilities. Commenting that Ireland since the 1970s has experienced a 'growing secular and liberal ... reality of life' for younger people that is 'not yet reflected at the institutional level', she points out that this new reality is 'just beginning to find expression in the artistic world'. She speaks about 'thirst for an expressive theatre, cinema, music and literature, which acknowledges and comes out of this second Ireland, this concealed Ireland, this Ireland which has up to now been silenced by emigration' (pp. 22–3). We shall see in subsequent chapters the ways Mary Dorcey's own remarkable lesbian poetry and fiction have been important agents for change in the 'second Ireland'.

Mention of emigration conjures up one of Ireland's most painful historical realities, and Chapter 3 examines women's fictional explorations of this experience. Political and economic pressures within Ireland have been the perennial cause for emigration, but the term can also evoke the experience of self-exile, the desire to flee what author Edna O'Brien calls the 'psychological choke', the need to leave because 'we beg to differ'.[9] To be sure, Edna O'Brien's sexually frank fiction no longer gets banned in Ireland as it did in the 1960s when a theocratic state censored the subversive, the sexual, and the heretical; in fact, her 1996 novel, *Down by the River,* offers her boldest challenge yet to what persists of patriarchal Catholic Ireland as she fictionalizes in the harshest of terms the infamous X Case of 1992.[10] Even with censorship lifted and freedoms abounding, however, enough of the political and religious conservatisms remain to prop up what Dorcey calls 'a bigoted Protestant state in the north and a bigoted Catholic state in the south ...' (p. 22). In other words, the 'second Ireland' on both sides of the border challenges a normative 'first' that still, despite significant change, has considerable power in the lives and minds of the Irish.

The struggle to imagine a country in which women can thrive – in effect, to create one in and through one's art – has been a difficult task for any woman caught in what Irish critic Ailbhe Smyth calls the 'closely meshed layers of the facts of femininity and Irishness.'[11] Here Smyth alludes not just to the suppression of the Irish language, culture and society via the centuries-long colonial domination by the English, and the traditional poverty that Irish women share, albeit unequally, with men. She includes as well the destructive elements of misogynist Irish Catholicism and Protestantism, and patriarchal, post-colonial nationalism that identified 'woman' and 'country'. Chapter 4 examines the ways women are using historical fiction as a strategy for recuperating androcentric versions of Irish history, a project of particular urgency amid the continuing struggles over ideas of 'nation' and the emergence of a newly hegemonic revisionist historiography.

When Mary Dorcey refers in the statement above to the younger generation of artists born since the 1950s to which she belongs, her careful reference to a 'concealed Ireland' allows us to recognize the persistence of a long tradition of resistant or occluded art that has until recently been almost invisible amidst the quasi-sacred canon of (male) Irish literature taught throughout the English-speaking world. It is only through the efforts of feminist critics intent on uncovering the lost – or honoring the devalued – voices that we are now becoming aware of the wealth of writing by Irish women both outside and inside the country. For example, Ann Owen Weekes's invaluable 1993 encyclopedia of women writers, *Unveiling Treasures: the Attic Guide to the Published Works of Irish Women Literary Authors* offers entries on 278 women authors, and many scholars of Irish literature are busily excavating and interpreting other lost voices.[12]

But it is not to historical precedents that I devote myself in the following chapters. I am interested in the work of the last generation, even the last decade, a time when in Ireland as elsewhere we have seen a prodigious growth in the number and diversity of women's public voices. Nowhere has this phenomenon been more apparent than in the works of fiction that women have, for the first time in history, published in huge numbers. This success is no accident, nor was it inevitable. It happened because large numbers of women have, again for the first time in their history, managed to acquire the necessary material conditions for creative expression: education; some time and privacy at their own disposal; newly available access to publishing houses, or, equally significant, the creation of such Irish firms as Arlen House in the 1970s and Attic Press in the 1980s and 1990s dedicated to producing women's writing; a measure of choice in their sexual and reproductive lives; worldwide feminist movements determined to value the lives and work of women; and women readers with the desire and money to buy books by women.

When Mary Dorcey links the emergence of 'this second Ireland' to the 1970s creation of the Irish women's movement, she also stresses how it is accompanied by a 'fierce backlash against the women's movement' (p. 22) which signals a continuation of states of oppression that dog Irish women's efforts at self-determination, creative expression, and group solidarity. So if a writer or critic draws a circle around women's writing, looks at it apart from the writing of men, this is not a denial of its connection to that larger shared literature. Rather such an exercise asserts that the conditions of a woman's work, the subjects of her writing, and the experiences of her life will be, inevitably if variably, connected to the two meanings of 'second' – the progressive changes of the last generation and the continuing oppressions specific to women's lives. 'I am neither a separatist nor a postfeminist', writes one of Ireland's most famous poets, Eavan Boland. 'I believe that the past matters, yet I do not believe we will reach the future without living through the womanly angers which shadow the present.'[13]

We find in contemporary women's fiction many of these contentious and contradictory elements. For numerous women this may mean an artistic existence as a kind of 'insider-outsider' as Mary

Dorcey puts it (p. 22). And it is an experience by no means unique to the younger generation. In my explorations of contemporary writing by women I find that some of the most radical, both in terms of experimental forms and in political perspectives, are by women born in the 1920s and 1930s: Leland Bardwell, Eithne Strong, Maeve Kelly, Julia O'Faolain, Mary Beckett, Edna O'Brien. All but O'Faolain and O'Brien are women who have chosen to live and write in the Republic of Ireland for most of their lives, although the territory they occupy as artists might well be described as a kind of borderland between the first and the second Irelands their lives have spanned.

There are critics, and not just in Ireland where this kind of critical project is somewhat unusual, who have questioned devoting an entire book to the writings of women. We discover an example of this critical bent in an essay by a young Irish critic and poet, Katie Donovan, who describes such an exercise as putting women into an 'outhouse'.[14] She decries, for example, the publication of women writers by feminist houses as the act of placing their 'protégées in a custom-made pool where they hover, maternal lifeguards, ready to buoy their charges' (p. 5). The charge that women are eager to promote shoddy writing is not worth considering. But the suggestion that women will easily and suddenly be allowed to swim with men requires a complete denial of the daily ways women's writing has been ignored and derided in the past, and how it might continue to be viewed pejoratively as long as women's places in the society are ones in which difference and subordination can coexist. For example, a careful examination of the reviewing pages of Ireland's most important newspaper, the *Irish Times*, will reveal an astonishing gender imbalance in the attention paid to the hundreds of works by women now actually being published, even as one of their literary critics can publish an article, apparently without irony, entitled 'And Let's Not Forget the Men'.[15] Over the years the great writers will emerge from among the less great; the first step is to make sure they appear at all. Thus when I am asked the inevitable question – 'Why only women's writing? Why not include those contemporary men, like John McGahern, Roddy Doyle, William Trevor and Brian Moore, who have written so sensitively about women in their fiction?' – the answer is both simple and complicated. It requires an appreciation of the ways in which some voices can have a blocking effect on others – a political argument that will appear briefly in these pages but which goes well beyond the scope of this study. The short answer might be that I do not need to write about contemporary fiction by men, because so many other hundreds of critics are already doing so. The longer one would require subtle explorations of the ways one woman's creativity can inspire or enable another's, and the cumulative effect of ever widening circles of creation, even where the individual choices of artists are very different. Three examples from three generations of writers speak to the importance of models. The first is from fiction writer Emma Donoghue, born in 1969, who tells of discovering at age 14 in a second-hand bookstore, Ireland's first lesbian novel, *Interlude* (Richards, 1982); despite its 'hilarious bra-bursting frenzies' it 'remains an important book', she maintains, 'because it was written, it was published by an Irish press, and it was goggled at by 14-year-old Irish lesbians who could find nothing else that told them they existed'.[16] The second example comes from the Northern Irish poet Medbh McGuckian (born 1950) who says of Eavan Boland's youthful poetry: 'I am not saying if or how much my life would have altered. I am just saying, I wish somehow I had discovered it or it me [as a 17-year-old]: it would have meant everything as an influence.'[17] Finally, and most poignantly, from the Irish novelist and poet Maeve Kelly as she approached her sixtieth birthday in 1990:

> . . . the finding of women's words has been among the great discoveries of my life. Women's writing has moved me and touched me in countless ways. It has given me endless pleasure and stimulation. But for more than half of my life I searched fruitlessly for these words. I did not know that they existed.[18]

If becoming a writer in a peaceful country poses formidable challenges, these proliferate for women living in a society at war. Of course, the 'Troubles' of the North affect citizens very differently, and it has been possible for some writers to ignore the situation altogether, often by going to places where 'life resembled life more than it did here', as Frances Molloy's protagonist puts it at the end of *No Mate for the Magpie* when she joins the stream of exiles.[19] One of the few writers to move against the tide is author Jennifer Johnston, who moved from the Republic to the North, and we find in some of her work, as in all the other texts examined in Chapter 5, the diverse ways that the 'war has gone into' the people of the North.

The last two chapters of this study return to the Republic and to types of story-making that particularly address themselves to women audiences. Chapter 6 is a study of the feel-good phenomenon of women-centered, mass market blockbusters, a burgeoning industry in

Ireland and, in a small way, in Northern Ireland. Although the popular fiction genres by Irish writers borrow some of the literary 'consumables' from a global market in women's dreams, some at-home elements remake the genres in (and for) Ireland. My study focuses on the work of the two most successful of these writers, Maeve Binchy and Patricia Scanlan, and explores the fascinating mixture of conservatism and subversion found in their novels.

The final chapter moves from the remunerative exercise of popular blockbusters to altogether more challenging terrain – feminist fiction. My essay opens with an analysis of the differences among the various 'women-centered' fiction genres, then examines some fiction that foregrounds political challenges to the status quo – work that bears a consciousness of itself as part of what Irish journalist Nuala O'Faolain wittily calls the 'time of the break-out'.[20]

A gathering of women's writing of the sort offered in these pages is not a project in compensation, although it is, to be sure, a 'phenomenon born out of past neglect'.[21] It is a celebration of women's creativity and an invitation to join the feast. But here I return to the image of 'torrent' with which I began. In the past few years, the creation has been gathering momentum and changing course. Many of the works studied here have profound concerns about the deep class/caste divisions, as well as the gender divides in Irish society. But very recently, as Ireland becomes a more multicultural society, new voices are emerging that have been absent in the past. Even as late as 1989 Traveler and African-Irish women could only be written *about* in Ireland, as in the remarkable stories of Maeve Kelly's 'Orange Horses' and Clare Boylan's *Black Baby*.[22] In 1998, the Trinity College Dublin's Second Annual Women's Studies Summer School offered a panel called 'Telling Our Own Stories' featuring the Traveler Women's Group of Tallaght (Dublin), while Ronit Lentin, a gifted Israeli-Irish novelist now publishing and teaching in Ireland, spoke on 'Racialising (our) Dark Rosaleen'. From such events one can predict that women's project of changing Ireland proceeds apace.[23]

2
Authorship, the Forbidden Country

> But you must take every step first
> along this passage
> we daughters follow after
> each one of us
> moving into the space
> cleared by our mothers.
>
> Mary Dorcey, 'Trying on for Size'[1]

Irish backgrounds

Getting published is, for any writer, a rare achievement. For most of the world's women novelists, it is something in the order of a miracle. External prohibitions that would prevent women's creativity are difficult to avoid internalizing, and even after publication, further barriers proliferate. Literary mothers may have cleared some space, but as Anne Le Marquand Hartigan, an Irish artist, dramatist and poet, asserts: 'Clearing the space is not something we do once in our lives. . . . The new space – canvas, paper, bed, stage – has to be re-made, emptied, re-formed in order to begin. We are always beginning again.'[2] This problem of 'occupying' space and forming it to one's own dimensions is one women of Ireland share with writers of other countries. But many Irish women authors speak of bogies particular to their culture. Ireland is a tiny country with magnificent literary traditions. Accordingly, the cult of the writer is a major cultural practice and export business, and attention to the artist's merit and life a national pastime. Entrance to the sacred precincts is jealousy guarded.

In 1985 the Irish journalist Nuala O'Faolain encapsulated these bogies in the most negative terms, thereby conjuring up the ghosts –

11

personal, social, political and aesthetic – that threatened to paralyze the woman who would be a writer:

> We inherit a country, modern Ireland, where the single imaginative construct we might admire – what Irish men did with words – is utterly at variance, in respect of images of women, with what the men who have power over us want us to be.[3]

The 'brilliant misanthropy' of Irish male authors, she argues, will 'radically and paradoxically' checkmate the self-respect of Irish women who cannot fail to admire and respect that great 'Irish national achievement' (p. 129).

This profound allegiance to the idea of the unquestioned, and nationally necessary, superiority of Irish male literature leaves Nuala O'Faolain herself checkmated in this article. She rhetorically asks if there is a 'single Irish woman writer in the English language whose work you would choose to preserve …? Can the catalogue be revised to prove there is?' (p. 128).

If an Irish feminist could offer in 1985 so chilling a view of Irish women's literary accomplishments, to say nothing of the monolithic fixity of the Irish canon, it is hardly surprising that a woman might falter at the notion of writing.[4] The artists themselves, of course, must – and do – resist such critical diminutions and erasures, but the pressures and anxieties are not easily banished. They, like women of other cultures, appear to spend inordinate amounts of public time explaining, defending, or denying sexual difference in writing and writers. In a familiar double bind, such explanations sound like too much protesting. Yet more damaging distinctions can be made; novel writers may be more disadvantaged than poets.

Eiléan Ní Chuilleanáin, a distinguished poet and daughter of prolific novelist Eilís Dillon, offers an apt analysis of this extra handicap: the 'novelist, who simply devotes so much more time and energy to the work than the poet, needs some kind of secure psychological base to launch so weighty a thing as a novel, and to be embedded in one's material must make it impossible to find the base.' She elaborates on the meaning of 'one's material': for a girl, 'the conventional stages of growth and aging … are inimical because they are not designed for her sex, and yet they represent the only recognizable patterns of progressive involvement with the whole of society.'[5]

In the psychoanalytic discourse of French critic Luce Irigaray, which provides one useful tool for articulating these patterns, this inimical position into which girls and women are forced is a process that has created what she calls an 'economy of the Same'.[6] In this economy the entirety of the dominant culture figures in, and is contained by, a monolithic discourse that constructs 'Others' (not just women) who are then excluded from the 'same', Others who are objects, not 'subjects'. 'But what if the "object" started to speak?' she asks. 'Which also means beginning to "see", etc.' What if the woman 'object' refuses to believe that 'in the beginning was the end of her story, [refuses to believe] that from now on she will have one dictated to her: by the man-father' (p. 43).

Even for the woman willing to take the risks, anxious to disrupt what Irigaray calls 'the discursive mechanism',[7] the methods are not self-evident. No matter how ill-fitting her position, a writer creates from within the language and culture that exclude her if she deviates from the norms, or can include her only as exception, mutant, or interloper. But the model and argument of Irigaray's own writing, as American critic Molly Hite argues, demonstrates that there is 'always the possibility of speaking through the gaps, of exploiting the contradictions within a system that cannot afford to acknowledge its own self-division'. If there is no clearly delineated 'Other' language, it follows that 'difference must use the language of the Same – if rather differently ... must write differently'.[8]

One important method of discovering significant models is to undertake the painstaking task of unearthing and valorizing a women's tradition of writing within Irish literature.[9] Because of course Irish women have been publishing novels for at least two centuries, poetry for even longer. As Ailbhe Smyth points out, 'Irish women writers, and all Irish women, urgently need a literary history which will restore to them the story of their creative expression. They need to understand why that story has not been told, or only told in fragments.'[10] 'Because so little is known of the tradition, nothing is known of the counter-tradition of resistance to submission and erasure.' Without this knowledge, the 'unsuspected, unsignalled and unanticipated surge of contemporary Irish women's writing' will be incomprehensible.[11] The importance of her argument cannot be overestimated; where women look back to and through literary mothers as in English fiction of the eighteenth and nineteenth centuries, one sees particularly rich possibilities for women writing in the twentieth. Only in very recent days have scholars begun the important unearthing work as in Ann Owen Weekes' valuable *Unveiling Treasures: the Attic Guide to the Published Works of Irish Women Literary Writers*.[12]

In the absence of such knowledge, women piece together for them-selves useful models; the cross-fertilization creates a stimulating eclecticism but may leave a writer cut off from the creative soil of her own land.

I asked all the Irish fiction writers I interviewed in the preparation of this book to name their most useful literary models. While a few named Irish authors like William Trevor, Michael McLaverty, John McGahern and Elizabeth Bowen, many named women writers from other traditions such as Alice Walker, Grace Paley, Toni Cade Bambara, Margaret Laurence, Toni Morrison, Joyce Carol Oates, Sylvia Plath, Alice Munro, Angela Carter, Colette, Katherine Mansfield, Fay Weldon, Anne Tyler, Clarice Lispector. They were not dismissive of Irish men's achievements, nor did they seem to be suggesting that these foreign women were free of the gendered impasses that block Irish women. Rather, they admired the fictional strategies and subjects these women devised in negotiating the impasse, in freeing them-selves to write. And yet every writer is contained within her local tradition, to some extent shaped by it. How can she then use it to her own ends?

Poet Eavan Boland offers eloquent descriptions of her own evolving perceptions of this process. As a young woman she realized that she was 'likely to remain an outsider in my own national literature, cut off from its archive, at a distance from its energy. Unless, that is, I could repossess it.'[13] Citing as analogy the swimmer in American poet Adrienne Rich's 'Diving Into the Wreck', Boland sought to discover the 'damage that was done and the treasures that prevail'. She has been aided in this search, she argues, by her marginality within the Irish tradition, a position that 'allows the writer clear eyes and a quick critical sense'. Citing another American poet, Alicia Ostriker, she declares that 'years of marginality suggest ... the real potential of subversion' (pp. 19–20).

In more recent formulations of this idea, Eavan Boland underlines the power of this position. She describes a sea change in Irish poetry, a fact missed by critics 'hooked on elitism and seeking lines of succes-sion from male poet to male poet'. As all national traditions are 'prescriptive and therefore oppressive', it is imperative that the artist disturb the 'conventional tribalisms'.[14] The woman poet has become in Ireland

the emblematic figure of the oblique or disruptive angle to the tradition, as was the romantic poet or the modernist poet in earlier times ... and their questions the ones central to poetry in our time, questions about voice and the self, about revising the stance of the poet and the relation of the poet to the act of power.'[15]

Eavan Boland thus manages to repossess and blend both 'Irishness' and 'femininity'[16] in her poetry, an artistic achievement that has resulted in her being, as the Irish poet and fiction writer Mary O'Donnell puts it, elevated to a 'grudgingly enough conceded status of one of this country's foremost poets.'[17] But O'Donnell notes that when Boland first published 'women's subjects' in her poetry in the 1980 volume *In Her Own Image,* most critics, male and female, in Ireland and abroad, bridled at her working within what one of them ... described as 'the Anglo-American feminist tradition', as though any attention to the 'socially untouchable effects of women's lives' makes for a 'narrow' or 'unsuitable' and derivative art, and almost anything to do with women's lives is liable to be termed 'feminist', a convenient mechanism perhaps, by which the actual poetry may be critically diminished (p. 41).

We see a similar kind of critical trajectory in the responses to Irish women's fiction. Continually judged against a canonized valuation of formal experimentation, this criticism remains too often oblivious of, sometimes even hostile to, women's radical experimentation in fictional subject and treatment. This is particularly the case with those writers who attempt to adapt the tradition of realism in their work – to place fictional women within a recognizable 'historical' environment while simultaneously attempting to revision that environment.

Consider, for example, the 1990 remarks of Irish critic Eve Patten in her special issue on 'Women and Fiction' in the literary journal *Krino.* Contemporary Irish women's fiction she describes as mere 'reportage', 'confessional and autobiographical realism', 'stylistically transparent, reactionary, anti-intellectual, anti-philosophical and realist to the point at which it slips easily into journalism or polemic'. She says more, and worse, and while she may not be the most dismissive of Irish critics, I quote her because this assessment gives such a vivid picture of one of the barriers fiction writers face: the assumption that a woman's focus on women's lives reveals nothing more than a non-artistic transcription of the 'identity quest'.[18] With particular kinds of male experimentation firmly in mind as model, one will fail to see how women's texts radically de-center and re-center the value structure of the narrative tradition, engendering the subject in language, and creating a wholly new relation among reader, writer and text.

In a witty revision of the traditional Irish writer/audience relationship, Irish novelist Mary Leland telescopes in two paragraphs the process whereby women shift from being men's best audiences, to men's imitators, to their own self-created presence. The context here is poetry; it could equally be fiction:

> 'Touch me,' the poet crooned, and every woman in the audience dreamed of touching him, every man dreamed of being touched. There were more women than men, Claire noticed. And maybe she was wrong. These were women who dreamed of being poets themselves.... No. Looking around even in the dark she could see that the attentive faces had a considering look, judgmental even. The women at this reading were feeding fantasies not of making love with the poet but of sharing the platform with him, or reading to an audience that included him.[19]

Self-begetting novels

One of the most inventive strategies by which fiction writers challenge the notion of women's inability to be writers is the creation of metafictional narratives in which women writers self-consciously reflect on the difficulties they are facing as writers, and the strategies they employ to overcome these problems. As obvious a choice of subject as this should be – it is, after all, a staple of male writing – it is a literary pleasure women novelists traditionally withheld from their protagonists and denied to their readers.[20] By pleasure I mean the experience of watching a woman character purposefully engaged in a creative act akin to that of her author, with that work creating an imaginative possibility for the reader.

Although women characters appear as 'writers' in some Irish women's fiction, it is still exceptional to find one who is a self-declared writer and not just a composer of private letters and journals.[21] One contemporary exception – and its recent appearance reveals the changing status of women in the Republic – occurs in the novel just quoted, Mary Leland's *Approaching Priests*, where the protagonist is a professional journalist whose increasing skill and success is an important line of the narrative. As Claire Mackey becomes more successful, especially when she begins producing elegant Irish tourist materials for foreign audiences, her writing increasingly diverges from her real concerns, her passionate engagement with the cultural, political and spiritual life of her country. At the end of the novel she describes herself as 'a journalist: justified lies were part of her skill, what she lived on. But not what she lived by' (p. 290).

While it may not be possible to speculate usefully on the ways Mary Leland's former career as journalist shape her novel, it is true that her insider's knowledge makes for a significantly different kind of public discourse within women's fiction and one that rewrites the experience of newspaper work. On one assignment, for example, Claire accompanies four IRA men on a recruiting trip and has to negotiate the shameful, secret discomforts of menstruation ('conscious of the itch of the pad with its weight of blood', p. 150) while the men cavalierly use the outdoors as toilet in front of her. Her job as journalist is to attend and judiciously respond to the men's talk with its implicit focus on bloodletting but her experience of female embodiment and later of terrorist violence, in which her sister (a mistaken target) is raped and killed, leads her to condemn any form of nationalism that depends on violence. 'She turned to him ... knowing that she had only to get through this day, and tomorrow's return journey, until she would be free of him and his mission. Of all their missions' (p. 151).

We do not watch the protagonist here construct the novel she inhabits. On the contrary, the reader watches Claire progressively relinquish such responsibilities: 'I imagined myself interfering in the stories I read, changing the end because I knew the end. Now I am living in a story, one of the stories that make up this country. And I want to change it – but I don't know what the end will be. How it will all turn out' (pp. 290–1). Claire's fictional life with its radical uncertainties, and her inability to make painful decisions, functions here as emblem of women writers' impotence in writing Ireland's story in the 1990s.

Another woman writer in contemporary Irish fiction, and one of the oddest and most memorable, is one of Mary Beckett's creations. Miss Teeling is a character whose own joyless and abused life results in her desire to destroy other people's. To this end, she sends letters to strangers accusing them of what she clairvoyantly perceives as their central weakness or secret crime. In more formal terms one can say Miss Teeling creates fictional interventions that literally restructure her environment. Mary Beckett neither romanticizes nor sentimentalizes this character whom she described in an interview as an 'evil woman'.[22] But in this discussion of the hostility of the Irish tradition to women writers, Mary Beckett's creation of a wicked 'literary woman' is a magnificent *jeu d'esprit*. 'I believe in God,' says Miss

Teeling. 'Only a fool wouldn't believe in God. So many nasty things could not happen accidentally.... Oh He is mighty and He can do great things but I am an independent operator. I can compete in my own small way.'[23] Compete she does, in an interconnected cluster of short stories in this volume, seemingly independent narratives, but all controlled in some idiosyncratic way by Miss Teeling's machinations.

Miss Teeling may be unique but women writers in Ireland are most assuredly independent operators even though they often labor in extremely difficult material conditions. That said, one needs to explore the formal means by which they exercise that literary independence. One particularly flexible and comprehensive device is the creation of metafictions wherein women authors 'write' themselves. This kind of narrative 'contains' its characters as all narratives must; but it also offers a commentary on narrative as 'containment' when it attends to the representation of women's writing.[24] It is both instructive and sobering to read works that inscribe at their center a woman who wants to be a writer, to watch her explore the strategies by which she can find the secure psychological base from which to launch her novel, to follow the ways in which she creates a new kind of relationship with her audience.

One of the most formally sophisticated of the contemporary Irish metafictions is Briege Duffaud's *A Wreath Upon the Dead* but its focus on the problem of historiography places its discussion more usefully in Chapter 3.[25] Here I want to focus on three novels that belong to a genre American critic Gayle Greene calls the 'self-begetting novel.[26] Works of this genre represent the protagonist attempting to write, and each concludes with the protagonist having composed the novel we have just read. Each explores generalizable problems about women writing fiction in Ireland.

Jennifer Johnston, Clairr O'Connor and Maeve Kelly have all created a central character concerned with how to be a woman and an independent literary operator amid the misogynist scripts for femininity within their specific social realities.[27] At the beginning of each novel is a character already capable of refusing inherited orthodoxies, and each chooses a form of self-exile from Ireland. Yet all three of the protagonist-writers are also aware that it is unwise, and in any case impossible, to attempt a simple escape from the personal and social legacies that have to some extent constructed them; such an acknowledgment requires a regrounding, at least for a time, in Ireland. Each novel chronicles the protagonist's search to find a suitable story among the unsuitable materials of a female life in Ireland. Each protagonist is offered, and refuses, a version of the 'heroine's text', the term American critic Nancy Miller gives to the heterosexual love plot so central to traditional women's novels. Each novel explores the relationships of the 'writer' to her parents and family, seeking to understand how those relationships enhance or hobble the creative process. Each inscribes a version of Ireland as inhibitor and enabler.

Despite these similarities among the three novels, we find important differences as well. First, their reception. Jennifer Johnston's novel *The Christmas Tree*,[28] elegantly crafted, was internationally reviewed and highly praised. It has a mainstream British publisher as does Maeve Kelly's *Florrie's Girls*,[29] which was reviewed less widely but, where it was, generally either savagely criticized or enthusiastically praised, with the *Times Literary Supplement* unusual in its careful, respectful notice.[30] Maeve Kelly's book, deeply intelligent although less polished than Johnston's, offers a far more interesting and challenging social canvas than does *The Christmas Tree*. Clairr O'Connor's *Belonging*,[31] published by Dublin's feminist press Attic, received virtually no reviewing attention outside Ireland, very little within the country. This novel, which occasionally falters because of its contrived plot devices, does usefully illuminate aspects of Irish women's writing. Jennifer Johnston was, by the time her novel was published, already an established novelist with a large international audience. Maeve Kelly, like Johnston a writer in her sixties, had published only one previous novel, one volume of poetry and one of short stories, while *Belonging* is the first novel of the much younger Clairr O'Connor, also author of a previously published volume of poems.[32]

Jennifer Johnston's novelist/protagonist, a Protestant Dubliner of independent wealth, is a woman in her forties dying of leukemia. Although her life has been devoted to the attempt to become a published novelist, her intense, apolitical individualism and obsession with private experience preclude any serious attempt to engage with the larger society. Maeve Kelly's writer, a young, rural Catholic woman whose narrative spans the ages of 17 to 21, is preoccupied with the question of how to enter usefully into a society she experiences as killingly hostile. Clairr O'Connor's West Cork writer has a family background that is a confusing (but finally liberating) combination of Protestant and Catholic, bourgeois and working class; a woman in her thirties, she has a useful public role but one that removes her from Ireland where, from earliest childhood, she had felt silenced and impotent.

All three of the fictional authors use the act of writing as part of their struggle to negotiate among the 'splits' and gaps in their experiences; each attempts to craft an art that has regenerative powers. Insofar as each succeeds in her project and 'begets' the novel we read, each can be said to have entered and recharted the forbidden country of authorship.

Jennifer Johnston's *The Christmas Tree*

In *The Christmas Tree* we are offered a portrait of a woman who chooses early in life to refuse marriage, motherhood, even female sexuality in pursuit of an ideal of artistic achievement. In Constance Keating we meet an artist as middle-aged woman with no explanations of where her aspirations came from, nor any sketch of a childhood environment in which an artist might have developed, nor any witness of the actual writing apprenticeship of her 25 years in London following her departure from her bourgeois Dublin family and 'boring' Trinity College. It is only many years later, after Constance has written and failed to find publishers for three novels, that her father tells her of his own youthful playwriting as a Cambridge student. Despite some success he 'had to make decisions .... The law seemed more secure. I have never been what you might call a daredevil' (p. 112). He then confesses to his daughter that 'it would have given me a certain satisfaction if you had become a writer. Had taken the idea seriously' (p. 113). He dies without knowing of Constance's ultimate success, *The Christmas Tree*.

Given that Mr Keating only shares his own literary past when he knows of Constance's failure, one doubts the sincerity of his stated hopes for her. He withholds the enabling support and assumes that her failure was akin to his, one caused by lack of commitment, apparently unaware that Constance, as a woman writer, might face certain psychological and social barriers different from his. The damning indifference of the 'man-father' (Irigaray's symbolic category) takes another form when she writes her first novel in London and submits it for publication. The treatment it and she receive at the hands of the man in the elegant blue suit and silk shirt offers a sobering portrait of the publishing gatekeepers who have godlike power over the writer's life.

> 'You have a small talent. Quite an original eye. To be blunt Miss ... ah ... Keating is it? ... Keating ... there is no point in us publishing a marginal first novel if we don't feel strongly that a second novel

will come along, and a third. Growth and development. No point at all. We are not a charitable organization. No.' He allowed himself a slight smile at the thought. 'You have, as I said, a small talent, but I don't really see you developing. In fact, I would be very surprised if you ever wrote anything else' (p. 95).

The experience of rejection is obviously devastating for any writer, but the subtle ways in which this female character is particularly diminished by the powerful male, the gendered inequality of their social positions, and the ease with which a woman's production can be cast as 'small' mark special barriers faced by women. On her way out of his office, Constance, temporarily routed, dumps the typescript into a dustbin, but she does continue writing, being a woman willing 'to have confrontations with men behind desks' (p. 132).

And yet her refusal to accept for herself what in Luce Irigaray's discourse is called 'true-life stories', or female scripts, leads her to adopt for her first 43 years 'a *masculine* narcissistic ideal' (p. 106, Irigaray's emphasis). Constance does not lack some 'master signifier', nor does she escape having one imposed upon her; but as a woman she remains an outsider, so her 'access to a signifying economy ... is difficult or even impossible' (p. 71). In choosing the masculine ideal, she fails to 'solve the problem of her relationship to her beginning, to her mother, to those of her own sex' (p. 106). From this first failure comes her second; she cannot make her mark as a writer. This is the problem the novel turns on.

Because Jennifer Johnston focuses so carefully on the ways powerful men intervene in a woman's life, and because the male characters cast such long shadows over the text of Constance's 'life', one tends at first reading to underestimate the more complex relations among women which form the core of Constance's narrative. These women include her mother, her infant daughter, her sister Bibi and Bridie May, the hired woman who will tend her child after Constance's death.

If Mr Keating had a vague desire to see his daughter succeed as a writer, to be the man he wasn't, Mrs Keating had an even more crippling (and within psychoanalytic explanation, quite predictable) desire for her daughter: 'I'd like to have had a son.' Constance recalls that 'she made it sound as if, somehow, it were my fault that she hadn't' (p. 49). Mother and daughter within this economy will be forever separated, yet always bonded in a shared biological destiny. To fail in so elemental a way, to be a woman, then to be a sonless mother – is there any way to repair such damage?

Everything I am summarizing here is presented through the mind and pen of Constance who is recollecting the past as she waits to die of leukemia in the Dublin home she had left 25 years earlier. On the first page of her novel she states her project: 're-creation. All that is left' (p. 1). What she seeks to recreate is her own life story, an 'eleventh hour comment on myself' which she characteristically disparages as 'a non-Odyssey if ever there was one', and 'not much of a story. No plot, no adventure, no love' (pp. 63, 122). She hopes that this exercise will produce a publishable novel at last, a book rich enough to warrant reading. Constance believes that a novel can change a reader's life, can produce a form of immortality in that other person, and for the author (p. 95).[33] But at another level Constance seeks to 'see the pattern. There has to be a pattern' (p. 85). Unable to accept the various ecclesiastical explanations available to her, her parents' comfortable Church of Ireland theology, her sister Bibi's evangelically stern Catholicism, her lover's Judaism, she still believes that there is a pattern and that it is a person's task to discover it. But she laments to her friend and doctor, Bill, that 'We're not given much to work on, are we? Just a few pieces of jigsaw puzzle and too little time' (p. 140).

Constance's emphasis on finding a pattern through recreation of the past is created by the metafictional devices of the novel. Meaning is never transparently obvious; the writer, or any observer, creates her own meaning which is endlessly displaced, never certain, requiring constant attention to the creation and recreation of significant narratives. Jennifer Johnston's decision to make her writer a woman on her deathbed makes for an extraordinarily poignant novel; it also suggests how illusory is the hope for deathbed (or end-of-novel) clarities; even near the end Constance confesses herself 'lost in a forest of irrelevancies' (p. 51). The reader is beckoned into the forest with Constance.

The method Constance devises to orient herself in the thicket is the use of memory which projects what she calls 'home movies' or 'movie stills' (pp. 8, 141) whereby she has another chance to 'see' and thus to understand. Chronological time, of which there are many examples in the book, for example the chiming of church bells throughout Dublin (p. 104), do not herald the significant moments. In fact it is in the moments when Constance is most confused through the ingestion of pain-killers and whiskey that her most important epiphanies, visions of her dead mother, intrude (p. 102).

But if Constance's memory seems to work at random, there is nothing random about Jennifer Johnston's narrative organization. She establishes three kinds of time: the present, between 19–26 December 1978, the last days of Constance's life; the past which appears unbidden, encroaching on Constance's self-conscious recollection and inhabited by the ghost of Constance's mother; and the events of Constance's entire life 'recalled' chronologically, although so interspersed with the other two times that at first reading the linearity is not apparent. This already complicated organization of times present and past is made even more complex by using the present tense only nine times in the novel, excepting of course in direct dialogue. In other words, even in the present time of Constance's last Christmas, the narrative is usually framed in the past, a device that gives a kind of authority to the narrative detail – a pattern to attend to, the pattern that Constance has created in this narrative she is writing in which past and present are no longer usefully distinguished.[34]

Constance's decision to return to her childhood house to die does not suggest a return 'home'; it offers a temporary residence in which to attend to the future of her baby and a place to write her novel. Significantly, Constance takes over her father's bedroom in which to die and his study in which to write her novel and to install the Christmas tree with its blue lights, a symbol throughout the novel of the life force trembling against the darkness about to engulf Constance. In the course of Constance's 'recreations' the reader learns that the 43-year-old Constance, still a virgin, had decided at her mother's death two years earlier to become a mother. The delivery of the baby girl coincides with her father's death. This girl, only provisionally named, her destiny still uncertain, reverses the usual Freudian family romance. Instead of a mother bearing what Irigaray calls the 'penis-product and penis-substitute' (p. 74), Constance has effectively displaced her father by bearing a daughter:

> 'Thank God', she said. 'She doesn't look like my father.'
> 'Her father', corrected the nurse.
> 'No, no. My father. She doesn't look a bit like my father. I was afraid I might have given birth to a ghost.'
> 'She's a pet. Mummy's little pet.'
> 'That remains to be seen' (p. 118).

This elimination of the father from the heroine's developmental course fits a pattern that American critic Marianne Hirsch describes as the 'feminist family romance' of the 1970s. 'Whereas in the nineteenth-century novel, mothers had to be eliminated or disempowered so that

heroines could have access to plot, in the texts of the 1970s, the elimination of fathers has become either a precondition or an important preoccupation of female plots.'[35] Within this new plot, the daughter
struggles to overcome her matrophobia, a term that means not hatred of
the mother, but fear of becoming one's mother.[36] According to Hirsch
this type of romance is not based on the separation from parents or the
past, but from patriarchy and from men in favor of female alliances.

> Yet, inasmuch as this romance is centered almost entirely on the
> experience of daughters, with mothers no more than objects
> supporting and underlying their daughter's process of individua-
> tion.... [the] woman as *mother* remains in the position of *other,* and
> the emergence of feminine-daughterly subjectivity rests and
> depends on that continued and repeated process of *othering* the
> mother (Hirsch's emphases, p. 136).

Jennifer Johnston's decision to have only the mother's ghost appear
would seem to suggest that this author is attempting to recuperate
that mother-daughter nexus as the one carrying most emotional
weight in Constance's life despite her earlier rejection of the feminine
in herself. But her continuing unease if not antagonism to the idea of
sisterhood and motherhood denies the possibility of a strong inter-
generational bond among the women of Constance's family. Despite
all the narrative movement towards this idea – Constance's longing
for her mother at death and her decision to become a biological
mother – the plot derails its own trajectory. In the final vision of
Constance's life the mother becomes the oceanic death force that
pulls her into the darkness: 'Mother smiled as I drowned. She sat in a
green velvet chair by the edge of the sea.... Mother, I called. She
smiled. Mother, the bright day is done. More weeds grasped at my
arms. Mother' (p. 156).

Eliminating the father and refusing to bestow subject status on the
mother, Jennifer Johnston presents yet another 'plot' which
Constance also refuses, this one offered by her Polish-Jewish lover,
himself a comic writer unable to face his own ghosts, his story of the
holocaust (p. 128). A loner like Constance, he wants her to stay with
him at least for a while. Recognizing that he too would teach her, tell
her how to live so as to have a life story worth writing, Constance
leaves him without telling him of her pregnancy. At the end of
Constance's life, when she summons him to rescue the child from her
probable future as a rich Dublin Catholic in her aunt's home, Jacob

Weinberg accepts her Annunciation (which is the beginning of this novel, the end of Constance's story) and comes to claim her, renaming her Zelda after his dead ancestress, thus obliterating her Irish genealogy. His fathering will give him the courage to talk to his own ghosts when he teaches his child what it means to have a Jewish heritage (p. 128). But that story goes beyond Constance's end and beyond the end of Jennifer Johnston's novel. In choosing to close with the flight of the Jewish-Irish baby with her father and foster-mother Bridie May into England (the Irish Egypt), Jennifer Johnston rewrites the familiar Christmas narrative. Its intertextual resonances suggest a rather bright future for the baby and maybe even for Bridie May, but little hope for a woman writer in Ireland. Jennifer Johnston may be recasting the story of the escape of the artist from the stifling Motherland, a familiar *topos* in male Irish literature, but in the latter, the artist's future shines with possibility. In this woman's narrative, our heroine's 'bright day is done and [she] is for the dark' (pp. 142, 148, 156, 167).

In a recent published study of the novels of Jennifer Johnston I argued that the friendship that developed between Constance and Bridie May is an 'intelligent, effective partnership', the first between women in Jennifer Johnston's fiction.[37] In the context of my present reading, I think this is too vague a description of their alliance. If Constance's mother even in her after-death appearances remains the conventional and truth-denying woman she had been in life, Bridie has never known her mother, having been left at birth on a park bench. This lack, however, is treated here as beneficial; unencumbered by a 'real' mother Bridie can construct her own to fit her needs, she can be self-generated. Constance befriends Bridie, encouraging her acts of independence and 'plotting'. After Constance's death, Bridie moves to England with the baby and the baby's father. Ann Owen Weekes suggests that the relationship of Constance and Bridie 'pays tribute to the ability of women to think and mother in common'. But the appeal to this cross-caste commonality of nurturing seems too positive a reading to apply in Jennifer Johnston's novelistic world.[38] Both women are so deeply damaged as daughters that neither can find a fit in a line of inter-generational women. Instead, their bond seems predicated on their shared rebellions as 'daughters', as religious apostates, as participants in the socio-sexual transgression of 'illegitimacy', and in their shared role as 'author'. Each act is an individual accommodation to a particular life, and makes no claims for the possibilities of mother-daughter identification even after the elimination of the father. On the contrary, Constance who had thought her mother's death would release her for the 'first time' into 'an identity', realizes that the death resolves none of her confusion. She must follow another path altogether to recreate herself as a woman, as must Bridie.

If Constance's story is to include her death, someone else must record the event. Wanting to maintain control of her own 'plot', she exhorts Bridie 'to write everything down.... Everything ... but, Bridie, no flights of fancy. Just straight, put it down straight. No flights' (p. 159). But in the final metafictional gesture of the novel, Bridie, although determined to obey the command about no flights, finds herself unable to avoid offering interpretation, shaping the plot. What is more, although she apologizes for doing it, presumably to Constance's ghost, she persists, and so the 'novel' is the work of two women authors, both straining to control the problems attending the act of *representing* women's writing. Given that one of them dies and the other leaves Ireland taking with her the child who is being protected from an Irish upbringing, *The Christmas Tree* offers a very bleak picture of women's writing in Ireland. To invoke once again the writings of Luce Irigaray: 'When the one carries life, the other dies. And what I wanted from you, Mother, was this: that in giving me life, you still remain alive.'[39] Despite the text's apparent ideological commitment to the idea of a new plot for motherhood, in fact, the mother is killed so that the writer may live. But not, it seems, in Ireland.

Clairr O'Connor's *Belonging*

The opening of *Belonging* resembles that of *The Christmas Tree* with a daughter of recently deceased parents returning home from self-exile in a foreign land, sitting at her father's desk, proposing to write. In what amounts to a parody of the narrative of Freud's family romance, Deirdre Pender sits reverently before her father's writing implements, his 'pipes, inkwell, fountain pen, letter-opener.... I look at them, touch them. I want them to be significant. In what way I'm not quite sure. They stand to attention like Stonehenge, relics of his past, while my cheap biro moves over the paper.'[40] Just to add to the reader's sense of discomfiture, O'Connor adds the detail: 'I'm wearing one of Mam's black silk dresses, relieved, as she herself used to say, from the funereal look by the white lace collar' (p. 10). 'Funereal' all too apt here as Deirdre recalls four paragraphs later the double burial of her parents, the 'pair of coffins, companionably side by side' and adds the cheerfully macabre detail, the 'funeral was a great success.... a jolly rouge, the last camouflage before the rot starts in earnest' (p. 11).

Like Jennifer Johnston's Constance Keating, Deirdre Pender is writing for her life, wielding her pen in a therapeutic exercise. But even these few quotations from *Belonging* reveal how dissimilar are the two books: the delicate, elegiac, imagistic prose of *The Christmas Tree* requires an act of sympathy and respect from its readers and any essay into humor by Constance marks her as a woman wittily in control. *Belonging,* at least in its opening, self-consciously defies us to take its heroine seriously.

Although 33 years old, Deirdre appears to be going through a delayed and very stormy adolescence, complete with sullen withdrawal, refusal of minimal sense of responsibility, self-mutilation, eating and sleep disorders – in short, a serious case of 'hysteria'. The ostensible reason for these reactions is her post-funeral discovery of what appears to be a revelation of a lifelong false identity: instead of being the only child of Irish parents, she now believes herself to be an adopted Hungarian orphan, a misreading that requires much of the novel to correct. However startling such news might be, especially when coupled with the trauma of her parents' deaths, Deirdre's reaction seems wildly out of proportion, although she does tell her readers that her 'entire relationship [with her long-time American partner Barry] is based on my ethnic authenticity. He fell in love with my Irish photograph albums' (p. 12). Deirdre adds: 'wanting this man has been both the centre and also the main confusion in my life' (p. 13). Desire and confusion presumably are immediately manifest in her curious admission of her twice weekly psychiatric/sexual encounters – every Tuesday and Thursday – with Mark, her New York therapist. This relationship has existed alongside that with Barry, a potent secret entrusted to Deirdre's lifelong best friend, Greta, who eventually and treacherously marries Barry herself.

The comic jauntiness of the tone, the disheveled quality of the prose, the muddle of the mind, to say nothing of the mess of the fictionalized life, are all part of a narrative in which the author's 'hands scrawl and race to tell all' (p. 10). 'Obedient as a schoolgirl' she writes everything down, as instructed by Mark, both the journal writing and the obedience habits of long-standing. But just as the reader begins to long to withdraw from this text, the writerly 'I' suddenly addresses her readers directly in a metafictional sleight of hand that reengages our attention, amuses us, throws us off balance:

> Mark ... actually said to me on the phone, before I left New York, that my parents' death was a golden opportunity. Heaven sent! I could unload all that stuff that has been crowding out my head for years. Send it to lost luggage and move on. His last book was called *The Halo Effect of the Cliché*. You can see why. I have been sleeping with this man, my therapist, for ten years. 'He should be struck off,' I hear you cry and you're right. In a crisis you hope for something more than a quotation (p. 11).

The 'you' here, saluting and thereby creating an audience, disrupts the realistic illusion of the 'journal'. But 'you' also implies Deirdre's knowledge of her audience as she predicts our disapproval of Mark's unethical practices which had, as we discover, been very destructive of Deirdre's health. By focusing on his misbehavior, Deirdre shields some parts of her own from our scrutiny, and her own. 'Deirdre' creates her audience, then uses us as confidantes in the subsequent pages. On one level this device plays havoc with the idea that this fictional writer is out of control; the hysterical quality of the opening pages is revealed as the fictional artifice it always was. But on another level, the blatant rupture underscores the thematic center of O'Connor's novel: the difficult necessity of learning to decipher such social constructions as 'home', 'love', 'trust', 'friendship', 'motherhood', 'work', and 'belonging'.

Deirdre's hysteria, although not her unhappiness and confusion, is short-lived. And Clairr O'Connor uses the moment when its dust settles into ironic self-consciousness and 'authorial' artifice to reveal the faultlines of Deirdre's personality; her task, and the point of the narrative, is the reintegration of those antagonistic selves.

One of Deirdre's earliest experience is of voicelessness. This manifests itself in painful stammering, a condition that was only brought under control after years of twice weekly speech lessons – every Tuesday and Thursday – with Miss Bateman (her first therapeutic relationship) and one in which a woman teaches her to find her speaking voice. Deirdre as a child experienced her wordlessness as a character flaw, and she recalls her childhood as a 'sepia memory' of a 'soundless movie' in a family that 'hoarded words carefully, taking them out and dusting them down on appropriate occasions, when politeness demanded' (p. 17). A small, undersized child, she wanted to be unremarked, unremarkable. But her mother, a genius at lacework, showed her love for her only child in creations of elaborate, heavy dresses that only made the child feel more helpless in her conspicuousness: '...

Mam's sewing. Love that had stitched and pinned me to inhibition and wordlessness' (p. 65). This inability to speak persisted through her university years. Only when she left Ireland to do postgraduate studies in the United States did she become a talker. 'Now I am positively spendthrift, throwing words to the wind, appropriately or not' (p. 17).

When Deirdre finally stops trying to interpret her father's cryptic journals and seeks enlightenment about her origins from an eyewitness friend of the time, she learns that her stammering was the result of her mother's *grand mal* epilepsy. Although the particulars of this illness were kept secret from Deirdre all her life (her mother would retire to her special bedroom to recuperate), Deirdre always felt 'guilty, responsible for her delicate state. Afraid to upset her in any way' (p. 91). Thus for the few brief months after her parents' death when Deirdre thinks she is adopted, she feels, after her initial hysteria, a kind of exhilaration, 'energized by these complications' (p. 91). 'I have found a mother indeed. Not Mam, the pale invalid. On the prayer list for the sick all my life. Pulling me to her heart by anxious threads. But Inga [the Hungarian refugee] who knew what she wanted and took what she could' (p. 79).

But in a curious move, when Deirdre discovers who and where this Inga is, she chooses not to seek her out in her adopted Canada, but to go instead to Hungary, to discover her cultural heritage instead of reconnecting to the presumed biological one. And it is in this exploration of cultural parentage that O'Connor offers a critique of Ireland's malfeasant effects on women's lives.

Although Deirdre never makes an explicit connection between her mother's invalid state and her own cultural maladaptation, she does explicitly realize that she must leave Ireland if she is to find an effective voice. Her undergraduate love of feminist literature, particularly the poetry of Sylvia Plath and Emily Dickinson, 'excited me' although it was the type of literature 'least valued when I was an undergraduate in Cork' (p. 75). So after graduation, she left Ireland to study further, eventually becoming a university professor in New York. But this adult competence exists only in her American persona; her Irish 'self' is as faltering as ever. Despite her active sexual life in the United States, it is clear that Deirdre's articulate voice remains cut off from its physical roots, disembodied, arrested at a pre-pubescent level. And as a way of exploring this phenomenon, O'Connor afflicts Deirdre with two forms of paralysis: fear of becoming a mother, and fear of becoming like her own mother.

When Deirdre becomes pregnant in the United States a year before her parents' death, she chooses to have an abortion. Urged by her lover

Barry and her friend Greta to have the baby, she refuses: 'There was no obstacle really except the enormous one inside my head. I knew this baby would never arrive, knew I couldn't possibly let it' (p. 58).

In her treatment of abortion, O'Connor shows a compassionate clear-sightedness about the many facets of this experience. This amounts to a difficult and courageous feat in a country which outlaws not just the act of abortion but even unambiguous permission to travel to a foreign state for abortion.[41] Deirdre's decision to abort 'Em' is seen by the character as a mistake, but not in the moralistic terms of her cultural conscience. Rather, her inability to mother – not the same as a choice to be not-a-mother – is part of her psychic invalidism, as is her flight from her mother.

In her landmark study of the institution of motherhood, the American poet and critic Adrienne Rich suggests that 'the loss of the daughter to the mother, the mother to the daughter, is the essential female tragedy' and adds that 'there is no presently enduring recognition of mother-daughter passion and rupture'.[42] According to Rich's analysis, the ways in which mothering is constructed in patriarchal culture result in the 'mother's bondage'. In such a condition, the young woman who would be 'individuated and free' sees the 'mother' as the 'victim in ourselves, the unfree woman, the martyr, the victim'. And so develops matrophobia.

> Matrophobia can be seen as a womanly splitting of the self, in the desire to become purged once and for all of our mother's bondage.... Our personalities seem to blur and overlap dangerously with our mothers'; and, in a desperate attempt to know where mother ends and daughter begins, we perform radical surgery (p. 236).

Using this analysis, one can argue that Deirdre's decision to flee Ireland was only in part a choice to leave a society in which her feminist awareness was not accepted; more fundamentally, it was a decision to flee the effects of that misogyny on women, on her mother, on herself. Any sort of rehabilitative process, then, requires a new kind of understanding and acceptance of her mother.

At the beginning of my discussion of this novel, I focused on the scene where Deirdre sits down at her father's desk days after his death and touches his pen and writing tools. When she reads his diary months later, she comes across a passage written when she was only seven, recalling the first time 'Dad let me fill his fountain pen .... I was delighted at my own expertise' (p. 173). This highly symbolic act, wherein Deirdre is apparently designated her father's literary heir, holds her imagination in thrall, but does not liberate her into authorship. Characteristically, while she and her father are engaged in this exercise, 'Mam was taking a rest in her sleeping-room' (p. 173). In her adult consciousness, Deirdre still erases the invalid mother from the creative act. And yet, when Deirdre reads her father's diaries, she realizes that 'this is no great work of literature' (p. 174), and recognizes for the first time the value of her mother's artistry. With her cousin, Marge, she decides to create a museum in which to display her mother's lacework. From her initial habitation of her father's study, she moves into her mother's two rooms, the sleeping room, scene of her mother's retreat, and the sewing room, place of creativity, which Deirdre makes into her own study. The two rooms which had apparently symbolized the tragic split in her mother's life, become the site of Deidre's own regeneration as the daughter reclaims her mother and thereby sutures her emotional wounds.

This novel luxuriates in one of the most drawn-out denouements in Irish literature, as problem after problem is unraveled and resolved. In its careful plotting, coinciding with Deirdre's birth at the time of the Hungarian Revolution and her eventual psychic cure at the demolition of the Berlin Wall, its symbolic framework creaks all too obviously. But if the novel is formally flawed, it offers illuminating possibilities for cultural analysis, as O'Connor works to show how the individual healing will ideally result in a greater awareness of, and involvement in, the larger society. But Deirdre is not integrated into what Irigaray, whom I quoted earlier, called the 'economy of the Same'. Instead O'Connor devises a bold but highly eccentric resolution.

Reconciled to her parents, Deirdre can also be at peace living in Ireland. But aware that she loves her teaching and 'there is no way I could get a comparable teaching post in Ireland' (p. 187), she decides to divide her life between her work in New York, and a different kind of work in Ireland. The fictional New York offers an invigorating (if fanciful) picture of a utopian feminist English Department. Ireland, site of a newly constituted 'home', offers her a domestic grounding and an adopted family of women, who will inhabit Deirdre's Georgian house. In Ireland, the year after her parents' death, she succeeds in writing a book about Emily Dickinson. In New York, she discovers her ability to write creative fiction. The last words of the novel are ones in which Deirdre describes the experience of writing short stories: 'They write themselves or so it appears to me. I do not want to interrupt their wholeness' (p. 204).

Deirdre is thus lifted by her author out of the 'economy of the Same' and deposited into two different sorts of very positive women's worlds. While Deirdre speaks of the 'wholeness' of her fiction, the reader of Deirdre's 'self-begetting' novel is only too aware of the rare privilege that allows her to enjoy the requisite freedoms of two cultures. She describes her time in Ireland as 'playing house but much more too. I walk the four fields of [her inherited property and of traditional Ireland] and I feel a sense of territory, of belonging, that's strong and positive' (p. 187). O'Connor's writer creates a 'doubled' subjectivity, competent in two worlds, but firmly grounded in Irish soil.

Maeve Kelly's *Florrie's Girls*

The authors of *The Christmas Tree* and *Belonging* created protagonist-writers whose ages approximated their own. Maeve Kelly's *Florrie's Girls* attempts quite a different strategy, offering a 'writer' 40 years younger than her author. Moreover, it does not employ the 'structure of circular return' used by Johnston and O'Connor to allow an older 'author' to circle back and revision the past as a way of reordering the present.[43] Instead the much older Maeve Kelly attempts to create a very young woman in the language and experience of the late 1940s.

As the journal/novel begins, 17-year-old Caitlin (Cos) Cosgrave from rural Kerry is six months into her nursing training in a Catholic Hospital in London. She nostalgically recalls her departure from Ireland, claiming that if she 'were a character in a book', she would have jumped off the train that was carrying her away from home. 'In the real world,' she adds, '... we get on the train and we keep moving because the train is on its tracks and it's easier to go with it than to get off.' And so, she adds, 'here I am six months later starting to put pen to paper at last' (p. 1).

With her heuristic distinctions here between fiction/reality, character/person, writing/written, Maeve Kelly self-consciously blurs the boundaries between novel and autobiography, problematizing such genre distinctions while embracing both. This 'border traffic' strategy, to borrow British critic Maggie Humm's useful term, extends to narrative time as well: the 'at last' of young Cos refers not so much to linear chronology as to the experience of cataclysmic life changes including emigration from her native Ireland into a society and profession where she is continually made to feel alien and clumsy.[44] But if the reader considers this statement through the generic lens of the novel/autobiography, she cannot fail to remark that 'pen to paper at last' refers as well to Maeve Kelly who writes of 'Cos' 40 years after the events narrated. This is a book that, as the author herself states, should have been written 40 years ago had she the opportunity to write it then.[45] If we read with such doubling in mind, we enter the consciousness of a very young woman while also experiencing the palimpsestic presence of the much older author whose political awareness, social knowledge and compassion inform the text. While this doubled consciousness is a central pleasure of the novel, Maeve Kelly's long literary silence raises questions I shall return to later.

Another feature that distinguishes this metafiction from Johnston's and O'Connor's is that this young fictional 'author' never offers an explanation of how or why she comes to write. Her writing is simply a given and her self-training in the art of writing follows a course parallel to her attempts to learn nursing during a three-year period.[46] Yet, as we shall see, in the end she feels herself balked in both areas. But if Cos closes her text (and the novel) by declaring herself as not-a-writer, we see her during her training period, which is also the duration of the text, addressing much more self-consciously than Constance Keating and Deirdre Pender, the formal problems she faces as writer, problems of narrative voice and persona in particular. For Cos, these are not merely formal questions; they reveal life struggles of primary importance.

An example of this struggle occurs when Cos finds herself unable to use first person narrative after witnessing the deaths of patients. Determined to 'kill' the vulnerable 'I' (p. 101) she experiments with third person narration that keeps at bay the unbearable pain, gives her world a different, more manageable shape. And yet, one pays a price for such a dispassionate distance, as one pays a price in aging:

> The other person that still is me is older, wiser and writes better. She leaps out of my skin and takes enough of my self with her to be able to interpret what needs to be interpreted. She says it all with more grace but no humour. This 'I' makes me laugh when I read what she has written. The other, 'She', sober-sides, is grave observer, not feeling any pain or mirth, not smelling any death. I-I-I-I-they are trying to steal it away from me (p. 104).

Being an artist is for Cos synonymous with being an effective, aware adult. She discovers during her training that becoming a nurse in the environment of a rule-bound misogynist medical hierarchy would require her to kill the artist/herself. As one of her more observant nursing instructors, a British intern also professionally miscast, ironically remarks:

> Oh, Cosgrave is at heart an artist and this is a big problem she has for many reasons. She is in the wrong profession, she is the wrong sex and she comes from a country dominated by the greatest obscurantist force of European civilisation, the Roman Catholic Church (p. 156).

Despite this dismissive reference to Irish religious colonization and misogyny, recurring themes in Maeve Kelly's long and short fiction, we find no antagonism to her natal country in young Cos. In fact one might venture to say that the element that most distinguishes this book from Johnston's and O'Connor's is the protagonist's relationship to home and Ireland. The novel inscribes a deep love of her family, Irish rural life, landscape, and history. To be away from Ireland, working in England is described by Cos as a 'strange exile' (p. 163), and her alienation from most things British can be explained not just by their inadequacy but by Cos's own rootedness in Ireland. Reflecting on the possibility of staying in England, she thinks: 'It would wear me out. And it would wear me out having to forget all that I am, all that I am rooted in and the thousands of years that went into making me what I am' (p. 162).

Cos leaves Ireland, as most emigrants do, for economic reasons. Her elder brother will inherit the family farm, and his siblings have to find ways of supporting themselves. The necessity of departure Cos simply accepts, but regrets her parents' unwillingness to write. But writing here does not involve bourgeois fathers sitting in their studies as putative artists, their daughters longing to hold their pens; when Cos complains that her parents 'aren't good to write', she is referring simply to their letters which 'give the same old news' instead of 'simple answers to simple questions' like 'Was the hay good this year? Did you cut the turf from the lower bog? Did you get the piped water in?' She guesses that they 'don't believe I mean it' (p. 2); how could the distant daughter concern herself with these homely details. But in submerging the details of their lives, they reveal a sense that their lives and world are not the subject of art, not even of a humble epistolary self-expression. Perhaps nothing reveals the class differences between the Keatings, the Penders and the Cosgraves so effectively as this detail.

If Cos's relationship to literary ambition differs dramatically from those of the other two 'authors', so too does her relationship with her parents. The figure of her father, for example, holds no particular bogies for her; a kindly and loving man, if reserved and somewhat distant, she is clear about the mechanics of freedom from paternal authority: 'I don't hate my father but I don't take too much notice of what he says' (p. 199). Furthermore, her strong, easy relationship with her mother reveals none of the matrophobia of the other two 'authors' examined above. The worst tension experienced in the parent-daughter relation occurs when, in her final year of training, Cos is wrongly assumed to be marrying an Englishman. The family, parents and siblings, combine to scold her during her visit home: 'They made it up with me before I left but I have a sense of their having washed their hands of me a little bit as if they have lost me at last. They didn't refer to me as the *sidheog* any more or even Cait or Katie but Caitlin. My full name.... It was painful leaving them' (p. 236).

But Kelly does not sentimentalize Ireland or Irish family relations. Using Cos's friendships with the other Irish nurses as a way of depicting different kinds of Irish lives (as well as creating remarkably funny dialogue), she has Cos contrast her own freedom from father-bondage with the situation of her friend and classmate, Hanly, who bitterly hates her father for his wife battering and sexual abuse. In a characteristic private reflection, she writes:

> Was it not [Hanly's] father who killed her mother? Supposing I said, Hanly, your father dug your mother's grave and put her in it, so why should you think he is right in his opinion about anything? A man who ran a funeral business and a public house [as Mr Hanly does] would learn about drunkards and the dead but what would he know about women? If Hanly hates her father as she says she does she should hate his opinions too (p. 199).

This passage reveals what I referred to earlier as the dual consciousness of the narrative voice. The slightly breathless and naive thought contains wisdom possible in an intelligent young woman, but the skillful, if lightly sketched, analysis about emotional/psychological bondage and freedom, destructive gender relations, suspect economic power, and its abusive potential in family life – this bespeaks the sophistication of a long life of observant political awareness. Behind this writing is the knowledge of Maeve Kelly who has spent the bulk of her working time since 1974 – not writing – but founding, then running, a battered women's shelter in Limerick.[47]

Feminist awareness shapes other significant parts of the novel. Kelly places at the narrative center of her work female friendship and friendship-in-work, one of the relatively few women's novels that meets the challenge made over 60 years ago by Virginia Woolf in *A Room of One's Own*.[48] There Woolf recounts her delight in reading an imagined novel called *Life's Adventure,* described as the first by man or woman that does not feel the need to show women primarily 'in their relation to men' (p. 79). As a kind of blueprint for women writing about women, *Life's Adventure* makes it 'evident that women, like men, have other interests besides the perennial interests of domesticity'. If a woman author can succeed in showing friendship between women, says Virginia Woolf, 'she will light a torch in that vast chamber where nobody has yet been.' But, as Woolf astutely remarks, it is not just the friendship, but friendship-in-work which makes their kinship 'more varied and lasting because it [is] less personal' (pp. 79–80). Although Woolf's essay used to function as a quasi-bible for white western feminist readers, it is curious how few books by women authors, even feminist authors, in fact manage to create female friends in the full and often difficult complexity of their relations with each other, and through the mediating experience of their shared work. It is this aspect of *Florrie's Girls* that marks its striking originality.

Accompanying the focus on female friendship is Kelly's reevaluation of women's traditional work and a celebration of its achievement as in this representative sample:

> Nothing in my books had prepared me [for the difficulties of orthopedic nursing]. I discovered movements and rhythms in myself as a dancer must. I bent and leaned and knelt, stretched and bowed and ran to the tunes played by imprisoned limbs and twisted bodies. I learned to give and yield and be pliable, not only physically but mentally and emotionally (p. 148).

Little resemblance here to *Cherry Ames, Student Nurse*, for over two decades a best-selling romantic pulp fantasy in Britain and North America, and set in the same period as *Florrie's Girls*.[49]

Cos does have a short-lived but lyrically beautiful, guilt-and-baby-free love affair – one of the few in Irish women's fiction. But just as heterosexual romance is not the central preoccupation of this narrative, neither are sexual relations. When Cos's lover declares her sincerity will get in the way of being 'good in bed', her response is 'it is not my most cherished ambitions' (p. 203). Yet when this man dies of cancer on her ward and in her care, her devastation with this loss and her own tuberculosis contracted in the hospital combine to make her despair about the possibility of nurturing life in the midst of so much apparently senseless death, in an institution so patently unfit to promote real health. A person who 'thinks about everything that happens and [needs to] work out why it happens' (p. 141), she feels that there can be no mitigating explanation adequate to the horror and she abandons her childhood faith: 'I don't really want to know such an individual [God], so pitiless and immune to prayers. Binks says it is blasphemy to say such a thing but you cannot blaspheme what you do not believe' (p. 244).

The novel opens with the simple, but radiant sentence: 'The day I left home was the sunniest day of the summer' (p. 1). The novel closes, three years later, thus:

> I don't seem to have anything to say any more. Nothing I say is of any importance. Nothing I read is of any importance. I would like to study Chinese and be a Chinese scholar in Peking. I would like to learn a language so different from my own that it would be like starting all over again, with different thoughts and different ideas. Perhaps I will marry Chris [the farmer back home who steadfastly woos her].... At night time I might be able to study Chinese by the electric light instead of the old oil lamp. I might be able to begin these diaries all over again so that they will end differently, I might be able to write in Chinese 'The day I left home was the sunniest day of the summer' (p. 246).

The almost dogged simplicity of this writing reveals the young writer's attempt to strip thought and style of comforting adornment. She knows that '[w]ords are dangerous. Sometimes I think that by writing it down I begin the process of destruction.' But she also believes that 'words make [experience] permanent and real' (p. 219). Thus the discovery that neither her words nor those she reads are 'of any importance' leaves her bereft.

Despite the crushing losses of the young woman, and the depictions of inevitable death, the writing in this novel does not, to recall Virginia Woolf's assessment of *Life's Adventure*, 'lower one's vitality' (p. 77). The repetition of the opening sentence at the novel's end is not a circular return; instead it marks a passage out of innocence into an apparent impasse that is, on closer inspection, illuminated by an awareness that there are other 'languages' to speak, other ways of experiencing the world, even other ways of shaping the world. Cos may declare herself silenced but we have the proof of Maeve Kelly's ability to create in our hands as we read. This contradictory situation takes us back to the considerations raised at the beginning of this chapter.

Between the 1950s when Maeve Kelly returned from nursing training in England to Ireland, married her farmer wooer and raised a family, and 1989 when *Florrie's Girls* was published, the life possibilities of the majority of Irish women, as well as of at least some women in many other countries, underwent a sea change. Maeve Kelly describes this in a 1990 speech at an International Congress on Women in New York: 'There is a huge increase in the numbers of women who receive higher education and who have access to libraries and sources which were denied our mothers and grandmothers. There are the women's presses and publishing houses.... there is evidence of a huge market for women's work. And most important of all there is the new found confidence among women, the daring belief that we can do anything we put our minds to.'[50] In this environment, women are creating a new literature, what she calls a 'great body of work different from anything that has gone before'.

Yet in these celebratory remarks she recalls as well the fruitless search during half her life for the writing that could speak 'intensely and recognizably with a female voice'. Failing to find it, or 'being led to believe that for reasons no one could explain these words were not as important as the words written by men', she started to write herself as a middle-aged woman, composing 'of course in longhand, like countless other women, making a space for [herself] at the kitchen table' on a farm in County Clare, 'in between washing nappies and cooking meals and mucking out the milking yard'. Her subjects were the lives of the traditional Irish women among whom she lived, and her short stories are, in my estimation, among the most remarkable from Ireland.[51] Her own success in creating this literature answers the question she raised at the beginning of her New York speech:

> How can we, so long accustomed to having our experience and our feelings made to seem trivial, our ideas either ignored or worse, plagiarized by our male colleagues, how can we invent a literature with which we can identify, of which we can be proud and which will owe nothing to the sacred traditions of male writing?

Or how can women, to echo the question posed by the fictional Cos, 'learn a language so different from my own that it would be like starting all over again, with different thoughts and different ideas' (p. 246)?

The answers will be as diverse as the authors writing. But according to Maeve Kelly, there is this commonality: 'each will lay claim to the words we have learned and use them to unlock all that is in our hearts and our minds. We create within this space a vision of the world which is uniquely our own. And then we try to share that vision with others.'

With these words Maeve Kelly claims the country of authorship for women writers, and for women in Ireland. The texts examined in this chapter explore the old terrain, and chart the dangers. The fragmentation that is the subject of each of the self-begetting novels is also a representation of the condition of women writing against an entrenched cultural domain. Yet if each of the fictional authors may have begun in that psychic space described by Irigaray – 'in the beginning was the end of her story', each writes herself out of this prohibition, using it as the material from which, and by which, to generate different kinds of stories.

3
Women Writing Exile

> Of course she paused, there,
> at the head of the pass, at sunset,
> looked back, thinking
> it over, then retraced her steps.
>
> Roz Cowman, 'Lot's Wife'[1]

> O the price of leaving,
> the cost of coming home.
>
> Mary O'Malley, 'The Price of Silk is Paid in Stone'[2]

> Here, in this scalding air,
> my speech will not heal. I do not want it to heal.
>
> Eavan Boland, 'In Exile'[3]

Finding voice, being seen: Irish women emigrants

The word 'emigration' has a plangent ring, especially in Irish contexts, where it evokes the experience of mass departures out of particular surroundings, those places ostensibly 'home'. But as a concept, 'emigration' is perhaps more germane to demography or historiography than to fiction as it has, at least at the literal level, a neutral content. It is only when the idea of 'exile' is superimposed onto 'emigration' that the human face emerges, marked inevitably with a sense of pain and loss. Exile, the *OED* notes, is banishment or expatriation. But all of these definitions have very particular resonances, I shall argue, when we view them through the lens of gender, when it is a woman leaving the *patria*.

Numerous narratives of emigration and exile occur in contemporary Irish women's writing and small wonder given how common the experience. But a surprising idiosyncrasy attended Irish departures historically. Unique among western European countries since 1870, Ireland has experienced in several decades a larger outflow of female emigrants than male, and many of these women left Ireland alone, neither accompanied by a man nor joining one in her new country.[4] What this means of course is that Irish women's emigration tales cannot be subsumed within a husband's story, although American historian Maureen Murphy established recently that many Irish women in the nineteenth and early twentieth centuries mentored younger siblings as a way of reforming a family unit in America.[5] As Irish critic and historian Grace Neville points out: 'Historians of Irish emigration have, to date, concentrated on male emigration and male experiences. Female emigrants, despite their greater numbers, generally flicker like shadows at the edges of their perception' (pp. 271–2). In recent years historians who have focused on women's emigration patterns have argued that emigration was not exile but opportunity, and that the chance to leave Ireland was a voluntary decision to opt for wider economic and social opportunities.[6] While the search for greater opportunity certainly would have been an important motive, the idea of 'voluntary' needs interrogation. In the absence of the women's actual voices, it is tempting to speak for them, as does American historian Hasia R. Diner in this questionable generalization: 'Not only did women [in the nineteenth century] leave Ireland more willingly [than men], but leaving involved very little emotional pining. They made the decision to leave with a relatively light heart.'[7]

The Irish sociologist Mary Daly wrote as recently as 1989 in her book *Women and Poverty* that when it comes to 'women who are emigrating now or those who have emigrated in the past – we have no idea why they are leaving or what happens to them subsequently'.[8] While this certainly remains the case with past emigration, this is not the contemporary situation. Even as Daly's book was being published, three books of contemporary Irish women's oral histories of emigration were also being issued by feminist presses in England, Ireland and Canada.[9]

Many of these oral histories recount the economic necessity of leaving an impoverished nation. Here, for example, from Irish-Canadian Sheelagh Conway's book, is the voice of an Ottawa Valley woman named Bridget Grealis-Guglich:

Going off with the little bag, that was the story of the people in and around Ballycroy, Co. Mayo where I came from. Life was hard .... We knew at a very early age that we'd have to be leaving and taking the bag. But there was nothing in Ireland for us. That I had to give up my homeland was maybe the saddest thing in my lifetime (pp. 123–4).

There is nothing particularly gendered about this description of emigration in the 1950s, at least in this woman's narration. But another of Conway's informants, this one from the 1980s, analyzes her emigration quite differently in an explanation that reveals highly politicized changes in Irish society and consciousness:

Anybody who comes abroad does so for a reason. If you're happy, why would you leave? You leave because you're discontented .... A lot of people come to Canada for money. That wasn't my reason, ever. I left Ireland because I was tired of the chauvinism, tired of women being tied to the kitchen sink (p. 167).

With this statement we move from a description of economically driven emigration to that of expatriation: not exile from a beloved Ireland, but the female experience of being exiled within Ireland by virtue of its patriarchal heritage, a situation with economic consequences. In the last decade particularly, many Irish women writers, northern and southern, have been exploring the meanings of exile. Women, their texts suggest, can never be absolutely at home in a *patria* – an idea of fatherland that devalues 'the mother' while paradoxically mythologizing the homeland as Mother.

'Ireland has always been a woman,' says Edna O'Brien, Ireland's most famous woman exilic writer in the opening of her autobiographical *Mother Ireland*; '[Ireland is] a womb, a cave, a cow, a Rosaleen, a sow, a bride, a harlot, and of course the gaunt Hag of Beare.' To O'Brien this Ireland is 'Godot land' and, with a characteristic shift from a private 'I' to a more inclusive and urgent second person pronoun, she declares 'you must get away'. Using geography as cultural and personal metaphor she reflects: 'to be on an island makes you realize that it is going to be harder to escape and that it will involve another birth, a further breach of waters. Nevertheless an agitation to go.'[10] This agitation to go, while not unique to women, has perforce in O'Brien's novels from the 1960s to the present, as in other contemporary women's writing, a highly gendered quality. With her choice of birthing metaphor, 'a further breach of waters', Edna O'Brien refuses the etymological possibilities of the word exile –

to leap out of – which have been artistically exploited by such writers as James Joyce and Joseph Conrad. These male writers, argues American critic David Seidel, find that imagination not only compensates for exilic loss but registers that loss as aesthetic gain.[11]

One finds a more difficult 'breaching of waters' with the women, an added burden of the cultural prohibitions internalized, or what Irish critic Ailbhe Smyth has called the problem of 'writing yourself up from under the closely meshed layers of the facts of femininity and Irishness'.[12] These facts are not more crushing in the present than they have been in the past. The expectations of a different, more equitable reality, however, expectations implicit in the 'chauvinism' quotation above, make especially galling the continuing misogyny and male control. But if Irish women may experience a social/emotional exile within Ireland, their situation as emigrants is also compromised. As Irish historian Ide O'Carroll explains:

> the profile and situation of the 1980s emigrant ... young, single, but most of all highly educated [meant that] this group brought comparatively higher qualifications to fewer opportunities. For Irish women the 'push' back to the kitchens and the kettles, to babies and making bread was a severe blow, since for most of those educated through the 1960s and 1970s the promise of equality of opportunity (hard won by the feminist movement in Ireland) had been dangled at the end of a long rope of education and training. In reality they were worse off [in their new countries] than their foresisters.[13]

Yet if leaving, or worse, having to leave, can be infinitely painful, the experience of returning may be no less problematic. Once gone, forever changed, and even a returned emigrant will be an insider/outsider perched uneasily in the place called home. This is not an uncommon experience in Ireland. Poet and fiction writer Mary Dorcey, herself an emigrant who chose to return to Ireland, says that 'half the country has lived abroad', a fact that 'adds to this general game of "genuine" Irish and "lapsed" Irish.' The reasons for leaving are varied, of course, and have changed over time, although Dorcey claims that 'most Irish people get pushed out of Ireland. Because of unemployment, because of social pressure to conform, because everyone knows about you and talks about you'.[14]

The experience of community Dorcey conjures up here has both positive and negative aspects, or, perhaps more accurately, reveals the deep ambivalences that can attend a return 'home'. We find one such example in Anne Enright's *The Wig My Father Wore*, a novel that deploys a brilliant fusion of parody and irony, from what the narrator calls 'that place where grief and joy are one'. The following passage in which Enright's TV producer describes her journey out and back, evokes several of the themes I gather together in this chapter.

> I left home. At the time I thought that it was nothing to do with my father. I thought it was a political thing, because a girl has to grow up any way she can. So I went to England, a country where women didn't bury their babies in silage pits, a country where people knew the virtues of stripped pine. Exile was mainly a question of contraception and nice wallpaper .... I woke up six months later with the feeling of a hand choking me in the dark. There was no-one in the room. I was in Stoke Newington and very little of it made any sense.

This heroine, Gráinne, who sheds her ethnically marked name with its echoes of tragic mythology for a more sanguine 'Grace', returns to Ireland: 'I came home to the country where you could tell if a man was married, and if you couldn't, then you could always find out. Not that I could care less, because I was in love, whatever that meant, with a man who rang one Saturday morning and asked me to have his child. Certainly, I said. In Ireland we have babies just like that. We have them all the time.'[15]

A typology of Irish women's exilic fiction

We discover this kind of bifocal presence, of uneasy sojourning in a contested 'borderland', in many recent women-authored documents, from occasional journalism to official reports. But women's creative literature offers the richest inscriptions of these experiences, particularly fiction which positions its characters within their social contexts. In the following pages I venture a typology of recent exilic fiction by Irish women as a way of showing how broad and nuanced is the phenomenon. Listing the titles is a crucial beginning point, because so many of them remain unknown outside Ireland, and deserve a wider audience. I follow this with a closer examination of several texts in order to illustrate how much of value this particular critical lens can discover. Of course none of the books can be contained within my classifications. This typology is offered simply as a basis for further exploration and discussion. The fiction includes the work of writers from both Northern Ireland and the Republic, metropolitan and rural settings, privileged and disadvantaged backgrounds. It is, therefore, marked by a wide variety of different preoccupations, to say nothing of very different political contexts both inside and outside the texts.

The first group are the *Bildung* novels, the recounting of early child-hood and young adulthood as a centrifugal journey that leaves the protagonist poised for flight at the point of maturity. Among these, from the North, are Frances Molloy's *No Mate for the Magpie*,[16] Joan Lingard's *Sisters by Rite*,[17] Linda Anderson's *To Stay Alive*,[18] Kathleen Ferguson's *The Maid's Tale*,[19] Mary Costello's *Titanic Town*,[20] and from the South, such novels as Edna O'Brien's *A Pagan Place* and the first two volumes of her *The Country Girls* trilogy,[21] Leland Bardwell's *Girl on a Bicycle*,[22] Jane Mitchell's *Different Lives*,[23] Moya Roddy's *The Long Way Home*,[24] Aisling Maguire's *Breaking Out*.[25] I would include in this group as well Eithne Strong's *The Love Riddle*,[26] although the narrator's migration is internal to the Republic, because her particular tale of expatriation from the Irish-speaking rural west of Ireland constructs Dublin as a 'foreign' country.

Related to this category is one that includes the narrative of the adult protagonist living in another country whose story inscribes her self-exile. This richly diverse group, which in some novels ends with a final page return to Ireland, includes such examples as the third volume of Edna O'Brien's trilogy and *The High Road*,[27] Ita Daly's *Dangerous Fictions*,[28] Julia O'Faolain's *The Irish Signorina*,[29] Margaret Mulvihill's *Low Overheads*,[30] Leland Bardwell's *That London Winter*,[31] Mary Rose Callaghan's *The Awkward Girl* and *Emigrant Dreams*,[32] stories from Dolores Walshe's *Moon Mad*,[33]– all these the work of women originally from the Republic – and from the North, Deirdre Madden's *Remembering Light and Stone*,[34] Kitty Manning's *The Between People*,[35] Polly Devlin's *Dora*,[36] Linda Anderson's *Cuckoo*.[37]

A third category presents narratives of women who depart from and then return to Ireland, a process that leaves them feeling strange in, or even estranged from, their natal land. This includes stories from Evelyn Conlon's *My Head is Opening*,[38] Mary Dorcey's *A Noise from the Woodshed*,[39] Helen Lucy Burke's *A Season for Mothers*,[40] Rita Kelly's *The Whispering Arch and Other Stories*,[41] Ita Daly's *The Lady with the Red Shoes*,[42] Angela Bourke's *By Salt Water*,[43] Briege Duffaud's *Nothing Like Beirut*[44] as well as such novels as Evelyn Conlon's *Stars in the Daytime*,[45] Anne Enright's *The Wig My Father Wore*, Leland Bardwell's *There We Have Been*[46].

Another grouping includes metafictional novels of exiled women writing what can be called a 'self-begetting novel' in which we watch the protagonist writing the novel we are reading.[47] Three such novels, each exploring the necessity of self-exile and eventual return, include Clairr O'Connor's *Belonging,* Jennifer Johnston's *The Christmas Tree* and Maeve Kelly's *Florrie's Girls.*[48]

A fifth category consists of works that inscribe flights from Ireland in explicit reaction to the horrors of the political situation. Among these are Mary Leland's historical novel *The Killeen,*[49] a cross-class republican novel set in 1930s Cork; Linda Anderson's *Cuckoo* (mentioned above) in which a Belfast *Bildung* tale is embedded in a 1980s exile narrative set in London; stories such as 'Five Notes After a Visit' in Anne Devlin's *The Way-Paver,*[50] also set in 1980s Belfast; Briege Duffaud's *Wreath Upon the Dead,*[51] a metafictional recreation of 150 years of 'history' in the 'murder triangle' of Crossmaglen, Armagh; and an almost gothic Belfast republican intrigue in Kate O'Riordan's 1995 novel *Involved.*[52] This category might include as well stories of flights from Northern Ireland to the Republic in the aftermath of the 1968 'Troubles' as in Fiona Barr's 'The Wall Reader'[53] and Jennifer Johnston's *Shadows on our Skin* and *The Railway Station Man.*[54]

Yet another type of exilic writing is the fiction of the descendants of Irish emigrants for whom the meaning of Irish womanhood acts as a troubling inheritance, a project of recreation and, perhaps, of reconciliation as, for example, in Canadian Jane Urquhart's *Away,*[55] British Moy McCrory's *Bleeding Sinners*[56] and Maude Casey's *Over The Water,*[57] New Zealander Fiona Farrell's *The Skinny Louie Book.*[58]

Finally, and most heuristically, I would include as part of women's exilic literature the often horrific narratives of internal/internalized exile, the loss of a sense of integral 'self' within Ireland due to abuses in personal relationships, often reinforced or perpetuated by systemic social structures that put women at risk. These include stories of unwanted pregnancy, criminalized abortion, wife battering, verbal and physical violence, rape, incest, poverty exacerbated by gender constraints. In these writings, the authors struggle to give artistic form to radically new content; the problem they face is how to give convincing verbal form to the hitherto unspoken and unspeakable. Not surprisingly, these narratives are often the subjects of short stories, although whole novels have also been devoted to them. The list here could be very long but would include such works as Leland Bardwell's 'The Dove of Peace';[59] Emma Cooke's *Wedlocked,*[60] Harriet O'Carroll's 'The Day of the Christening';[61] Maeve Kelly's 'Orange Horses',[62] Jennifer Johnston's *The*

Invisible Worm,[63] Frances Molloy's *Women Are the Scourge of the Earth,*[64] Éilís Ní Dhuibhne's 'Midwife to the Fairies',[65] Dorothy Nelson's *In Night's City* and *Tar and Feathers,*[66] Lia Mills's *Another Alice,*[67] Edna O'Brien's *Down By the River.*[68]

Ideology of gender

In all these categories, the narratives reveal the many ways in which women's (and men's) lives are shaped by an ideology of gender that ascribes to women the position of subordinate, an ideology that shapes and limits women's possibilities in Ireland or abroad, no matter how skillfully and successfully many strong women subvert the control in their private or public lives. All of these narratives have inscribed the experiences of exile, yet to none of these writers would Richard Kearney's phrase 'migrant minds' – his term for Paul Hewson (Bono), Paul Durcan, Neil Jordan and Robert Ballagh – be appropriate as a description for women's emigration/exile stories.[69] While the term 'migrant mind' seems a curiously disembodied evocation even for men's cultural explorations, it is impossible to think of it as adequate to the trajectories of women. To state the obvious, which almost never appears in male-authored texts but is ubiquitous in the female-generated ones listed above, women ignore the 'realities' of the female body at their peril, which is not, of course, to suggest that they are determined entirely by and in those constructions.

Grace Neville, in her study of oral histories referred to above, points out how early-twentieth-century Irish male informants interpreted women's departures according to the 'dowry theory of emigration' (p. 286). According to this theory, 'Women are depicted largely as one-dimensional characters with just one aim in life: to get married locally, i.e., to someone not unlike the informant or collector.' This view, she asserts, is 'reassuring to men: it confirms their image of themselves as the center of the universe, their view of single women as incomplete beings seeking through marriage and pocketfuls of dollars to buy their way in from the margins.' The dowry theory puts men 'effortlessly on a pedestal,' a view preferable to the 'alternative suggestion that the woman's decision had nothing to do with men in general or with them in particular or, worse still, that it had ...' (pp. 285–86). This final acerbic comment speaks volumes, and while late-twentieth-century women emigrants have many reasons other than profitable marriage as their goal, it would be true to say that at the center of many of their published stories is some troubling fact of life associated with marital, sexual or reproductive experience. This is to say that they leave Ireland as women, and sometimes *because* they're women.

But the women writers also face the added hurdle of being the 'other' to that normative Irish male artist, of struggling to create new areas of artistic expression in a culture that prides itself on already having achieved a superior form of (male) literature, designated as the generic Irish. Evelyn Conlon puts the point trenchantly in a *Graph* article: 'I sometimes wonder if any of these men ever blush, even in private. Some of us are still reeling from a collection called *The Irish Mind*. The Irish Mind my ------- ---- we say in private. Thirteen essays by men about men, one essay by Elizabeth Cullingford on W.B. Yeats. Perhaps indeed a true reflection of the Irish male mind.'[70]

This statement poses the dilemma many Irish women artists have spoken about. As we shall see, relocation to another country does not necessarily solve any of these problems. What is demanded is an even more taxing struggle; recreation of the 'self' in terms that refuse cultural and internalized misogyny. For this task, women need different stories, different forms of representation. 'Representation' here does not mean some reflection of a transparent reality; instead it refers to what British critic Stuart Hall, theorizing from a racialized position, describes as 'the task of constituting "identity" not outside but within representation … not as a second-hand mirror held up to reflect what already exists, but as that form of representation which is able to constitute us as new kinds of subjects, and thereby enable us to discover places from which to speak'.[71]

In the following pages I examine specific examples of such artistic 'reconstitution'. The first set of texts comprise tales of leaving home, the second, of returning. All are remarkable for the ways authors struggle to create a form adequate to the experiences of loss and recreation.

Leaving home

While it is unwise to construct hierarchies of pain, it would be difficult to find bleaker accounts of exile than the *Bildung* novels that take us through the early lives of girls trapped in poverty, sectarian violence, blinkered orthodoxy, dead-end possibilities, or abusive families to a moment of exile that is coterminous with the end of the novel. To be sure, this bleakness sometimes reveals the experience of impotence endemic to childhood. Important Irish versions of this occur in Clare Boylan's brilliant comic novels *Holy Pictures* and *Home Rule*.[72] Here we discover versions of family life in which the parents perform antic contortions to protect their secrets; their behaviour creates, from generation to generation, a sense of bewilderment and betrayal in their children who are unable to fathom the cultural oddities, dysfunctional behaviours, and deliberate lies of their parents. These two novels, carefully researched from documents such as newspapers and advertising copy that reveal the preoccupations of daily life, offer an eccentric slice of Dublin social history from 1893 to 1925. But while the main female characters of these novels move in, out and about in Ireland and England, they do not finally choose exile. The girls may be abused but achieve quirky buoyancy, as Boylan's comic treatment – a 'wild rampage, sternly managed' – resolutely deflects any sense of the tragic.[73]

In other works by Irish women, the helplessness of childhood is far more ominous, a claustrophobic entrapment that is the fate of those too young to live independently of their 'protectors.' The fact that those adults who abuse are themselves often at risk in the larger society does little to lessen the pain of the children; if anything, the impotence of cruel adults adds to the pain of the children who see little to encourage them in their own push toward independent adulthood. This kind of impasse is at the desperate heart of both Dorothy Nelson's novels, *In Night's City* and *Tar and Feathers*. The secrets here are as evil as anything in Irish literature, including incest, brutal sexual abuse, wife battering, assault, and actual murder. So intimate and pervasive is the evil that the reader could hardly stand a frontal view. Nelson makes possible the reader's approach by creating a veiled, experimental style as code one must break. *In Night's City* opens with the abuse of a three-year-old girl: '"I see your colours, Daddy," I said. "I see them." He laughed down an' all the colours grew bright an' came runnin' down his face' (p. 7). The rest of the book inscribes the experience of exile from one's own being, as the abused central girl breaks into a schizophrenic doubled persona who suffers incest in one 'life' but flies away from it in another. The experimental form created by Nelson for this experience is, in my estimation, the most successful 'version' of incest in a growing body of incest narratives in the English language. Only Edna O'Brien's *Down By the River* and Leland Bardwell's 'The Dove of Peace' in her collection *Different Kinds of Love* approach its frightful power. Other Irish incest narratives, like Jennifer Johnston's *The Invisible Worm* or Lia Mills's *Another Alice*, come at this subject via adult narrators (re)membering their early lives, an angle that has the merciful effect of distancing the intensity of the experience as it focuses instead on the possibility of 'cure'.[74]

Readers find the reading of such emotions difficult, yet it is a certain fact that the *Bildungsroman* genre exerts a perennial fascination for readers. When the reader is a woman, and the protagonist a girl, a whole different set of expectations and concerns come into play from those at work in a male *Bildungsroman*, as the traditional mainstream cultural expectations for women are so different, ideas of 'success' so curtailed. A husband? A home? Motherhood? 'Women's' work? So the woman reader reads with pleasure and fear as she watches the protagonist navigate multiple levels of danger and hope. Those works that end at the beginning, so to speak, with the girl-woman alone and leaving the world of her childhood, offer particular challenges for an author, who must find a way to create a sense of coherent 'character' while ensuring that the 'character' remains unfinished and frangible. The three novels discussed below all create this kind of paradoxical balance. In each work, the leaving signifies a kind of rueful victory.

Frances Molloy's *No Mate for the Magpie,* Leland Bardwell's *Girl on a Bicycle,* and Eithne Strong's *The Love Riddle* create young women still under 20 years old at the end of their books. Each of the heroines emerges from the pages as remarkable and highly memorable, even though each is being created in a narrative form that resolutely ruptures any sense of a unified or autonomous subjectivity in the young protagonist. Beyond these similarities, we find few resemblances among the three novels.

Frances Molloy, born in 1947 to a poor Catholic family in Derry, published just one novel and a few short stories before her tragic early death from a stroke in 1991. Her novel, set in the 1950s and 1960s of her own youth, ends climactically at the time of the civil rights explosion in the North. It is, at a literal level, the bleakest of tales, in which caste-created poverty, religious intolerance, and civil injustice combine to ruin the hopes and material possibilities of its heroine. But the novel does not admit the literal or the 'realistic', choosing instead a comic form of satire. Molloy writes in a northern dialect speech whose extraordinary oral vitality and precision were celebrated in 1992 when the famed Druid Theater of Galway presented a dramatic presentation of the novel.

What the reader 'hears' throughout is the voice of the apparently guileless but all observant Ann Elizabeth McGlone whose first-person narration sweeps up lives and voices into her own story which thus becomes emblematic of many others. Born, like her author, to a poor, working-class Derry family, Ann Elizabeth gets off to a bad start and never recovers: 'Way a wee screwed up protestant face an' a head of black hair a was born in a state of original sin. Me ma didn't like me, but who's to blame the poor woman, sure a didn't look like a catholic wain atall' (p. 1). In this breezy satiric style, Molloy charts the growth of her Catholic wain, who may look like a Protestant, and indeed has a Protestant grandmother, but has none of the social benefits that this affiliation might bring in the North. Class deprivation is exacerbated by gender discrimination: 'It was discovered early on that a had a natural aptitude for washin' dishes, cleanin', cookin', nursin' an' changin' nappies so a wasn't sent to school at the usual age' (p. 9).

Using episodic vignettes that illustrate a wide range of social situations and political assessments, the narrative propels Ann Elizabeth through Catholic and Protestant sectors in the North, humorously noting the perfidy and (occasional) generosity of both, whether they be in a Catholic school, a republican jail, a Catholic council house development, a Protestant factory or butcher's shop, a Catholic convent, a mental institution, or a parish rectory, her last job in the North before she joins the Belfast civil rights movement of 1968. Here Molloy, playing with the political rhetoric of the movement in which northern Catholics are described as 'second-class citizens', pushes the satire to its limit:

> Well, when this news broke, a lot of ordinary people were surprised te learn that they had been citizens all their lives, an' not only citizens, but second-class citizens too at that. My God, they were sayin' te wan another, te think that all this time we have been only wan step down from the tap an' didn't know it. They were delighted so they took te the streets in their droves, an' a went way them (p. 127).

After being viciously beaten by the police during a supposedly peaceful demonstration – a fictional reenactment of the People's Democracy march from Belfast to Derry in 1969 – she spends weeks in bed recovering. With characteristic gallows humour she describes her recovery in a way that limns both police brutality and her own dead-end possibilities in a war-torn, caste-riven society:

> A stayed in bed for a wheen of weeks an' wheniver a got up a started to prepare mesel' for the future be practisin' some basic skills that a thought might come in useful if iver a went te look for work again like, combin' me hair, moving me head from side to side slowly, an' noddin' it up and down a bit, sittin' down an' risin' up from a chair without bein' helped, puttin' on me own clothes, tyin' me shoes,

walkin'. After a was satisfied that a'd acquired sufficient skills, a set out again in search of work, but a decided not to go back to Belfast, as it was clear for all te see that me an' Belfast weren't made for each other so a allowed that a would give Dublin a try instead (p. 139).

Dublin turns out to be no better; months of unemployment end in imprisonment when she enters an anti-American Vietnam war protest. In the final paragraph of the novel, Ann Elizabeth sets about leaving Ireland, but she does so with little education and few skills other than her wits. These material limitations set her a long way from the preparation for exile provided for that more famous fictional exile Stephen Dedalus, whose author Ann Elizabeth conjures up in the final paragraph of the book as she looks outward, looks back, the exile's fate. Unlike James Joyce's Anna Livia with its (literary) circular return, Molloy's river offers a one-way passage: 'A could see "Anna Livia" movin' beneath me, resolutely, determinedly, headin' outa Ireland, an' a knew then that a too must do the same an' go to a place where life resembled life more than it did here, but that like "Anna Livia" my mind would never quite escape the compellin' god-forsaken shores of my fool-driven land' (p. 170).

Molloy's satiric mode is unique in the literature of Northern Irish women. Writers such as Joan Lingard, Anne Devlin, Mary Beckett, Linda Anderson, Kathleen Ferguson, Deirdre Madden, Fiona Barr, Janet McNeill, Barbara Haycock Walsh, Stella Mahon, Una Woods, and Brenda Murphy invent styles that experiment with forms of traditional realism in their depictions of northern life and its effects on women.[75] But if Molloy's work is unusual in the context of Northern Irish writing, her choice of genre puts her in the company of many postcolonial writers – although a poor, northern Catholic writer may not have reached the 'post' of postcolonial. Like those other ironists, she chooses satire as a subversive tool to rethink and rearticulate her history. As Canadian critic Linda Hutcheon points out, this kind of doubling-talking, forked-tongue address is a 'rhetorical strategy for working within existing discourses and contesting them at the same time'. Irony's doubling, she argues, offers a 'complicitous critique', inevitable when one is working within a postcolonial 'doubled identity and history'.[76] Ann Elizabeth may have sailed out of Ireland, but her author, who also left for England at that age, may not have succeeded so well in her escape. Molloy is eulogized thus by Irish writer Tom Morgan: 'We take our baggage with us always and everywhere. I don't know what hell [Frances Molloy] inhabited but her work is alive and humorous, brighter colours informing the grays round the edges.'[77] The brighter colours may need to be taken on faith here. In my reading, Molloy's satire resembles the neutron bomb. It may level the inhabitants of the fictionalized Irish institutions she has laboured to construct, but the novel's ending and the need for exile make it clear that the institutions remain standing, ready for rehabilitation.

The pain of the struggle against/within this situation, even though deflected by the hilarity of the satire, remains the palpable achievement of this work. Despite the prestige of its Virago publication, it is a work too little known outside Ireland. Ruth Carr, herself a poet and editor from the North, claims Molloy as 'Sister' in an elegy that calls this novel the 'touchstone book'. This elegy, included by editor Victor Luftig within a collection of other tributes paid to Molloy by Irish writers, may illustrate the respect she earned among her peers, but Evelyn Conlon, one of those writers, complains that literary reviews in Ireland were 'lamentably unforthcoming ... in informing us of her work while she was alive' (p. 39).

The next two books I turn to are also very little known outside Ireland, although their authors, Eithne Strong, born in 1921 and Leland Bardwell in 1928, have distinguished reputations in the Republic where they were born and continue to publish. Both mothers of large families – Bardwell has six children, Strong nine, the youngest mentally disabled – they nevertheless have managed prodigious literary outputs. Both are primarily poets, with Strong writing in both Irish and English, but both have also written several books of fiction, Bardwell a good deal of drama. Both have also enabled others' writing, for example, by co-founding poetry journals in Ireland: Bardwell, the journal *Cyphers* in 1975, Strong, the Runa Press in 1943.[78]

Leland Bardwell's *Girl on a Bicycle*, published by The Irish Writers' Co-operative in 1977, is now out of print and cries for reissue. Set in the early 1940s, it offers a protagonist unlike any other in Irish literature or in women's literature, and has a superb style almost minimalist in its poetic economy. Unlike Molloy's rollicking tone, *Girl*'s is intensely serious, with a clear-eyed, politically astute but maniacally reckless young protagonist, and a narrative tone that gives away none of the intensity with deflecting humour. Where Molloy's novel self-consciously crosses Irish political borders as a way of showing how similar are the injustices of cross-cultural 'differences', Leland Bardwell's *Girl on a Bicycle* uses the idea of liminality as its central trope. Perched, yet in motion, a figure on a bicycle, running from what seems a no-home, to an unnamed and uncertain future, Julie de Vraie, aged 18 for most of the novel, suffers from more than Edna O'Brien's 'agitation to go'. Julie 'bowls along', 'buckets', 'flies' head-long through various border 'states', straddling several worlds, belonging to none. One of her characteristic stances, in fact, is looking in through windows or doors, to rooms she has some claim to inhabit but for various compelling reasons cannot enter. In this condition, movement is crucial. As Julie reflects after resisting a temptation to suicide late in the novel, '... if God exists, he is surely two wheels and a rickety frame; my only friend!' (p. 132)

This kind of frantic self-propulsion speaks of the infinite longing of a gifted and dislocated girl, one who cannot and will not 'fit' in what is presented as the repressive and philistine Protestant Anglo-Irish society of the 1940s. Worse, she chooses to live as a young man of her age might – hitting the road ('And on a boy's bike, too'), earning her living as a groom, questioning authority relentlessly, drinking heavily, having sexual relations, refusing the social and religious mores of her class and gender (p. 91). Julie is trying to live in the wrong life and the wrong literary genre; a half century ago the picaresque novel still belonged to men. Her choices cost, of course, and her behaviour appears at first reading merely self-annihilating. But to refuse the risks would kill just as certainly. What we find in this novel are the lineaments of a life that cannot – no matter how imperative the requirements – approach the ordinary. Young Julie, in refusing to obey class and gender rules, is radically exposed to horri-fying dangers, among them sexual predation at every turn from men who assume she must be universally available because she is so hungry for intense experience. As Julie says, opening hotel doors on the sleeping bodies of 'pretty boys and girls' from Dublin: 'These bodies make no mistakes. They sleep in organized fashion, their beds paid for in advance. They never sleep in their clothes or do anything that might cost them something afterwards. Caution. Sensible caution displayed while they nevertheless enjoy themselves. How do they do it?' (pp. 158, 160).

Like her creator who was a member of the distinguished Hone family, Julie de Vraie was born into a wealthy Protestant family in the Republic.[79] A rich, horsy life notwithstanding, Julie's childhood life is so appalling that it is sketched and buried in fewer than 100 lines in Chapter 1 of the novel. Unloving, unreasonable parents, a beautiful older sister ('huntress, dancer, Artemis', p. 12) who overshadows and controls her, no chance for further study, and no way to escape the

Republic during World War II, Julie manages to find temporary employment as a groom for the Earl of Girvan, symbol of all that is awful and desiccated in a dying but still privileged Anglo-Irish aristocracy. His estate, in a fictionalized version of the border county of Cavan,[80] occupies a thousand acres in a 'county of unqualified hostility', with 'its lumpy hills, scanty farms, small squares of fields, awful with poverty, lean, stony, uncultivated' (pp. 77, 35). The world within that county, as in Dublin, that is available to Julie is of the Protestant minority, who whether rich or poor, are locked into a regimentation meant to ensure their survival in the Catholic Republic. But Julie's choice of friend among the servants is Catholic Nellie, servant to the servants, a woman Julie tries to protect in a break with caste privilege and a concern for class justice that earns her nothing but scorn and anger among the other servants.

When Julie first arrives in the land of Girvan, she still inhabits a green world of innocence, roaming the roads on her bicycle, eager for experience. 'The gaps in the hedges flashed past. Dark and light. Light and dark. Blackthorn, blackthorn and more blackthorn. Beasts lumbered in the fields. The corncrake rapped out its message. Crr. Crr. Like an unanswered telephone' (p. 35). But she wants someone to answer, and one of the first, and only suitable, interlocutors she connects with is the Earl's elderly spinster sister, Miss Emily. She, however, is virtually incarcerated in a crumbling domicile on her brother's estate, watched over by a nurse for the mentally disturbed. In Miss Emily, Julie finds a friend and kindred spirit, but Miss Emily is not allowed out and her forays into freedom are considered proof of her madness: '"I had to fetch her in once. Dripping wet," [says May, the nurse, to Julie.] "Stayed out in the rain all night." I stopped laughing, I looked beyond May, beyond the small Sheraton desk which contained Emily's [horticultural] notes, beyond the window and the tall yellowing grass and all the sunny centres between trees and shrubs and I saw a tall woman walking. In the dark. In the rain' (p. 32).

Emily's home has its own version of a green world, the greenhouses where she tends her orchids, but it is a claustrophobic jungle that stifles Julie. Emily had once struck out for freedom as Julie does. As a young woman she had spent four years in South American deserts, indulging her passion for 'grubbing around for strange growths'. When she and her male guide and fellow horticulturist disappeared into the Chilean hinterland, she was pursued and apprehended by alarmed Irish relatives. 'I went into the desert. Yes. I had a great piece of luck. Yes.... But it didn't work. I didn't go far enough' (p. 35). These words Julie attends to, especially when Emily, worn out and despairing, finally hangs herself in her greenhouse.

Julie is devastated, in part because she had been so powerless to help the other woman escape. But Julie's helplessness finds a parallel in her doomed attempt to shield poor Nellie from the abuse or neglect of everyone above her, including all the servants whose lack of any *useful* sense of class consciousness divides them terminally from the clairvoyantly aware Julie. Emily and Nellie – 'two prisons; the one surrounded by cold gentility, trees and winds, the other by hurrying brutality, bare boards, cracked porcelain sluices.... No difference really' (p. 149). The novel ends with Julie, after another disastrous copulation, pissing in a toilet, hoping thereby to prevent a pregnancy. The narrative voice, which has shifted between third and first person speech throughout the novel, asks here: 'Who is this person, shivering on the porcelain, sitting there with her elbows on her knees? What is she doing?' The non-answer comes in a new second person imperative as Julie talks to herself: 'You must pedal hard now. No loitering. Hurry up. Faster, faster ... Do you hear the corncrake?'[81]

If Bardwell's heroine has no one to answer her and nowhere to go but England,[82] Eithne Strong's heroine has an intellectual companion and lover to whom she talks throughout *The Love Riddle.* Set, like *Girl on a Bicycle,* in 1942, this novel offers Una Normile, Julie's contemporary, choosing her own version of flight, and figuring out how best to build a nest. The core of the novel takes shape as an extended eight-month 'conversation' she has with the 30-year-old, upper-class English Protestant, Nelson Forterre, who in the course of the novel becomes her friend, then lover, finally husband. Unlike the first person narration of Molloy's *Magpie* with its wild address to an audience in need of its didactic possibilities, the narration of Strong's *Riddle* moves between the first-person conversations of Una and Nelson, and the third person biography each constructs for the other. The reader is allowed to eavesdrop from outside the magic circle of this confederacy. Instead of the apparently breezy satire of Molloy or the pared-down, evocative language of Bardwell, we find in Strong's novel a compacted, mannered precision of language that labours to find the expression of an ethic worthy of directing what will be Una and Nelson's shared life. The ethic they struggle to create is one that will refuse many of the orthodoxies of their childhood training.

Although the dialogue is structured as a conversation, it is the conversation of therapy which the two lovers use for mutual knowing and their own self-analysis. Sharing the significant 'bits and pieces' of their young lives, they 'make pictures', fit the pieces into a 'jigsaw'.[83] Unlike most novels, the conversation here is the primary text, its progress the 'meaning' of the novel. But the linearity of the primary text, what narratologists would call the *fabula*,[84] parallels another series of events, an embedded text which in this novel appears in disconnected fragments with no closure, the reader needing to do her own sympathetic listening and piecing. 'Come on' urges Nelson, 'paint me pictures.' 'Well, we can both paint, can't we?' (p. 22), replies Una. And they do. So, for example, when Nelson asks, 'Your father, tell me about him' Una's response is that 'Any telling about him will have to have mixed in other people: my mother, and certainly more about Jack – Jack, of enormous importance to my parents, the first-born, the boy, you see – he's the one who, taken for granted, is now getting the university course. Mind you, I don't grudge that but I'd make better use of it' (p. 21). What follows such an exchange is a conventionally constructed third-person omniscient passage in which the father is created, but also the mother, the brother Jack, Maggie the 'girl', neighbours, friends, and strangers. In other words, Strong's narrative strategy seems designed to show how lives are created within relationships, then endowed with meaning through interpretation in conversation – the latter exercise being the significant achievement, and the interest of this narrative structure.

While both the speakers employ a self-reflective tone, it is Una's struggle that is paramount in the text where she is cast as the learner to the much older Nelson. Yet he too is a student, apprenticing to the psychoanalyst, Penn Reade.[85] Together Una and Nelson set themselves the task of understanding the meanings of love offered by Reade: 'love is sustained volition and action, willing the good, carrying it out' (p. 13). Cast in this light, love is not just personal connection between people but a form of social healing that 'concerned itself with all people, not just lovers, with the nature of jealousy, with murderous rages, the urge to kill, how to confront and contain these titanic forces in the self, how to transform into constructive ways the energy that otherwise meant flooding blood and destruction. It had to do with giving' (p. 251). These pronouncements have immense power for the young people, struggling to make decent lives and a new society amidst the horror of World War II at Ireland's doorstep. What the lovers explore, in the community of Reade's circle, are experimental ways of living and loving which fly in the face of traditional Irish (and English) behaviour, but which promise a hope of transformative social relations.[86] On one level, the novel contains an extended analysis of ideas. How does such a gnarled offering succeed as a novel?

Surprisingly well, in fact, because of Strong's ability to make stories; because of the interest of Una's struggle, epic in her time; and finally because of the intelligence of the examination of the 'love riddle'. The nub of the riddle for the young Una lies in her erotic/intellectual desire for the urbane Nelson and a life of 'unfettered' exploration; this desire her family and church construct as perverse and forbidden, a conflict that forces her to choose between the life he offers and the deep, emotional love she has for her family and for the rural, Irish-speaking land of her youth. The spectrum of colours she paints for Nelson covers the breadth of Ireland, but always, at the centre of the story, is the daring, deeply ethical Una struggling to transcend a constrained, censored girlhood. 'I've seen you rushing against the wind,' says Nelson to Una, 'a wild thing – that's how you are really.' To which she answers, 'The flesh is a hellish vileness – that is what I've been made to feel as long as I remember. I have told you about it all. With my head I know it is false but it's as if I have been frozen up against this hellishness' (p. 194).

The burden of this Jansenist Catholic heritage notwithstanding, Una manages to go 'many places now, accountable only to herself. A huge appetite for doing. For knowing' (p. 98). It is her infectious daring that we witness and in which we see the possibilities for a changed Ireland. Pioneering a new kind of sexual morality, Una (and her author) are decades ahead of her time. Yet, rebellious as Una is, she is intent to sift out the good of her past, to use it to make a new shape for living. She brings to the task many skills, one of which is the ability to be silent and alone, another, the belief that one must have a 'vocation'; thus, her growing up amounted to what she succinctly calls 'deep times' (p. 134), But the road to that self-making requires flight from the west and her family when they attempt to imprison her in their home, a bicycle journey, across the width of Ireland with a punctured tire, from Co. Limerick to Dublin. That journey carried her from her home, Catholicism, her childhood, into the experimental world of erotic love and intellectual exploration, so many bridges burned, another 'country' to be created.

The conquering of the self-hatred involved in denying the body is not one achieved in this novel. Judging from Eithne Strong's subsequent writings, both poetic and fictional, that task requires a lifetime. In 1980 she published a long poem entitled *Flesh, the Greatest Sin*, in which a narrative parallel to this novel figures the same struggle. Strong's poem and novel, both autobiographical,[87] together form an extraordinary record of one way of remaking an Irish legacy without having to jettison those things of value.

There is no doubt that in the writing of Irish literary history, the work of these three women should be seen as very significant. Eithne Strong says accurately that 'I may have been the first Irish woman poet to confront certain themes pertaining to women's situation. I think ... I have a place in the transition of English written by women in Ireland from the 40s on.'[88] I would make the same claims for the fiction of Bardwell, Strong and Molloy. They offer astonishing fictional worlds of danger and daring, of passionate work in truth-telling. These writers may have left 'home', but their form of leaving is a precious gift to those never left behind.

Writing 'home'

The fiction that takes its heroines off to a new land only to send them back again offers particularly rich possibilities for exploring the meanings of exile because both the homeland and the destination are put under intense comparative scrutiny. The meanings and relative values of 'home' become the focus, the decisions made and unmade, the obsession. When a character has the possibility of choice, the necessity of choice can be paralyzing – or liberating. The two writers whose works I examine in this section, Evelyn Conlon and Mary Dorcey, are both writers who declare themselves to be feminists and are thus particularly attentive to the political aspects of women's personal experience. Both left Ireland for extended periods of time, both have resettled in Ireland and are engaged in the struggle to create what Dorcey calls 'this second Ireland ... which up to now has been silenced by emigration'.[89] They also write of the experience of exile in the foreign place that is never home. Furthermore, both experiment with form, using highly self-conscious narrative strategies. Their narrative forms delineate personal experience intersecting with public structures that affect (and effect) the personal. The result is a discourse that is both public and private, as it shifts our attention from one process of structuration to another which, like a gestalt experiment, can be 'read' two ways.

Both Conlon and Dorcey were founding members of Irishwomen United, the second organized feminist group in Ireland, formed in 1975; this means that both are very visible feminists in a society that, even two decades later, still distrusts such a political orientation. In fact, Mary Dorcey, an 'out' lesbian writer in a society where (male) homosexuality has only been decriminalized as of 1993, says that

> just the label 'feminist' on its own may threaten as much as the label 'lesbian'. I think many women writers in Ireland have deep fear within this virulently misogynistic literary culture of being considered feminist writers or of being seen to identify in any political way with their own sex (p. 21).

Both of these writers put women's sexuality at the center of their work, Dorcey lesbianism, Conlon autonomous female heterosexuality. With these overdetermined subjects, both authors foreground the reasons why women have particular feelings of alienation in their own country where, as Dorcey puts it, 'the Catholic Church puts the full weight of its authority and political genius into the repression and control of women's sexuality' (p. 21).

In a short story entitled 'Home – What Home?', (*My Head is Opening*) Conlon inscribes the experience of needing to leave, needing to return. Two years into her sojourn in Australia we hear the protagonist Ellen thinking about why she had left Ireland:[90]

> She had been reared in that house with three symmetrical eyes looking out on the small hills. There was nowhere else to look. They were in the way of other visions. They were all right in themselves, but if she could just move them back a little from the front door her expanse of view could be better. Yes they were much too near the window. She had spent her teenage years reading books and looking for men, boys. There was nothing else to do (p. 96).

The wavering, homogenizing drift of her musing shifts to observations of the social snobbery endemic in the island, memories of hated neighbors' faces. But then it finally includes as well comfortable memories that the narrator adroitly subverts in the final sentence here: 'But still there was something to be said for home. She knew the fields. Every hedge of them. Every tree that stood to give shelter. Every voluptuous hedge that could hide and seat two adults and six children during the haymaking showers. They would still be the same. Or so she thought' (p. 97).

Departure from her 'wet gray' island brings her into the company of other Irish emigrants in Australia who 'had come to make new lives, new money [but also those, like herself] who had secret passions for self-communion, [who] had chosen red dust, bindies and startling heat as their life surroundings rather than softer familiar places.' As a tour guide she can luxuriate in continual movement, satisfying her 'agitation to go'. But as Ellen learns the secrets of the Australian landscape, she also studies the human history of racist colonization which she, unwillingly, enables with her presence and knowledge. Political awareness informs her every experience; although an alien in a strange country, she does not pretend that she can elude its political complicities. With such engagement, self-imposed exile is not a leap into freedom, but a prison of its own, like the Wentworth Prison, a stop on her tour, where nineteenth-century Irish prisoners had first to make the bricks, then to stack them into the building that finally held them captive. Reconnecting 'with a former self', she recalls the rejected landscape of her youth, but this time her imagination lifts the focus above the hills to the evening skies

> stretching forever ... Would a different job help? No. Ellen would have to go home. Adam did not understand. Hadn't he been good to her? He wasn't impotent any more? What did she want? Ellen took off her halter top and the sticker 'Make love not babies' from the back of her trousers and went home (pp. 104–5).

The words 'went home' close the story, although its title 'Home – What Home?' destabilizes the closure of the final sentence. But Conlon's novel *Stars in the Daytime* takes another female voyager with 'an agitation to go' beyond the ending, delivering her, pregnant, back to Ireland. It is not a felicitous reentry:

> The telling was a long bad day that wouldn't end with waking up. A day which had to do exclusively with that special contradiction – menless mothers – telling them at home. Have you told them at home yet? About whatever.... And Rose kneeling down before their venom, falling with them at their horror, weakened by the unrelentlessness of their rage. God could never have thought sex such a sin – Nothing a man could do would ever be such a sin – murder was not even as dirty. What came out was bile. The sick of catholicism, the vomit of the religion of unmarried men, the fear of the religion of all men. She left, covered in spew and blood (pp. 154–5).

Such an experience is not an unusual one in contemporary Irish women's fiction, but Rose's use of it may be. The novel ends five years after the scene above, when Rose and her son have survived and made a life in Ireland. The life is still problematic but usefully so:

> [Rose] was outside, where she had always been most comfortable. It was a good thing to have had a child ... She had come to learn that having him had indeed been a form of escapism, but then it is gaolers who most despise escapism. The form of escapism was her valid ticket into a twilight view of mankind (p. 168).

Achieving a twilight view of mankind, with all the ironies implicit therein, may be an achievement in Conlon's fiction, but is one that ensures a continuing sense of unease at 'home – what home'. Turning from Conlon's (outlaw) heterosexual world to Dorcey's lesbian territory the reader and author face an even more radical challenge to 'home'.

In Mary Dorcey's short story 'Nights Underground', (*A Noise From the Woodshed*) the reader meets a group of women who have made the break from the confinements of Ireland, yet what Dorcey chooses to inscribe is not their sense of liberation but their experience of stalemate.[91] The author moves her Irish émigrées into the underworld of the London tube for a Civil Defence exercise where they wait out the night cheek by jowl with other Londoners. At one point, having just encountered yet another instance of anti-Irish racism, a character named Juno wishes she were back in Dublin. Her friend and ex-lover Aoife scorns such sentimentality about Dublin, claiming that the absence of racism in Ireland just signifies the absence of the occasion, with so few minority people. 'Yes, dear old Dublin – not much chance of racism there. Who have we got to threaten us, after all?.... a couple of hundred Jews, some Indians at the College of Surgeons and a handful of Italian ice-cream families!' (p. 189). Notwithstanding this dismissal of Dublin, both women talk about returning – without doing it, endlessly criticizing England yet dug in deeper every year. In an interior monologue notable for its creation of dialogic experience, Aoife thinks about return:

> You came over here to make a living, to escape the neighbours and the Catholic Church and then, before you knew it, you had become an emigrant – crying into your pint and singing 'Comeallye'. But you couldn't go back. When you went for a visit you felt like a foreigner – the place seemed so small; a parody of itself – or was it that you grew too rigid for its inquisitive, garrulous ways? Aoife had seen it happen to so many – half her friends were living in London

or the States, talking of going back when they had enough money or the right skills or whatever. She and Barbara had come for the summer – four years ago! And Juno and Zoe too. Zoe had moved on, but to Paris, not home. And now that her mother had died she'd probably never return. Would any of them, come to think of it, even manage the annual Christmas pilgrimage, if not for mothers anxiously waiting?[92]

In the purgatorial state of exile from Ireland, from family and from her lover, Juno finds no psychopomp to lead her into a different realm. She vainly searches the underground world throughout the night for another former lover Zoe only to discover as morning returns that Zoe had been arrested during the night for resisting police harassment.

This personal state of exile is set against, and needs to be read as, a correlative representation of the global exile experienced by the Londoners who inhabit the underworld with Juno and Aoife, preparing for a collective and ultimately futile gesture of escape from the man-made disaster of nuclear war whose perceived imminence is the cause of the citywide exercise. In this story, the whole world is in exile and the only buttress against despair is friendship, community and political action of a separatist, and very fragile, nature.

In another story, 'Introducing Nessa', (*A Noise From the Woodshed*) the protagonist Anna has made the difficult break from her adopted country, Canada and has returned to Ireland. She has left behind a husband and, on her return, becomes a closeted lesbian. The vague sense of alienation inscribed above takes a much more precise feminist focus:

It was a shock coming back [to Ireland] after five years of married life in Canada. I had forgotten how women were treated here: the patronage and contempt that were part of daily life, how the smallest social exchange could become a set battle. It infuriated me to have half grown boys call me 'dear' and 'love'; to tolerate the gauntlet of innuendo and abuse one had to run ordering a drink in a pub or simply walking down a city street. I had forgotten all this. I had not realized that I could be made to feel a schoolgirl again because I had taken a ring from my finger (p. 135).

Mary Dorcey's fiction, radically separated from the heterocentric world of all the works cited in this essay, is in places much more hopeful than most. If Conlon's characters, for example, seem marooned on a desert island, and Edna O'Brien's 'you' is desperate to escape the island, Dorcey's lesbians, at least in one utopian journey, cross over the river of 'normalcy' to reach a lush island of erotic and creative freedom. The following passage from the title story of *A Noise from the Woodshed* combines in one onrushing torrent the ecstasy of sexual communion and female friendship with a litany of the struggles and dangers that make the island of exile within Ireland into a challenging but desirable new center:

> So that day, when she came along, it was almost too late for you. When she swept you up in the nick of time, and carried you over the waters, and laid you down in long grasses, and committed love with you, and staggered home drunken and laughing, shouting for joy and just for the sake of it, and did not stagger out again for days, being so busy, preoccupied with bodily surfaces and passages, and all that talking to be gone through – that day was no commonplace day – rest assured. If it were, even you out there in the wilderness would have heard by now.... She had come like a woman, a savior, in a white hatchback and saved you from doubt, tired eyes and wet feet, set fire to your loins and carried you off, coming for you as you had for so many in the past, come as so many have come for you and each other; women wandering highways and byways, saving the whales and the clinics, coming upon each other and lending a helping hand, or foot, or breast or mouth or whatever seems most useful at the time, snatching each other from boredom and flood in mountains and lakes and housing estates, from lies and inertia, from getting on and keeping up, from bearing up and saving face (pp. 9–10).

The 'you' addressed here is the woman writer who tells the story; it could also be the reader invited to recognize the possibilities in the lesbian island and the utopian genre, to join in the creative work of rebuilding the battered self and world.[93] What is remarkable about the story is the assumption that women's creativity can be fostered within Ireland, that marginality need not be exile. As Dorcey said in a 1995 interview:

> I want to be one of the first generation to say 'We are different. We dissent from the consensus. But we are staying here'.... I have a dream of Ireland in which all the troublemakers have come home to roost. But for that to happen some of us have to refuse to leave. To make a roost for others to return to. I think this is now happening.[94]

We find in contemporary writing a good deal of evidence that Dorcey's hope is becoming a reality. But, as we have seen, not all Irish women writing of the creative process are so sanguine. Although Irish novelist John McGahern may be right that younger writers (like Mary Dorcey) need no longer leave the formerly censorious Ireland, we still discover in many contemporary texts the attitude of Edna O'Brien's 'you' with her agitation to go and her unalterable sense of loss in the leaving.[95] At the end of *Mother Ireland* O'Brien names both the power and the defeat of exile: 'But I had got away. That was my victory ... That is why we leave. Because we beg to differ. Because we dread the psychological choke. But leaving is only conditional. The person you are is anathema to the person you would like to be' (p. 87).

Emigration is not self-transformation; one carries 'home' abroad, then carries the foreign back. As Mary Dorcey puts it, living abroad 'makes us feel when we return forevermore a visitor in our own country, not quite "truly" Irish' (p. 22). An inevitable fact of exile, it may be an uncomfortable reality, but it is also a borderland state that offers unusual opportunities for psychological and social movement within the still emerging 'second Ireland' – and a position from which to aid that other birth.

4
Returning from the 'Ghost Place': Recomposing History

> Her history is a blank sheet,
> Her vows a folded paper locked like a well.
> The torn end of the serpent
> Tilts the lace edge of the veil.
> The real thing, the one free foot kicking
> Under the white sheet of history.
>
> Eiléan Ní Chuilleanáin, 'The Real Thing'[1]

> Make of a nation what you will
> Make of the past
> What you can –
>
> There is now
> A woman in a doorway.
>
> It has taken me
> All my strength to do this.
>
> Becoming a figure in a poem.
> Usurping a name and a theme.
>
> Eavan Boland, 'Anna Liffey'[2]

Historiography and historical fiction

In her discussion of the uses of history, the British historian Carolyn Steedman remarks that 'written history is the most unstable of written forms'. It is an account, she says, that will last only a while, a 'story that can only be told by the implicit understanding that things are not over, that the story isn't finished, can never be finished, for some new item of information may alter the account that has been given'.[3] But while the historian's account is temporary, the reader, the teacher, or the citizen may choose to canonize a version of history that denies this textual instability. And if not just a single citizen but a whole citizenry colludes in this canonization, the resulting univocal explanation of historical time creates imprisoning distortions.

Such is the experience evoked by the Irish poet Paula Meehan who recalls how 'all this talk of the people, of who we are,/ of what we need' becomes 'sub-melody, sonic undertow,/ a room of children [in the Central Model School] chanting off/ by heart a verse.'

> I wind up in the ghost place
> the language rocks me to,
> a cobwebby state, chilled vault
> littered with our totems;
>
> a tattered Starry Plough,
> a bloodstained Proclamation,
> Connolly strapped wounded to a chair,
> May blossom in Kilmainham.[4]

The 'ghost place' referred to here is one no Irish person needs glossed; the 'totems', enshrined in spellbinding art, song and literature, retell the story of the Easter Rising of 1916, the prison executions of Irish revolutionaries by the British, the beginnings of the Irish Republic.

This compelling story the Irish critic Declan Kiberd calls the 'Yeatsian view of history' and he decries its use as the sole foundation for nation-building, as well as its insertion into the school textbooks of the Irish Republic. As he sees it, this form of historiography is a 'bleak revenger's tragedy, in the course of which this generation will get even with England on behalf of Ireland's patriot dead'. He insists it is 'not really historical at all, based as it is on a rupture of chronology by the endless repetition of familiar crises, with no hope of resolution'. In one of his most disparaging descriptions of the effects of this version of history, he describes the Irish electorate of the 1930s and 1940s as consistently reelecting to the national Dáil [Parliament] 'ex-gunmen who talked repeatedly about past gunplay'.[5]

While different mindsets may exist in the 'troubled' North – a question I return to at the end of this chapter and in Chapter 5 – many people in the Republic now question the historical practice of recycling a romanticized version of the story of revolutionary Ireland struggling against the ancient British oppressor. For example, Irish historian R.F. Foster, one of the most important 'revisionist' scholars, describes this practice thus: 'the writing of "the story of Ireland" as a morality tale, invented around the seventeenth century and retained (with the roles of hero and villain often reversed) until the twentieth.... '[6]

But Irish women's historians are critical of the ways this newly hegemonic revisionism creates other distortions. Margaret Ward, for example, describes it as a

> political controversy, largely conducted by men, fueled by those who want to distance the profession [of academic historiography] from any taint of nationalist sympathy, but what does all this mean for women? We seem to be invisible whatever the ideological view of the historian.

Maria Luddy and Cliona Murphy offer an even more trenchant judgment: 'And what is history in Ireland? A narrative account of the doings of men, carried out by men, written by men and taught by men.'[7]

Edna Longley, a literary and cultural critic from the North, suggests that the urge towards revisionism may be a painful withdrawal symptom of 'lapsed Nationalists' needing to react to the loss of belief in a nationalism 'internalized as God, Nature and Family'.[8] This criticism of nationalism and revisionism forms part of her larger argument that the Irish need to examine *all* the ideologies that have sustained both Northern Ireland and the Republic. Not only have these lost their usefulness; they have 'withered at the root'. While she considers the consequences dire for both genders, her focus in *From Cathleen to Anorexia* is on the lives of Irish women whom she sees as starved and repressed 'by all the Irish patriarchies...Unionism, Catholicism, Protestantism, Nationalism' (p. 3). In a condemnation of North and South, she claims that the 'ideological clamps that have held both Irish entities together' have 'distorted ethics, politics, social and personal relations, the lives of women, education, what passes here for religion, and our whole understanding of Irish culture' (p. 5).

Other women critics query Edna Longley's argument, finding in her apparent neutrality a reassertion of the Unionist status quo.[9] But the intensity of this debate reveals not just the diversity of approaches to these questions; more importantly, it underscores the political potency of historiographic revisions in Ireland, North and South.

The act of revision, however, is always partial in both senses of the word. For example, in the revisionist discussion by Declan Kiberd referred to above, it is instructive to see what strands of 'history' remain occluded even after the 'Yeatsian view of history' has been expunged. Kiberd argues passionately for a new take on the old 'fathers and sons' story, one in which young Irish men will find in their fathers a 'true image of authority'. 'Weak fathers', he says, 'lead to clutching mothers who raise rebel sons. If the father does assert himself, the child may begin the task of achieving a vision of society as a whole and the even more exhilarating challenge of framing an alternative' (p. 51).

Women might well quail at the thought of male 'assertion'. Or query where the female child will find her story in this homiletic revision with its disingenuous construction of 'child' as gender-neutral. Or wonder how women, clutching or not, can escape this newly shaped ghost place where men are still the only historical actors.

Edna Longley, in the text quoted above, expresses her belief that 'literature remains the primary place where language changes' (p. 5). While this may be the literary critic's too sanguine hope in this age of mass media (a problem considered in Chapter 5), most would agree that literature has played a crucial role in the formation of the political imagination in Ireland. There are good historical reasons, argues Longley, why Irish Nationalism so often reads like bad poetry and Ulster Unionism like bad prose. 'Cathleen [Ní Houlihan, symbol of Mother Ireland] of course has been muse as well as goddess' (p. 5). Given that Irish literature has so often been site of conflict and creator of meaning, Edna Longley is no doubt correct in thinking literary artists have a particular role to play in exposing the fallacies of inherited ideologies. She urges a return to 'origins in 1922' where one can go back behind the revolution's ideology. 'Rather than start a new literary and political clock, I think we should try to tell the time accurately' (p. 13).

Tempting as this time metaphor may be, I would question the possibility of recovering some originary moment whence one could undo the failures of the past. Better, I think, to argue, as does the Indian critic Homi K. Bhabha, that we need to see 'the nation's "coming into being" as a system of cultural signification' that represents 'social *life*, not the 'discipline of social *polity*'. If, as he argues, the idea of the nation emerges as a form of narrative and in the form of narrative, then we need to explore the 'ambivalence of the language' that constructs the narrative, we need to examine the 'image of cultural authority' in the (linguistic) 'act of being composed'. This is an exercise that creates the space where marginalized or suppressed realities may be reimagined.[10]

It is my contention in the following pages that the historical fiction of contemporary Irish women offers a heuristic way of destabilizing authoritative, distorting notions of nation. In their narrative constructions of sacralized historical sites, they often focus on the woman-blindness of the old ideologies and the effects on women and men of this blindness. Chief among the texts I shall consider is Julia O'Faolain's *No Country for Young Men*,[11] but dozens of other women have been busily revisioning this old and important genre in Ireland. Among the ones I find most compelling are those offering a doubled perspective that focuses self-reflexively on troubling continuities and thereby calls into question historiographic practice in Ireland. While there exist interesting depictions of the past which do not use ironic doubling, such as the work of Eilís Dillon (see pages 71–2 for discussion of Dillon's work) and Kathleen O'Farrell,[12] the novels that play with multiple layers create an intense querying of the pieties of history. Sometimes the doubling consists of synchronic cross-class/caste narratives like Mary Leland's *The Killeen*, sometimes they work with diachronic parallels wherein the narrative of one age is set against that of another as in O'Faolain's novel or in Briege Duffaud's *A Wreath Upon the Dead*, a northern novel I turn to at the end of this chapter. As the Irish critic Anthony Roche argues, 'Reading the past in the light of the present acknowledges the processes involved in the writing of history and relativizes the claims made in doing so.'[13]

In the only published monograph devoted to the study of the Irish historical novel as a genre, the American critic James M. Cahalan chooses as his generic model the work of Walter Scott as articulated in Georg Lukács's *The Historical Novel* and Avrom Fleishman's *The English Historical Novel: Walter Scott to Virginia Woolf*.[14] Cahalan decides that, for his purposes, the genre will be restricted to those works that deal with 'political events in modern Irish history prior to the author's own experience'; and he excludes those novels that lack a 'public, political focus, or that deal with minor, internal controversies rather than famous national events'. In line with Fleishman, he decides as well 'that a historical novel ought to contain at least one real historical personage, an actual "big name" from history'. Not surprisingly, given the long-standing hegemony of the 'Yeatsian view of history' in the Republic, he finds that his qualifying novels all focus on events of 'nationalist history', those events that form the 'chronicle of Irish struggles for independence from Britain'.[15]

Given the wealth of possible choices for inclusion in his study, Cahalan of course had to find some way of limiting the selection. But his sub-title is *The Irish Historical Novel*; the authority of the definite article makes claims the study does not support. So too his description of 'the hero of the Irish historical novel' who he declares is 'meant to be representative of the Irish people as a whole and reflecting the author's own views' (p. 204).

Quite apart from the questionable appeal to authorial intention here, one rejects the proposition that any single hero can represent the 'Irish people as a whole'. In saying this I mean to suggest many varieties of difference beyond those of gender, but it is worth noting that he devotes fewer than ten pages to three historical novels of two women, and is somewhat dismissive of the only ones that actually include women's stories, Eilís Dillon's epic diptych *Across the Bitter Sea* and *Blood Relations*.[16]

In a dissertation study of Irish women's historical novels, the Irish critic Leah Watson challenges Cahalan's discussion of Eilís Dillon's *Blood Relations*. I quote her at length here because her analysis points to directions I wish to follow later in my discussion of the uses of 'history' in Irish women's novels and the uses of 'women's lives' in historical narratives. Watson rejects Cahalan's assertion that the 'trouble with the history in Dillon's novels is not its accuracy but rather its uneven integration with the private plot. Chapters of love story alternate with chapters of public history' (p. 204). Watson argues that 'such a statement encapsulates the very essence of Irish andro-centricity' wherein 'the history of male activities is the only history.... Cahalan's dismissive "love story" is itself a misreading of the novel for the love chapters are as much about economic relations as they are about sexual ones':

> Far from being a narratorial fault, as Cahalan suggests, this separation between the public activities of men engaged in revolution and the private activities of women engaged in surviving provides a vehicle to capture and convey that very complexity and ambiguity in history which unilateral explanations, such as the nationalist one, write out .... The very sharpness of the divide carries an implicit critique of the assumption *that revolutionary activities were necessarily of much benefit to Irish women* [my emphasis].[17]

Leah Watson does not point out that the mixture of private and public is an essential feature of the Walter Scott-inspired tradition in Ireland and elsewhere. As Georg Lukács puts it, the 'maintaining' characters [of historical fiction] who live 'close to the ground' reveal in their immediate emotional responses the meaning of historical change in their time (p. 46). But if Watson does not attend to that particular contradiction of Cahalan's argument, she does suggest that the nationalist narrative celebrated on one level of *Blood Relations* is problematized on another: while the 'male chapters' talk of the freedom that will come as a result of the Anti-British struggle, the 'female chapters depict an economic and emotional enslavement of women to their male relatives', an enslavement condemned by only one male nationalist character, drawn after James Connolly (p. 144). Using the historical study of revolutionary Irish women by Margaret Ward, Watson also points out that Eilís Dillon herself erases the activities of female revolutionaries from her narrative, never mentioning the active role women played in the Easter Rising, nor the 22 rebel women who were also imprisoned in Kilmainham Jail after the Rising.[18]

Thus James M. Cahalan's observation that Eilís Dillon's heroines are 'traditional passive [ones] ... true to the average woman of the time' (p. 194) begs several questions. What is an 'average woman' of any time or place? What other names might we give to 'female passivity' in the time of famine and war? Why has women's participation even in the 'male' activities of war been written out of the narrative? How might women rewrite an androcentric, if not to say misogynist, nationalist history? And finally, if contemporary Irish women choose to use fiction as a way of rethinking or critiquing historical tradition, what shapes might their fictions take? Would they, for example, accept Lukács's ideologically based assumption that it is only the 'leading personalities', the world historical actors, who manifest 'historical consciousness' while the 'masses' reveal at most 'spontaneous reaction' to the 'major disturbances of life' (pp. 36–50)?

The following discussion of women's historical fiction in Ireland does not attempt to be all-inclusive. I exclude, for example, Julia O'Faolain's superb historical novels, *The Judas Cloth*, an exploration of Italian-based nineteenth-century papal history, and her *Women in the Wall*, set in a convent in sixth century Gaul.[19] Instead I have selected a few recent novels which use an Irish setting as a way of exploring how certain *ideas* of history have shaped the cultural spaces contemporary Irish women and men inhabit. In each, I would argue, the author has anticipated the ambiguous injunction in Eavan Boland's poem quoted above: 'Make of a nation what you will'. Equally important, each has struggled to create tools with which to

'Make of the past / What you can.' Boland's own sense that this act is a form of usurpation recalls the power of those able to define what matters in historical narrative. Women's presence in the writing of Irish historical fiction and history may not be a new one, but it is only now beginning to be large and important enough to effect revisions in historical imagination and historiographical practice. But before turning to these novels, I consider briefly two texts that cling to the version of Irish history as 'morality tale'.

Versions of 'the Irish soul'

Chapter 3 of this study examined the range of Irish women's fiction devoted to the rendering of emigration and exile. For millions of Irish, including many Irish artists, leaving Ireland has been the method of dealing with Irish history and its contemporary manifestations. One of the most famous of these exilic writers is Edna O'Brien who left Ireland when her sexually graphic fiction was banned in the 1960s. Her love/hate relationship with Ireland has always been a central theme of her work, however, and with it a tendency to essentialize the Irish and the Irish 'soul'. She inscribes a version of Irish history in her novel *The High Road* where the narrator and protagonist Anna offers in a lecture to her American audience a 'summoning up of one's land, battle-haunted, famine-haunted land'.[20] She is self-conscious about her interpretation, knowing that 'even as I said these things, delivered these gleanings of history that the soul of a race cannot be transmitted any more than the soul of a person and in trying to bring this past alive, I was both adulterated and adulterating' (p. 14). But as the reader registers this reminder of the fictiveness of historical telling, she notes that O'Brien's narrator still assumes the possibility of a racial 'soul'. We see in this example an 'image of cultural authority' in the act of 'being composed', as Homi K. Bhabha put it, when we read the rest of the passage:

> How could [the non-Irish audiences] know what it was to walk roads and byroads where nature was savage; a landscape shot at times with a beauty that was dementing, indigo, fuchsia but for the most part permeated with an emptiness redolent of the still greater emptiness, giving a sense of having been stranded, left behind by history and by the world at large, a severed limb of a land full of hurt and rage; a rage that enters and transmutes the way moss and the damp soak into the tombstones (pp. 14–15).

Not only do the Irish share a common 'soul'; this soul has now been rendered immutably tragic as Anna identifies soul, body and landscape through images of emptiness, physical mutilation, rage, and death. Faced with the enormity of this emotional landscape, Anna, like her author, chooses self-exile.

For those fictional characters kept at 'home' by their authors, the choices necessarily take different forms from those who choose to leave the island. Some who stay may choose a kind of internal exile. This is a pattern we find explored again and again in the novels of Jennifer Johnston. Her readers are always offered historical insight via the vehicle of personal relations that bridge class/caste chasms and propel the central characters into heroic refusal of tribal orthodoxies. But the achievement of empathy Johnston portrays with such sensitivity is always helpless in the face of massed social resistance, and the characters capable of such emotional and intellectual independence are left isolated and impotent. No social or political consequences follow the empathy; if anything, we find almost a vindication of the necessity of solitude when faced with such a hopeless populace. The great preoccupation of the novels would seem to be that one can maintain an essential 'purity' only within such isolation. Any attempt to enter the social stream would require compromise, loss of ideals, sullying of the perfection of spirit achieved only in a private haven free from tribal exigencies. As such, Johnston, who often writes historical fiction, offers scant sense of the actual workings of the historical process.

Fool's Sanctuary[21] offers an illustration of this characteristic dynamic. I choose it because it offers, at first glance, the model of the doubled perspective I earlier praised, in this case parallel plots of past and present in the life of another Miranda whose Brave New World never materialized. But because the novel zones in so exclusively on the dying consciousness of a single character trapped in a private construction of the revolution, the novel's doubled temporality does not take the opportunity to explore the historiographic construction of the failed revolution.

The events occur at the time of the Anglo-Irish War of 1919–21, events that are 'replayed' repeatedly 60 years later in the memory of Miranda, who lies dying in her family home, the eponymous Sanctuary, one of Ireland's doomed 'Big Houses', property of an Ascendency landlord. In the earlier time of the narrative, Miranda falls in love with a university student, a new recruit to the revolutionary cause, and son of her father's steward. When he receives the order to kill Miranda's brother and his English friend, both officers in the British army, he shows what is treated narratively as selfless heroism by refusing to execute the orders. This act ensures his own execution for betraying his political cause and colleagues. Miranda remains for the rest of her life in this house, refusing to move, to marry, or to act, rehearsing again and again her 'play', a 'romantic ruin full of ghosts' (pp. 2, 132), her tormented memory its own form of sanctuary. The narrative of the present time occupies itself entirely with her final rehearsal of the events.

The title of the novel may point to the folly of this history or perhaps to the folly of believing one can remain apart from it; in either case, it appears that the choice of sanctuary is doomed to failure. And yet the novel's melancholic wash of nostalgia gilds that choice with a kind of glamour that if anything valorizes it, rein-scribing a sense of the multiple ways in which the political and historical problems exceed the will and the imagination of the Irish. The fact that Johnston characteristically demonizes the IRA in her novels, for example, may make for a comforting 'truth' but does little to unpick the complex motivations, material conditions and emotional experiences of such characters. When she does choose to create a sympathetic portrait of a violent nationalist, Major Angus Barry of *The Old Jest,* he is a privileged, anomalous 'West Brit', and his tragic death tends to defuse any troubling considerations about his political choices.[22]

Reconstituting the Irish Republic in the fiction of Mary Leland and Aisling Foster

Mary Leland's *The Killeen* also offers flight as the textual resolution to the problems of her three main characters, Margaret Coakley, her brother Michael, and her employer Julia Mulcahy.[23] But in *The Killeen* these unresolved 'endings' avoid the kind of sentimentalization we find in some of Johnston's novels. Far from avoiding textually inscribed politi-cal analysis, this novelist relishes it, sometimes to the destruction of believable dialogue, which is not to say that it might not be drawn liter-ally from life, of course. Both *The Killeen* and *Approaching Priests,* Leland's second novel, evince as consistent an antipathy to revolutionary nation-alist politics as the one found in Johnston's novels, but Leland's novels are careful to enact the reasons for this stance.

The Killeen narrates the lives of two women who have loved violent revolutionaries but who come to condemn their violence and the revolution that requires it. It also sketches the lives of two other women who are thoroughgoing revolutionaries themselves, even to the point of offering up the lives of the next generation in the service of their nationalist dreams. Thus, while Leland's novel explores the political meaning of nationalism by considering its effects on the lives of women, she also eschews an essentialist position that would assume solidarity and innate pacifism among all women. In characterizing women revolutionaries, she draws from life in historical Cork and its environs, also the setting of the novel, although she adjusts the facts to make a more emphatic condemnation of the violent nationalists. In fact, the book savagely attacks its various targets.

The novel opens with the story of young Margaret Coakley, a poor country girl from Adrigole west of Cork who is taken from school by her widowed mother and sent to skivvy for a convent in Cork. There she is seduced by a young IRA irregular on the run who is sequestered in the convent grounds by his brother, Father Costello, a republican priest who is chaplain to the nuns. When she becomes pregnant, she is sent away to stay with Julia Mulcahy, a young widow whose own husband has recently died on a politically motivated hunger strike in prison. While both young women earlier had fallen prey to the powerful aphrodisiac of militaristic masculinity, both become thoroughly disillusioned when the lovers abandon them for republican ideals. Furthermore, both have infant sons who are being fingered by the monstrously portrayed aunts of Julia's dead husband. These aunts plan to train the children in a special 'school' for 'freedom fighters'. 'Who can interfere with a man's right to fight for his country?' (p. 87) they ask in a parody of Yeats's *Cathleen Ní Houlihan*.

These aunts are modeled after a famous Cork revolutionary, Mary MacSwiney, whose brother Terence, Mayor of Cork, died in a 1920 hunger strike.[24] But the historical MacSwiney died during the Anglo-Irish War – Ireland's 'good' war; Leland's character dies in the 1930s. By shifting the scene forward in history, the novel highlights the most extreme and discredited of the rump republicans, those women and men – Mary MacSwiney their 'stern guardian of conscience' – who had first refused to accept the Treaty of 1922 creating the Irish 'Free State', then, in 1927, broke with other anti-Treaty republicans led by Eamon de Valera when he finally accepted the Treaty as a way of entering the Dáil and gaining political power.[25] Those who refused to follow de Valera were outlawed by him in 1936 when their IRA organization was declared unlawful. They found acceptable, as do the aunts, various forms of fascism, including Hitler's, sometimes ending up as petty criminals.[26] Such is the ideological and political stripe provided for Maurice Mulcahy, Julia's dead husband, regarded by his aunts as hero, by his widow as monster. Having the freedom wealth can bestow, Julia escapes to France with her son, determined to keep him free of the republican mystique which might entrap him in his native land.

It is worth noting tangentially here that in her treatment of Julia as well as of other characters of this class Leland reveals her own 'ideological clamps'. Her narratives consistently valorize the beautiful, the elegant and the rich as though the *aesthetics* of those conditions might have a transcendent existence free of political meaning.[27] To what extent this somewhat uncritical attitude toward the privileged shapes the author's own ideas of a 'possible Ireland' (p. 56) is, of course, foolish for me to speculate about. The text does, however, make clear the practical wish that, instead of de Valera, the murdered guerrilla fighter, Michael Collins, might have led the new Irish Free State. As we shall see, both here and elsewhere in Irish women's historical fiction, the consequences for women of de Valera's absolute victory is constructed as a social nightmare, although Irish historian Sighle Bhreathnach-Lynch judges Michael Collins' romanticized vision of western Ireland's shawl-clad traditional women as model for modern women to be equally 'myopic'.[28]

Leland's task of discrediting these republicans is almost too easy, based as it is on incontrovertible historical evidence which sounds simplistic, wrong-headed and silly when presented baldly in the novel's dialogue, stripped of its historical contingencies. Considering the possibility of imminent outbreak of war in Europe, Miss Bina Mulcahy, for example, repeats a standard Irish adage: 'England's difficulty is Ireland's opportunity' with which Father Costello agrees, both of them being convinced that

> Ireland could be kept pure, unsoiled by what was happening outside. That purity would itself eventually produce a nation, strong, inviolable, racially untarnished, Catholic from Bantry to Belfast, the envy of whatever Europe would emerge from the rearrangements now being dreamed, discussed or witnessed in Berlin, Paris, London, and Rome, even in Madrid.

These pieties rehearsed, Miss Bina searches in the news 'the references to Germany for further signs that the rise of National Socialism offered some helpful guidelines for aspirant and dedicated Irish nationalists' while Fr Costello reflects on his abiding passion, the achievement of

Irish 'Catholic unity that would be a barrier to alien vices like socialism' (p. 43). The fact that these bigoted attitudes were at least partially shared by de Valera's government and much of Irish society in the Free State of the 1930s is one of Leland's more convincing narrative touches. Her domestication of political dogma into parlor chat makes it seem both outrageous and more ubiquitous.

But the novel focuses on another dominant political narrative of the 1930s – the political romanticization of the land itself as emblem and guarantee of the worthy 'Nation', and it is here that Mary Leland's novel is particularly interesting. In its attempt to demythologize such a belief, the novel places as its center the horrifying image of the Killeen. Refusing a homogenizing political 'meaning' for the land, the novel explores that which is most 'other', most alien to the sacred icon. The Killeen, also part of the Irish moral landscape, is the place where babies who died without being baptized were buried without blessing by the Catholic Church – eternal banishment from Irish Catholic society on earth and barred entry to the heaven of the faithful hereafter.

In the opening pages of the book, devoted to Margaret Coakley's story, a kindly nun who has befriended the lonely girl teaches her to read the contemporary prose of Daniel Corkery because he writes about Margaret's part of rural Ireland.[29] She reads: 'For me [Corkery] to gaze thus into that rambling distance where the little wind-swept hamlet, trees and all, fades into the light of the sky, is to sink softly, and with, perhaps, some gathering wistfulness, into the Gaelic world of the eighteenth century' (p. 12). Corkery's gently misted telescopic focus reveals at closer reading what Irish critic Terence Brown calls the 'conservative and authoritarian notes' of a man venerating an idea of 'national life' and offering a 'highly prescriptive sense of Irish identity'.[30] The nun counsels Margaret to listen, not to Corkery's interpretation of the landscape, but to his advice to Irish readers that they attend *themselves* to what the landscape means. She adds, 'We can't all be so sure that he's listening to it even himself, Donall O Corcora, and we'll never know' (p. 14). Her reference to his Gaelic-assumed name points to a deliberate policy of re-gaelicizing Ireland, as well as to Corkery's apotheosizing of the rural west as the true Ireland. Both of these ideas were crucial tenets of the republican faith and practice.[31]

Thus Margaret's republican lover, a city boy named Ernest Costello, proudly renames himself Earnán de Coisdealbhaigh while Margaret, herself an Irish speaker, is at first ashamed of her accent and bilingualism.

Having been urged to listen to her native landscape, she makes the mistake of listening to Earnán's version of its meaning and 'falls'. 'Her yearning mind succumbed to his references, to the sensual pull of his knowledge, and she began to look with the eyes of love not [yet] at him, but at her place, the countryside, the sources of literature and song, of language' (p. 32). But it is significant that Margaret never returns home to test this construction. She manages the only escape open to her – to England – with another Cork man willing to marry her despite her fallen state. But in a horrifying journey, *The Killeen* takes the reader to Adrigole and Margaret's family in Part Three of the novel.

Although Part Three is titled 'Thomas' after Margaret's son, the almost exclusive focus of this section is Michael Coakley, Margaret's brother, who agrees to raise Margaret's son when she finally manages to prise him from the grip of the Mulcahy aunts. Leland refuses the telescopic, romanticized view of the 'land'. Instead, she walks her reader through it with the farmer Michael, who knows every field and hedge of this landscape. 'He knew them all, their smell, texture, yield and crop, tilled or meadowland. His mind could knit them up like a calendar, the brown ribs of spring, the warm lush softness of the wettest of them in summer, the field that dipped down like a hill so that sometimes the cattle looked as if they were drowning in grass'. (p. 113).

But this beloved and beautiful land is also harsh and demanding. The American critic Catherine Ward, in a study of the use of land and landscape in this novel, claims that 'the land itself is an active agent of destruction ... evil ... sadistic ... a killer'.[32] But this interpretation mythologizes the land in a reading the novel does not support, failing to see how the humans who inhabit this land, with their benighted religious superstitions and their mean-spirited practices, *construct* the land – which, to be sure, can be brutalizing – into a killer force. It is Thomas's grandmother, crazed at the shame of illegitimacy, who kills Thomas, and it is the Catholic priest who refuses the child a Christian burial on the assumption that a bastard must be unbaptized and the unbaptized not worthy of humane treatment – these are the kinds of realities that finally make country life unbearable, drawing Michael away from his beloved fields and into emigration to America:

> He had lived with his back to the ocean all his life. He had no fondness for it, no knowledge of it, yet now the sea was his journey .... Michael let the sea move slowly into his mind .... For the first time he felt, faint as the lighthouse beam, the mysterious glisten of excitement. His course was set (p. 134).

Another reviewer of the novel criticizes Leland's use of discrete stories and separate(d) lives, seeing such a strategy as a failure in plotting. She also states that there 'is no political overlay' in Michael's story, which she sees as simply that of a 'man being turned away from God'.[33] In such a curious interpretation one can only wonder what is meant by 'political', and how the reviewer can fail to see the value in a narrative that so scrupulously shows the failed connections among characters of various classes and locations while maintaining a tripartite structure that refuses a false homogenization of their lives in an Ireland that 'means' so differently to different people.

Father Costello's plan in *The Killeen* for Catholic unity as ballast against the perils of socialism forecasts the historical triumph of conservative ideology in the Republic. In the aftermath of the 1916 Rising came the death or marginalization of key leaders in the pro-labor and pro-feminist branches of Irish nationalism, paving the way for the 1937 Constitution framed by Eamon de Valera.[34] Here are enshrined the 'reactionary values of Catholic social teaching, particularly in its insistence upon the primacy of women's role within the family'.[35] Aisling Foster's satiric novel *Safe in the Kitchen* is a very witty send-up of this process, a fiction-based form of the historical revisionism she shares with her historian husband, R.F. Foster.

The novel narrates various focal points in the years 1916 to 1970, also the span of de Valera's political career. The punning title evokes women's proper sphere in the new dispensation as well as the place where the Russian crown jewels are hidden in the suburban kitchen of Frank and Rita O'Fiaich. In a collaboration de Valera and his confederates erase from the official record, the novel fictionalizes in highly comic form the joint fundraising efforts in 1919 in the United States by de Valera, Frank and Rita with a group of Bolshevist revolutionaries.[36] When the Irish collect a few too many millions and the Russians too few, they strike a deal whereby the crown jewels are entrusted to the Irish revolutionaries as security against a loan given to the Bolshevists. In the ensuing decades, the fey and thoroughly unreconstructed Rita passionately tends, and occasionally wears, the jewels. But as the years pass, the memory of the former fellowship with the godless communists in the increasingly conservative Catholic state is also a secret that must be kept safe. So when the last of the Soviet comrades comes to claim the remaining jewels in 1970, he comments to Rita: 'You, I think, are not keeping ideals? You Irish do not want more revolting. Is like concrete, this place. This inspiration to Russian peoples, is corrupt puppet of capitalist West.'

Rita deflects his threats to expose her theft with this skilful counter-thrust:

> I have no claims on these items. I am only their guardian. They belong to your history, which I suppose you, like many politicians here, would prefer to bury. They will be returned to your government on my death. A letter to that effect is in the hands of my solicitor. I should add that I have read accounts of the Soviet Union in the *Reader's Digest* which make me a little nervous. You seem a surprisingly vengeful people. But should anything untoward happen to me, I have given instructions that a more detailed explanation of how the jewels came into my care should be sent to a journalist.... Of course if I die a natural death, that memoir will be passed on to the Taoiseach, and, I feel sure, incinerated for the public good, like much else in Ireland's time-honoured tradition.[37]

This adroit response masks her killer desire to keep the jewels for herself and as she outmaneuvers her old comrade, he chides her for 'not understanding these things, you Irish, not reading Marx or Lenin' (p. 346). Indeed, as her husband Frank had banned them while serving as minister in the Dáil, a deft recollection of the 1929 Censorship of Publications Act.

Rita, who began her adulthood hoping to be Frank's comrade in the struggle to create a new nation, meets only one true revolutionary in her life, a Russian Bolshevist lesbian sage who initiates Rita into the kinds of intellectual freedom and erotic pleasure that de Valera and Frank spend their whole political careers suppressing in the new state. Foster uses the comic but prophetic Nina to point out the parallel pitfalls of their revolutionary ventures; Nina's critical honesty of course eventually results in her being scapegoated in the USSR by her male comrades when things get hot for the old Bolshevists. 'You understand me, Rita,' says Nina in 1919,

> you same, like me, educated woman, cultured woman [Rita isn't, of course]. So, me, I speak dialectic. Your mans say me potatoes, my mans say dead souls! Then I speak new society. Your mans say me poets. Hah! And my mans tell me Marx and Engels – which they not read – never! I tell you truth, *chérie*, such mans is peasants, ignorant fools! (p. 41).

The trouble is Rita may see the value of such fundamental questioning of male authority, but remains emotionally attached to the idea of conventional love, which her husband fails to deliver, and respectable marriage, which she gets in spades although psychologically and physically abused by Frank whose violent public career persists into 'peacetime'. By 1937 the fate of Rita and her female compatriots is sealed when Article 41 of the Constitution declares the indissoluble family as the fundamental unit of the society, and domestic 'life within the home' the sphere and duty of women. Safe in the kitchen and locked up tight.

As the Irish attorney Mary Robinson, President of the Republic from 1990–97, stated in an article published in 1988: 'Who has been making the law? Who has been interpreting the law? Who has been administering the law? Who has been enforcing the law? Who has been providing legal services? The answer is the same in each case: either exclusively or predominantly, men. No woman had a hand in drafting the Constitution.'[38] Foster's novel creates a comic narration of this process that Irish critic Gerardine Meaney describes as follows: 'Women [in newly emergent postcolonial states including Ireland] become the guarantors of their men's status, bearers of national Honour and the scapegoats of national identity. They are not merely transformed into symbols of the nation, they become the territory over which power is exercised.'[39]

To be sure, Foster gives Rita her revenge. She outlives her husband, and even as she buries him rejoices that the 'past was dead, six feet down in the brown earth' (p. 347). She walks out of the end of the novel a free woman, if well-upholstered materialism counts as freedom. The novel chronicles the triumph of the Catholic bourgeoisie.

Julia O'Faolain: reconstituting Cathleen

Aisling Foster's novel satirizes a central character's lifelong trajectory as a way of charting the stillbirth of a nation; she focuses not on the leader of the nation but on those close to him. Julia O'Faolain's novel, *No Country for Young Men*, uses a similar strategy except that she creates a mirroring text wherein two nodal moments in modern history, 1922 and 1979, are set into parallel narratives as a way of tricking out the distorting flaws of a 'people' and their leaders, flaws reproduced from generation to generation.

> 'The 'people' are clay. You can do what you like in their name but, as Aristotle said of men and women, the formative idea comes from the male and the clay is female; passive, mere potentiality. The clay here is the people who have no self and no aspiration towards

determining anything at all until we infuse it into them. We are their virile soil,' [said Owen O'Malley]. 'We are they.' (p. 314)

The 'people' in this quotation are the Irish who, in 1922, had just voted to accept the Anglo-Irish Treaty in which the 26 counties of southern Ireland became the Free State of Ireland, with six northern counties remaining part of the United Kingdom. The virile 'we' are the Irish revolutionary leaders or 'Diehards' who refused to accept this Treaty, and were about to launch Ireland into a bitter Civil War rather than accept the partition of the island. The character who speaks these words is an amalgam of recognizable Irish leaders, most notably Eamon de Valera. Not surprising, perhaps, that this novel was short-listed for the Booker Prize in England.

The 'people are clay' quotation above is so baldly self-serving that the reader scents a satire; yet, as the novel progresses one sees the speaker's behavior unabashedly follow this declaration. Much is made in the novel of the effects of education on the young Irish, and Owen O'Malley's Jesuit training appears to give him sacerdotal permission to seize control of the body politic. The novel explores the interdependence of Irish education and socialization, Irish nationalist politics, Irish patriarchal culture, and Irish Catholicism: a lethal brew of realities that persists in the 1979 plot.

In this novelistic world, Ireland is not the country of young men invoked in W.B. Yeats's 1927 poem 'Sailing to Byzantium'; by 1979, the Irish Republic is a country maintained by and for old men. But O'Faolain has Owen O'Malley speak his lines in 1922, and his patriarchal message of political and sexual control of a formless and yielding 'people' reveals in the young Owen a patriarch in the making. The novel, then, examines the ways in which the Republic's postcolonial politics reinscribe – even as they contest – the political attitudes of the former British masters in a gendered discourse that has disastrous effects on the material lives of the ruled 'people'. Needless to say, there is a tragic irony here in the replacement of one master narrative, British imperial history, with another totalizing plot, that of a masculinized Irish nationalism that depends on the constitutionally-based colonization of women.

This colonization works within an articulation of nationhood enshrined in the Republic's 1937 Constitution, an articulation that revealed an 'image of cultural authority' in the 'act of being composed.' With Articles 2–3 the writers erased the reality of the 1921 Partition with a claim that 'the national territory consisted of the whole island of Ireland' even though the legal state included only 26 of the island's 32 counties. Even though the 1998 Peace Agreement relinquishes the claim, these articles remain a sacred promise for a Nationalist, or conversely, as an act of unforgivable aggression to a northern Unionist.

Raised in Ireland and Europe, and living most of her adult life in Italy, England and the United States, Julia O'Faolain occupies a privileged insider-outsider perch from which to view Irish nation-building. But as a member of the Irish Diaspora in North America during the time of writing this novel, she was clearly well aware of the ways nostalgic celebration of Irish republican history (the 'old morality tale') in the United States plays a crucial part in maintaining virulent nationalism in Ireland, North and South.

The novel is framed, beginning and end, by the murder of Americans who had gone to Ireland as observers of the nationalist scene. The first murder, of Sparky Driscoll in March, 1922, is a historical event reported at the time in a New York journal called *Gaelic American*, reproduced by O'Faolain as opening intertext of the novel. Assuming that British agents were responsible for the death, the journal proclaims Sparky Driscoll a 'new martyr to an old cause' and predicts that the murder will spur the Irish to intensify 'the onward march for the regeneration of their [female] country' (pp. 7–8). The second murder, of the fictional character James Duffy, takes place in 1979. The meaning and consequences of these deaths – in their contradictory significations – are used by O'Faolain to call into question the orthodoxies of twentieth-century Irish history. Although we do not see beyond the moment of James's death, the novel has taught us that this death will be used, as Sparky's was in 1922, by ambitious Irish leaders eager to promote their own agendas.

Significantly, the only witness to both the deaths is Judith Clancy, a woman whom no one believes because she is, in the first instance, 1922, a school girl who went into catatonic shock for several years after Sparky's death, in part because her brother-in-law Owen O'Malley ordered shock treatments to destroy her memory, and who in the second instance, 1979, is considered certifiably mad when, as an old nun, she sees James murdered. The choice of the Cassandra-like Sister Judith as history's witness is a brilliant metafictional device. She tells truths no one believes and forgets facts that would challenge received political orthodoxies. Incarcerated by Owen in a convent – a radical act of patriarchal colonization – she has spent 55 years trying to recall the night of Sparky's murder, a narrative trope that reveals how the deliberate mastery of the historiographic process will force marginal or dissident stories out of circulation and out of 'history'.

The year 1922 marks the year when the Irish revolutionaries attempt to suppress the differences among themselves; the civil war that follows this suppression creates such a volatile and unstable situation for the new free state that only the most conservative of tried-and-true orthodoxies can be entertained. When Judith Clancy remarks to the American Sparky Driscoll that her sister Kathleen's fiancé, Owen O'Malley, will 'be in the Dáil for sure. It'll be a country run by young men', Sparky asks the obvious suffragist question of the time: 'What about the women? They'll have a say now, too, won't they?' Judith's response to this, borne out by subsequent history, is 'the men in this country would never let a woman have a say' (p. 213). But this suppression of gender difference is just one symptom of the determination to refuse any of the heterogeneities existing at that time in Ireland. This ruthless suppression of difference, and the blocking of women's public agency, are political habits of mind that persist in the 1979 sections of the novel.

Here, as in the 1922 section, the characters are types borrowed from Irish myth and literature, a move self-consciously emphasized by O'Faolain as she has the characters quote from Irish texts in ruminating about the legendary or literary resonances of their names.[40] One of the first and most potent intertextualities is the recollection of traditional Ireland as the 'four green fields', the four ancient provinces of Ulster, Leinster, Munster and Connacht, a centuries old battlecry for the expulsion of Britain from Ireland, as in W.B. Yeats's 1902 play *Cathleen Ní Houlihan*. In the 1979 plot of the novel, the term has been appropriated as title of a Hollywood-made film that will be used as a front for IRA fundraising. The American producer, Larry O'Toole, is an ex-college football player now millionaire businessman, still dreaming of epic battles and manly prowess. When he hires his ex-quarterback chum, James Duffy, to do research in Ireland for the film, James happily sets out, blithely unaware of the dangerous bog he traverses. From the moment he enters Ireland he is put under surveillance by the Irish immigration police, who discover a seditious message from an American IRA funding raising organization called 'Banned Aid' in the box of cigars he was given at his departure by Larry O'Toole's lethally daft old father. [41]

At the end of the novel, after James has fallen in love with the Irishwoman Gráinne O'Malley (granddaughter of Owen O'Malley, niece of Owen Roe O'Malley), he is deported on the charge of sedition when the Irish secret police, acting out their own understanding of the meaning of clandestine, assume that James has been playing IRA revolutionary games when in fact he has been playing at adultery with Gráinne. Although there are comic elements in James's story, there is nothing comic about his assassination at the hands of Patsy Flynn, a demented old IRA warrior in the employ of Owen Roe O'Malley. Like Sparky Driscoll a half century earlier, James is the victim of a personal and political mistake that has to be textualized as a pro-British enemy attack if Irish politicians like Owen O'Malley in 1922 or his nephew Owen Roe O'Malley in 1979 are to protect their own Dáil careers. But unlike Sparky and the dominant O'Malley men, James has no sure plan in his work; we readers watch James as he collects historical facts, then attempts to make narrative order. As we watch, we learn that any such historical reconstruction will be provisional at best. In fact, when James, who has questioned Sister Judith and believes her story, discovers a version of Sparky's death that the reader knows to be 'true', he tries to convince Larry O'Toole that the film *Four Green Fields* must show the ambiguity of historical interpretation. To this suggestion O'Toole replies: 'Jesus, man, I took you out of academe. Even if your nutty nun's got the truth, we don't want it …. We're constructing a myth…. We don't give a goddam about truth. It does not set you free. It dissipates energies. Myths unify. They animate' (p. 320). Predictably, the marginalized characters, who are in the best position to challenge received versions of history, have the least power to convince others of the value of their questions.

In the 1922 plot of the novel, Sister Judith's radical isolation leaves her no one with whom to communicate. The assassin in the 1979 plot should be a character with an audience, after his yeoman's work with the IRA. But that kind of heroism is an embarrassment in the modern, Europeanized Republic of Ireland, as is the gun-running of his boss, Owen Roe O'Malley. The political ambition of this younger O'Malley is as ferocious as that of his famous uncle, and his disdain for women as intense, but where the earlier O'Malley practised a kind of sexual asceticism in marriage which 'he suffered in a Pauline spirit' (p. 192) the younger O'Malley with his 'jutting genitals' (p. 145) is a brutal philanderer who preaches a modern gospel of sexual libertarianism. The sexual perversity of these and other Irish men, the narrator tells us, is the product of a clerical tradition that posits women as the source of evil, the Eve or Pandora or Gráinne or Dervogilla from whom destruction flows. As Gráinne O'Malley, the central woman of the 1979 plot, enunciates it: 'Men in this country had been educated by clerics and, though they might react for a while against these mentors, sooner or later they could be relied on to start talking about love-making the way [her husband, Michael] just had. Whether they were passionate men like Owen Roe, or frigid ones, like Michael, either way, they needed the tongs of humor to pick up the subject at all. Monastic tradition described women as a bag of shit and it followed that sexual release into such a receptacle was a topic about as fit for sober discussion as a bowel movement.'[42]

This fundamental divide between the sexes results in the eroticizing of violence and the brutalizing of sexual love. It also equates women's bodies with the territory of the nation, both possessions of the Irish men. In the equation of 'cunts and countries' (p. 361), women are made particularly vulnerable because of their straitened roles and possibilities. The 1979 heroine Gráinne may have none of the sexual frigidity of her aunt, Sister Judith, but she finds herself trapped either in a sexual role or in a maternal/domestic role. Accused at one point by her American lover James Duffy of continually 'reconstituting [her]self' to fit male definitions of 'wife, mother, civic entity' (p. 254), she finally chooses flight from Ireland as solution to her impasse. But as the novel ends, she has been stopped in this flight by the gratuitous assassination of her lover, just as her great aunt Kathleen Clancy has been halted in her flight by the bizarre murder of Sparky Driscoll two generations earlier. At the moment Gráinne O'Malley walks away from her home, her husband and son reenter it. Once inside, they will find Owen Roe O'Malley already in possession. Like the Clancy home in 1922, this Irish home, emblematic of the ruling dynasty of Irish political families, remains secure as a 'male territory' (p. 20).

O'Faolain uses an obsessively recurring image of the Irish bog throughout the novel. This rich metonym finally suggests everything about Irish history and memory that threatens to suck the nation under. But the bog can also function as fuel, a recycled supporter of life. Significantly, only two characters in the novel can negotiate the physical bog, Owen Roe O'Malley and his great nephew Cormac, a 14-year-old republican warrior in the making. Their negotiation is a form of domination, however, as they gallop over its 'unfathomable layers' (p. 12).

The novel's American narrator, James Duffy, is impatient of what he calls the Irish 'parodying themselves and others', looking backward like 'pillars of salt' (pp. 217, 174). Like the other characters, his partial vision undercuts his authority to interpret. But the narrative positions certain characters 'between worlds' (as Gráinne describes herself), using them to reveal the ambivalence of language that constructs the dominant narratives and the images of cultural authority. Lacking such a perspective, the citizens will be chained to a destructive past, immobilized in the present, apparently unable to reconstitute themselves for the future. Lest the reader miss the point, the novel ends with the deadly parodic cycle in motion again.

Briege Duffaud: on the edge of a different bog

The historical novels examined above, all set in the Republic, focus on the inextricable connections between republican misogyny and conservative nationalism. Neither state can be changed without a radical reconstitution of the Republic. Putting women 'into' history is not a matter of adding an extra element but of redrawing the entire configuration. There are those who believe this can be done – indeed point to the changes of the past generation in Ireland as proof that it is being done. It has been my contention here that the best writers of women's historical fiction contribute hopefully, if very critically, toward that project. When we turn to an important recent historical novel by a woman originally from the North, that hope is dimmed. If I were to summarize the salient difference between the works of such writers as Mary Leland, Aisling Foster and Julia O'Faolain and that of Briege Duffaud, I would say that the former insist that there are not just other stories to tell but possible other ways of telling the common story, whereas Duffaud's *A Wreath Upon the Dead* inscribes the near impossibility of finding a usable common story.[43]

The novel is a very cleverly wrought exercise in historiographic metafiction in which the reader watches the 'writer' attempt to write the novel that keeps slipping beyond her grasp. Believing she can use legends from her childhood town to write a historical romance, Maureen Murphy finally becomes convinced that the northern writers and historians can possibly do no better than retreat 'to the safety of ancient monuments and defunct Gaelic families' (p. 449). But the events of the novel, which stretch out over 140 years, prove how potent those monuments can be, how alive and dangerous the supposedly defunct families.

The novel's primary setting is the little town of 'Claghan', drawn after the actual town of Crossmaglen near Duffaud's childhood home, and situated near a bog along the border country of South Armagh. One of the local characters in the 1960s describes it as 'a dead parochial Irish town. Two factories, a creamery, Catholic Bingo hall, Protestant Bingo hall, Catholic dance-hall, Protestant dance-hall, 99 pubs and twice as many churches and chapels!' (p. 347). This bland list reveals the sectarian fissure that will explode with seismic force by the end of the 1960s, a force reverberating into the present of the novel (and of contemporary history in the North). But Duffaud's literary creation of this town is not the first; Irish journalist and novelist Colm Tóibín describes Crossmaglen as 'famed in song and story' and quotes a 1852 police report calling Crossmaglen 'probably the worst part of the country.'[44] Certainly it has the reputation as the island's most republican town, and it is that heritage that the novel puts under scrutiny.

At the center of Duffaud's version of the town, and of the novel, are two poor Catholic girls who grow up there after World War II. One is Kathleen O'Flaherty who serves on one level as symbol for the hapless country with its violent progenitors and monstrous progeny; the other is Maureen, eldest of 13, bright, ambitious, and harboring fantasies of escape. By the age of 16, Maureen, 'with moment of truth arteries pulsing' knows she has 'found her vocation' – to become a writer of romance wherein to 'convey the infinite pathos of life' and by which to earn the money to buy herself a world where 'all would be accustomed and ceremonious, where innocence and beauty could be safely born, unblemished both by the Quarry Street hysteria [of Kathleen's home] and by the pathetic zinc-roofed decency of her own townland' (p. 116).

The narrative follows Maureen's fairy tale as she marries her Carnaby Street boss (who makes a fortune in the rag trade of London), buys a chateau in France, and becomes a successful writer of romance novels. Casting about for a new subject for her fifth novel, she decides to write a book about a pair of mid-nineteenth-century lovers still famous in her old hometown, Cormac O'Flaherty, a poor but ambitious peasant, and Marianne McLeod, daughter of the rich Protestant landlord. But Maureen is not the first to mine this particular story. It has been an important local legend fueling Catholic Nationalism as well as the occasional efforts towards cross-religious rapprochement. The legend changes shape to fit the tenor of the times, appearing in the 1950s as a publication of the Catholic Truth Society of Ireland, for example, and in the 1980s as a country and western hit by one Cuchulain McCool.

The *Wreath* opens with a '198–' letter from Myrna McLeod to Maureen in France, answering Maureen's request for a copy of the diary written by Marianne McLeod between 1840 and 1842, just before the Great Famine and her seduction by Cormac. It is not until page 419 that the reader is offered the letter from Maureen that prompted Myrna's response, although the diary makes its appearance by page 47, followed by a variety of contradictory responses to it. By the end of the novel, this supposedly certain historical document has been dismissed as a forgery. Such labyrinthine turns are characteristic of the *Wreath*'s narrative structure in which the reader is continually forced to negotiate among contradictory or disconnected fragments narrating 140 years of village life with its tribal certainties about unblemished heroism or unconditional victimhood. Although the London *Times* reviewer of the novel in an otherwise positive review calls it a 'stylistic nightmare', that surely is the point: the novel's kaleidoscopic structure creates the experience of traversing the layered and treacherous bog of human affairs and historical 'explanations' in the North.[45]

But letters, diaries, songs, newspapers and legends are not the only historical and ethnographic sources used by the fiction-writing Maureen and offered to the reader. In an attempt to get the facts straight about Marianne and Cormac – or at least to render the local color accurately – she collects public documents contemporary to their lives. Most of the documents are sent from Claghan to Maureen in France, accompanied by some kind of commentary that supports or debunks the document, a strategy that creates an extremely attenuated connection between explanation and 'reality'. While the reader struggles to follow the 'plot' – the stories of the lives of the descendants of Marianne's and Cormac's families – Maureen decides all the sources are hopelessly biased or 'folkloric', that is, compounds of folk memory spiced with local hatreds, fears, superstitions, and self-justifications. There is a nice irony here in that all the documents are in any case creations of Briege Duffaud (who also lives in France).[46]

But the folkloric is immensely powerful and Duffaud takes the opportunity early in the novel to set up a discursive exposition of folklore in action. In this narrative scrap, four-year-old Maureen is being 'formed' by her Catholic Granny who leads her to the edge of 'Claghan Bog whose bottomless pools were stiff with dead men holding pikes and scythes and pitchforks' which, Granny explains, 'was th' oul' English, darlin', drove them backwards into the bog and them after surrendering'. At this point Granny's tale begins to conflate potent religious/political narratives as 'Cromwell's mad dogs of Protestant soldiers … who was given the poor Catholics' land after, in place of wages' transmute into the Roman soldiers who crucified Christ, 'Cromwell's iron-headed soldiers stripp[ing] every stitch of clothes off him and play[ing] dice over who'd get his coat' (pp. 19–20).

Add such distortions to the daily rub against children free of rural superstitious Grannies in floor length black skirts and men's boots and the result is that Maureen 'hated hated hated' not the few liberal-minded Protestants she encounters, but the middle-class Catholics who have 'gombeen blood in them' (p. 21). These are the ones who persecute her for her poverty throughout her childhood, especially when she wins a scholarship to the rich Catholic girls' boarding school. Driven by such resentments, and writing from a distance across place and time, Maureen herself is constructed in the text – at least in my reading – as an unreliable narrator, a situation which forces the reader into radical uncertainties about the tales.

Maureen finally decides she must abandon her efforts to make an escapist romance out of a sectarian tragedy which has taken on new life in the 'Troubles' in contemporary Claghan. When her friend Kathleen then suggests she write a realistic novel about the place instead, 'Telling life as it is, like' Maureen's response is that she doesn't even know what realistic means. 'Could you leave out the folklore and still be honest? The recent Irish fiction Maureen read might be about cool Trinity graduates discussing Chekhov over a feed of escargots with lean, liberated blondes who knew all about birth control, but the parish priest, the Pope and the Provos [as well as the immorality of Edna O'Brien's novels] were still the stuff of her mother's weekly letters' (pp. 106–7, 326).

Even the possibility of 'telling life as it is, like' leaves Maureen spluttering: 'I wouldn't. I couldn't. I don't think I could ever write anything that sort of questioned their values. It would break their hearts. I could never go home again' (p. 327). In other words, cynic that she is, she cannot play the heretic.

For heresy it would be, it seems, to question the 'folkloric', the sectarian tale of good Catholics persecuted by evil Protestants. Yet even if one wished to question the orthodoxies, there is 'no true story', says Maureen, 'just a mess of ambiguities and lies and more or less guesses. And it doesn't matter, it doesn't change a thing. Claghan will make up whatever truth suits it. Don't we all?' (p. 448). But if the author within the novel meets this impasse, the author outside the novel, Briege Duffaud, composes a different image of cultural authority in her historiographic fiction by focusing on class relations. Here, it seems, is the real enemy, the class privilege which is not unique to the Protestants and which corrupts Catholics as well as Protestants, dwarfing the problem of gender inequality. Duffaud's single IRA Provo terrorist, for example, is a wealthy, beautiful young woman histrionically determined to assume the role and stature of Maud Gonne or Countess Markievicz. Here is her first attempt at a recruitment speech: 'I mean is there any reason why a girl can't make up her mind to join the IRA? Without having to be inspired by a boyfriend? I mean I'm as fit as any fellow to shoot B-specials or put a bomb in a wooden hut' (p. 247). In other words, that particular struggle is reduced to a self-aggrandizing charade, while the character who emerges as close to heroic as this novel can manage is a poor, working-class Protestant man who struggles for civil rights for Ulster's workers. Although the *nouveau riche* Maureen jeers at his efforts, Briege Duffaud, moving here uncharacteristically into the authority of third person narration, describes Dave Jenks thus: 'an unarmed civil rights marcher trying hard to keep fear at bay, [who] put his head down and counted every dogged step he achieved between two rows of Reverend Abe Clyde's jeering taunting parishioners who lined the route at intervals between Claghan and Belfast. Stones thudded and crunched on skulls and cheekbones and shoulder blades, sending gushes of blood over banners and jeans and anoraks' (p. 359).[47] Dave, for his principles, is blinded by a stone but continues his tireless, if fruitless, political struggle.

As Briege Duffaud allows various contemporary characters to tell their stories in internal monologues, reported dialogues, journals, letters, short stories and a one-act drama, what emerges is a vision of despair. The last 'take' on Northern Ireland is a scene in which a slum house – carefully preserved by liberal Protestants as a museum depicting the effects of sectarian bigotry – collapses in upon itself, symbolic of the North, when inhabitants within and enemies without blow it apart (p. 436). Significantly, one of the victims who dies in the explosion is the Protestant who set up the museum; he is also father, although he does not know it, of the young woman terrorist who is his killer. These inextricable interconnections between Protestant and Catholic who are trapped together in a collapsing house is no new phenomenon in Claghan. This house in Quarry Street, where Kathleen had grown up, was also the bolt-hole for Cormac and Marianne, the nineteenth-century lovers whose story Maureen had wanted to exploit. Recreating their home as a 1980s museum was to serve as a 'message of hope for the future', a place where Catholic and Protestant could reach across the divide and build 'a completely socialist state' (pp. 290–2). Like all the projects undertaken by characters in this novel, excepting only Maureen and her husband's ability to make money, this socialist vision too is doomed.

When Maureen finally abandons the idea of 'romancing' her natal town, she resembles her creator. Briege Duffaud says that the story of the nineteenth-century Cormac figure, the jockey who married 'up', occurred in her own family. Her father repeatedly asked her to write Cormac's story, asking one last time six weeks before his death. So she undertook to do so and we have the effort in Chapter 4: 'Frost in a thin sun: November. A fat crow heaves itself off the graveyard wall and trails aimlessly into grey shabby sky.... Crow. The emblem of these hungry townlands' (p. 32). This is the beginning of another famine novel, but one its author could not manage.[48] While Duffaud's Maureen claims 'there is no true story', the novel Maureen inhabits suggests that the people of Northern Ireland are telling the wrong story, recreating past miseries which distort future possibilities. The ghosts of all 140 years live on in the little town, making a return from the 'ghost place' impossible.

All the writers in this chapter have removed themselves from Ireland, excepting Mary Leland who lives in the Republic, and Jennifer Johnston, who in her second marriage moved from the Republic to Northern Ireland. Physical distance might create a liberating vantage point, but, like any position, will certainly create its own distorting refractions. Yet each of these authors is 'making of the past' what she can. None pretends to be telling the 'real thing'; each is engaged in replotting the inherited narratives. Like the 'one free foot kicking/ Under the white sheet of history' quoted at the beginning of this chapter, these women's historical novels work to destabilize Irish history as it has been written. By means of this strategy, they work to create the space for narratives that reimagine the past. From such a place, it may be possible to envisage a better future.

5

'The War That Has Gone Into Us'[1]: Troubles From the North

> In this land
> where the law is like a public bar
> with no toilet –
> the men pissing out the back yard –
> women live lives
> of even quieter desperation.
>
> Ruth Carr, 'Parity'[2]

> Before there were helicopters
>   there were dragonflies.
> And will be, after.
>
> Ann Zell, 'Nature Programme'[3]

Media lives

The lines above by women of the North hold the discussion that follows like bookends. On one side, the tragic contingencies of war, on the other a cry of defiance and hope. But these pieces are not really separable. If Ann Zell's dragonflies evoke the hope of a peaceful future for Northern Ireland, the poem cannot extricate images of nature from those of a militarized landscape: owls probe the night 'with infra-red eyes'; seagulls circle like 'spotter planes'; even 'tele-ported fauna' of South America reshape in the poet's dreams into the military presences of 'armoured cars', 'soldiers' and 'helicopters'. Reading the social 'text' beyond Zell's poem, we know that the tele-porting of foreign images into Northern life has its double in the broadcasting of images out, then back in, the people of the North watching themselves being watched – making war or attempting peace, all in a technologized landscape.

Against, and within, such a landscape, Ruth Carr's poem adroitly shifts the reader's gaze from the violent spaces of Irish men to the unnamed locations and unarticulated experiences of Irish women. But even as she evokes two separate spheres for men and women, the comparative notion of 'even quieter desperation' forces an oscillation between the spheres, urging a reconsideration of both. This self-consciously doubled focus – holding men's lives and women's in a taut, often dangerous, embrace – is a recurring structure in the contemporary fiction of northern women. Put another way, one can argue that women's fiction, as well as such 'border' genres as oral history and fictionalized memoir, are preoccupied with constructions of gender, particularly the construction of masculinity, in militarized zones.

But another issue is also frequently inscribed in the most recent texts. Again and again one discovers a concern about the distorting effects of media representations that search out episodes of violence for public consumption. Just as nature itself becomes in Zell's poem a 'programme', fictional characters in many novels watch as northern lives are reduced to cartoons in the TV images, radio reports and newspaper stories that flow into their homes, even as they flow outward to an aghast world. As Irish educator Eilish Rooney points out: 'censorship and the "sound byte" have reigned insidiously supreme in British and Irish media coverage of the past and the present in Northern Ireland' with the result that it is 'easy to lose sight of even the living memory context of the current conflict. This [present recurrence of] conflict has been going on for over 26 years. Long enough for the present generation to remember nothing but conflict.'[4] She points out that the occasional newsblast about northern violence cannot hold the attention of the world, 'crowded with bloodier, newer, more exotic conflicts', then adds that in the absence of more sustained and committed attention, 'the conflict is "contained". For people who live here the human costs of that containment are enormous' (p. 40).

These media productions support a state-authorized monologue in which the violence of a particular group, the IRA, can be constructed as uniquely lawless and barbarous, a narrative that legitimizes the violence of the state and the dominant order. That narrative, of course, can be challenged in so small and porous a territory as Northern Ireland. But women's experiences, political voices, movements, and history have traditionally been occluded or subordinated to the demands of the conflict, a condition which homogenizes and falsifies the 'sides' and promotes ever greater sectarian division.

Even for those attempting to attend – and our numbers are legion – 'reasons' are elusive. One foreign journalist humbly admitted in 1989 that with 'an American's belief in the "quick fix", I looked for logical solutions in a situation where logic has ceased to exist.'[5] But such a judgment seems to miss the point. Logic still exists, but in more than one form and in competing systems of self-proclaimed legality and rationality. The best way to fight one's corner in such a prolonged and painful struggle is to induce internalization of the group's belief system which in turn ensures daily practice of the group ideology. As Irish critic David Lloyd argues:

> ...the desire of nationalism is to saturate the field of subject forma-
> tion so that, for every individual, the idea of nationality, of
> political citizenship, becomes the central organizing term in rela-
> tion to which other possible modes of subjectification – class or
> gender, to cite only the most evident instances – are differentiated
> and subordinated.[6]

Those of us attempting to understand women's particular places and participation in this intractable situation will have trouble peering in through of barriers of 'armed patriarchy'.[7] While unionism may be the official state narrative, nationalism has been the deafeningly loud oppositional voice.

For this reason, recent historical studies that explore the multiple ways in which northern women have lived and attempted to inter-vene in the main lines of historiographical development are extraordinarily important. In the work of such northern writers as Monica McWilliams, Eileen Evason, Margaret Ward, Madeleine Leonard, Nell McCafferty, the Women's Committee of the National Union of Public Employees, Celia Davies, Eithne McLaughlin, Hazel Morissey or in the films and videos of Pat Murphy, Margo Harkin and Anne Crilly, we find what David Lloyd calls the 'superseded and over-loaded residues of history', 'history's inassimilable' whose very forms are incommensurable with statist historiography p. 264.

Great as the differences might be among different groups of women in the North – and they are – their attempts at cross-sectarian debate and shared action have characteristically been undermined in this state of emergency, among other reasons because it is difficult not to make common cause with the men of their tribe or class with whom they share personal and political experiences.[8] As Monica McWilliams comments, women have 'to expend extraordinary energy and imagination in order to put themselves into the

> 'big picture' of political conflict in Northern Ireland. In the trade union movement, in community development, in the umbrella and single issue women's groups of the voluntary sector, they have become the unofficial agents of change making representations to the various government departments and demanding resources for the wide range of work in which they are involved (p. 29).

This work is largely undocumented, because of the sheer physical and psychic impossibility of doing the superhuman – combining the Political, the political and the private.[9] This burden has made the 'piecing together of women's lives particularly hard' (p. 29).

Because of this absence, there is an intense need for narratives that work against the grain of history and against the cultural constructions of that history in contemporary media.[10] Despite the over-narrativization of tiny Northern Ireland – one of the western world's most 'articulated' regions – it is not always easy to find works that avoid the polemics of simplifying sectarianism. Obviously no text can transcend politics; a pretense of neutrality or political innocence generally masks, however unconsciously, a reassertion of the status quo. But even a very sophisticated observer might find it difficult to avoid using the oppositional categories at hand, as when the Northern Irish critic Edna Longley designates 'artists and writers as Protestant and Catholic' not 'in a sectarian or divisive spirit, but simply with reference to the kinds of cultural conditioning to which they might have been subject.'[11] If this conditioning is so thorough, then the writer who can work against the grain of such categories – which at the very least have strong historical and contemporary meaning – is all the more remarkable a phenomenon. While not unique to women's writing, important sites of resistance can be found among the growing but still too little known body of publications by and about women in the North.

Writing lives

Women's drama, particularly the work of the Charabanc Theatre Company, is emerging as a strong cultural force, if one difficult to export, short of carrying the company to foreign stages or publishing the dramatic texts, something still too little undertaken.[12] Women's poetry is more exportable, but only a few women, pre-eminently Medbh McGuckian but also Janet Shepperson, Joan Newman, Ann Zell, Ruth Carr, Janice Fitzpatrick-Simmons and Sabine Wichert have succeeded in publishing volumes of poetry from the North, although two anthologies composed entirely of northern women's writing have been published, *The Female Line* and *Word of Mouth*. Other anthologies of women's poetry and prose that include work from both North and South are now also available, for example, *Wildish Things*, *Writing Women*, and *Pillars of the House*.[13] One needs to seek out these women-only anthologies, and the occasional special issue of women's writing in Irish journals, because so many of the collections remain overwhelmingly Irish men's writing.[14]

Among the non-fiction writings of women, we find that a primary method women have employed to destabilize dominant discourses is to publish life writing and oral history (or to use these ethnographic methods within larger studies). Such personal testimonies allow space for voices otherwise ignored or denied access to publication. Because of the politics of the recorders, these works often focus on the most dispossessed and vulnerable. In such works as *I am of Ireland: Women of the North Speak Out*; *Peggy Deery: a Derry Family at War*; *Shattering Silence: Women, Nationalism, and Political Subjectivity in Northern Ireland*; *Women Divided: Gender, Religion and Politics in Northern Ireland*; *Only the Rivers Run Free: Northern Ireland: The Women's War*; and *Women's Voices: an Oral History of Northern Women's Health (1900–1990)*, we find the stories of women and girls who bear the pain and loss of the war and all those conditions that emergency situations preclude attending to: the daily effects of poverty and unemployment; sectarian violence and emigration; lack of education and positive opportunities; violence in the home by men against women and children; multiple pregnancies with limited access to contraception and abortion (in either sectarian group among the poor); obscurantism and prudery about sexuality; even the experience of prostitution, an established phenomenon 'many Irish people refuse to admit exists'.[15]

We find a few other books in which the single voice of a writer offers descriptions and analyses of women's lives in the North. Two of these are *All of Us There*, and *The Price of My Soul*. The first is a remarkable 'family' memoir by journalist and novelist Polly Devlin, in which the author describes and analyzes the growing up experiences of six Devlin sisters in the isolated village of Ardboe in 'the most remote region of a remote county – Tyrone', this memoir serving as a cultural biography.[16] The second, a well-known autobiography of Bernadette Devlin (MacAliskey), elected in 1969 at age 21 to the British parliament, recounts the saga of the northern civil rights movement of the late 1960s and her role therein, a book which she describes as an 'attempt to explain how the complex of economic, social, and political problems of Northern Ireland threw up the phenomenon of Bernadette Devlin.'[17] In both of these, the writers locate themselves carefully in their own historical narratives and make it clear how formative their class, gender, religious and geographic roots are to their own experience and understanding of the world they record. Although both women come from Catholic backgrounds (one urban, one rural), each in her distinctive way works to problematize at least to a degree her tribal subjectification.

These prose works may use the materials of actual lives but, like women's fiction, they refuse genre boundaries in their narrations. Northern writer Mary Costello notes, for example, that 'truths, untruths, misunderstandings, myths and rumours "ferment" into history' in Ireland, so she creates a novel/memoir form she describes as the 'disremembrance of time past'. This, she claims, is the method that best 'accommodates the natural and necessary exaggeration attendant upon the recounting of any Irish story....'[18] But hopes of representing 'reality' are not so easily discarded among writers whose existences were never meant to be written, unless in men's creations.

Polly Devlin notes in *All of Us There* that, as young children, she and her sisters 'could sometimes abandon the reality of our lives through reading, but we rarely lost ourselves in others' fictional imaginings, for our world was too daily, too palpably with us to be readily displaced'. As she grew older, though, it 'was books that began to show me a way out, although I was persuaded that even finding such a route to reality was probably bordering on sin, especially as Father Lappin constantly exhorted us to be on our guard against the written word. It was not just that the devil had all the best tunes, he also had control over the printing presses of the world' (pp. 148–9). When women could, as Polly Devlin did, break loose of that control and start writing their own tunes, they still needed access to the presses. The last generation has seen a remarkable flowering of men's literature in the North, but when I turn to women's fiction to see how northern women are imagining their respective communities, I find just a handful of published books – no doubt because of the class, gender and sectarian straitjackets mentioned above. The majority of contemporary works focus, not surprisingly, on the Troubles and their effects in women's, men's and children's lives. So it is to these I turn rather than to those contemporary works by northern women set outside the North or in the past, as in the novels of Caroline Blackwood, Polly Devlin, Kitty Manning, Kathleen Ferguson or, with the exception of two of her novels, Deirdre Madden. I bracket as well the work of Janet McNeill, Anne Crone and Kathleen Coyle, who wrote prior to the late 1960s, although Coyle's treats an earlier era of the Troubles, and Crone's is a remarkable mid-century exploration of the ways habits of sectarianism shape lives in the North.[19]

Northern contemporary fiction by women reveals a preoccupation with the ways authors 'write' conjunctions between the public and the private in people's lives, especially as these are mediated by social and media constructions of the Troubles. Each of the works discussed below offers a representation of the physical, familial, psychic reproduction of northern life. As northern novelist Linda Anderson put it in a description of her work: 'A recurring obsession in my work is the link between public and private kinds of violence, the way "public" violence seeps and deforms and creates what a man says to a woman in bed, for example, and the reverse situation, too. The way all our "privacies" create the mutilating world.'[20] In a time and place where newspapers and television offer too much and too little 'reality', is it a vain hope that perhaps artists can 'begin to free Irish images from the tyranny of stereotypes'?[21]

David Lloyd, modifying Bakhtin's theory, argues that the novel genre offers opportunities to create a 'heteroglossic' reality, a representation of the 'multiple social languages (or sociolects) of a given linguistic community'. The creation of competing modes of utterance will serve to destabilize or disintegrate 'an officially monologic national culture' but will also leave out a huge volume of 'inassimilable residue that it can neither properly contain not entirely exclude.' The formation of the novel requires its own careful 'regulation and hierarchization of sociolects' if it works to establish a 'normative ethical aim'. As the novel gives voice to some formerly voiceless groups, it disenfranchises other possible voices. Quoting Renato Rosaldo, he asks, 'Who isn't invited to the party?' (pp. 152–4). This is a question I shall return to at the end of this chapter.

War lives

In 1995, for the first time in my 20 years of visits to that region, a superficially peaceful Belfast wore giddy holiday colours under a blazing sun.

I was in that city, as were hundreds of other foreign and Irish scholars, for a conference with the sanguine title: 'Ireland: Island of Diversity'.[22] Our task was to discuss those multiplicities behind and beyond the traditional oppositions of Protestants and Catholics, nationalists and unionists, British and Irish. We were there to learn how to rescue the 'Other' from the realm of the exotic, to discover how many 'others' existed, to explore the conditions of the multiple sites of living, to examine and share the 'heteroglossic' reality. As northern novelist Frances Molloy put it in a speech reported after her death in 1991: 'If you look at a magpie closely it isn't black and white.'[23]

But since that summer, the 'Peace Process' – so hopeful, so fragile, and so flawed – has been broken again and again, the worst bomb explosion of the Troubles in Omagh in 1998 at the moment of highest hope for reconciliations. In such a history, polarizations can be difficult to resist. And so we discover, for example, in the 1984 fictionalized diary of the young female protagonist of Una Woods's *The Dark Hole Days*, this way of framing her writerly task: 'I'm looking down on the estate now. It's a weird sort of wilderness, yet in every house there's a story. I think about the stories. Sometimes they are sad and then there's a white flash. It might be a wedding or a christening and white laughing teeth. I think of blacks and whites. If I wrote stories, some would be black and some white.'[24]

In this formulation, black and white are emotional states, not political positions. Yet the novella ruthlessly forces the several stories possible at the beginning of the narrative into a single converging story of sectarian violence in which Colette, a young Catholic woman plotting her escape from Belfast and a career as writer, is balked from doing either when her apolitical father is killed as a randomly chosen victim of loyalist paramilitaries.[25] Another dead end closes the novella's parallel story of the teen-aged Protestant male protagonist, part of the group responsible for the death of Colette's father. In this 'plot', Joe ends up hiding out in a 'black dugout' under the floor in his mother's house, 'sinking in [his]own darkness' (p. 63). Although these two young people have never met, their fates link together inescapably. Colette, who had hoped to become author of her own narratives, becomes a statistic about whom 'all the usual statements have been issued'. The result as she sees it is that 'we're stamped as victims now, we'll always be victims of the Troubles' (p. 58).

This is perhaps the most extreme representation of the ghastly effects of civil war in the women's fiction that follows, yet all contemporary writers who would write about the North face a grim task: how

can one write of the 'Troubles' without falling into rhetoric or dema-
goguery or hopelessness? How can one *not* write of the 'Troubles' if
one chooses a contemporary setting? While most of the works I will
look at in this chapter offer resistant readings that do not make
women more victims than men, most inscribe the experience of Ruth
Carr's lines: 'women live lives / of even quieter desperation'.

Women writing the war in Titanic Town

Medbh McGuckian, Ruth Carr and Una Woods, whom I have quoted
above, all live in Belfast. This is not so common among women writers
whose subject is Belfast; most write of that place from elsewhere,
'where life resembled life more than it did here' as the narrator ironically states in *No Mate for the Magpie* by Derry writer Frances Molloy.
Molloy, Briege Duffaud and Jennifer Johnston, important northern
writers whose novels are discussed in Chapter 4, do not use Belfast as
their primary setting. In this chapter I limit my scope mainly to Belfast
fiction; as capital and largest city it is the most important site of narrative and conflict; moreover, in some of the fiction, the city itself
becomes a metonym for the civil unrest and divisiveness. Although I
refer to the works of several writers, I pay closest attention to *Titanic
Town, Sisters by Rite, To Stay Alive, Give Them Stones, Hidden Symptoms,*
and *One by One in the Darkness*,[26] all of which offer particularly challenging examples of resistant art. Although most of the works
discussed below are complex constructions of many aspects of
northern life, I shall focus primarily on how they inscribe the ways the
war 'has gone into' the characters, and how their 'privacies [in turn]
create the mutilating world'.

This focus generally involves as well narratives about characters
living on the poor side of a brutal class divide. As one of Elizabeth
Shannon's informants reports, as a middle-class Protestant, she is
'very little affected' by the Troubles because 'it's very much a
working-class war' (p. 136). Jennifer Johnston's *The Railway Station
Man,* set in Derry and Donegal, attempts to subvert such a view in a
novel inscribing the effects of random violence and mistaken identity
in the life of a middle-class Protestant woman who before the violent
deaths of her husband, son and lover thought of her life as one 'filled
with safety' (p. 4). But if the war can intrude into anyone's life, the
sheer *presentness* of its force is inescapable among the metropolitan
poor. This means Catholic poor and Protestant poor; as the wry
narrator of *Titanic Town,* Annie McPhelimy puts it: 'At the time we

lived just around the corner from what was to become, comically enough, the Peace Line – a half-hearted and in places permeable Berlin Wall, thrown up in the seventies to prevent impoverished Protestants and oppressed and impoverished Catholics from knocking the shite out of each other' (p. 9).

Back in 1969, when Bernadette Devlin and the People's Democracy group were still hopeful that James Connolly's socialist republic would be born on the island, she confidently stated that 'our system is one in which the basic divide is thought to be along religious lines, in which it is quite rational for a man to believe he is sentenced to unemployment for the crime of being a Catholic. But he is not. He is sentenced to unemployment because there are not enough jobs, and there are not enough jobs because investment is made on grounds of profit, not on grounds of people's needs. The crowd at that first-ever civil-rights march [on 5 October 1968] was interested in people's needs' (p. 96). But as the civil rights movement – variously inscribed in the fiction of Molloy, Duffaud, Costello, Madden, Beckett – disintegrated in the face of, among other factors, a violent loyalist backlash, class issues were increasingly shadowed by ethnicized 'religious' difference. In *Northern Ireland: a Chronology of the Troubles 1968–1993*, Paul Bew and Gordon Gillespie argue that the People's Democracy march on 1 January 1969 'marks the pivotal point at which the Troubles changed from being primarily about civil rights to the more ancient disputes concerning religious and national identities.' The aftermath of the loyalist response to what was perceived as a Catholic march unearthed 'layers of animosity and hatred which had remained at least partly buried [but obviously not dead] over the previous decades.'[27]

But if class and sectarian difference seemed paramount in the late 1960s and early 1970s, another systemic problem became prominent by the mid-1970s, the effects of skewed gender relations. So oblivious to such matters was Bernadette Devlin back in 1969 – a state she shared with radical left women of other cultures – that she, along with her colleagues, fought for universal adult suffrage (and still needed to struggle for this basic right in the late 1960s!) under the slogan 'One man, one vote.' And just in case her reader shrugs off such a construction as a non-toxic 'neutral' generic, she also articulates the need of the working-class Catholic as one in which 'fathers and husbands should be able to live and work in Ireland with decent wages and something like human dignity ... ' (p. 164). Such a demand is all the more ironic in that historically it was the working-class women in the North who were often the family bread-winners with their mill work, a condition Mary Beckett explores in her novel *Give Them Stones* and Mary A. Larkin sentimental-izes in her very successful Belfast romance novel, *The Wasted Years*.[28]

The problem of gender construction is one many northern women address, perhaps because it is so often occluded in a masculinist society that both causes and is reinforced by blatant militarism. In one of the first Irish publications devoted entirely to feminist discussions of Irish society, a special 1980 issue of *The Crane Bag* offered an article that suggests two important preconditions to this masculinist tradition that enables the reproduction of particularized gender roles: 'Within Irish families there has always been a rigid separation of roles between husbands and wives .... Although women may control the family in terms of maintaining it and holding it together, essentially it is men's and not women's interests which are served. The control of the family gives women merely the illusion of power; the reality is that women are confronted by immense burdens as they attempt to provide a reasonable standard of living.'[29]

Polly Devlin offers a personalized example of this argument in her own family memoir, one that she then applies more generally in Northern Ireland:

> We [six sisters] danced around our father, small Salomes, and believed fiercely, passionately that he was the only pivot of that ring, that he was the source of strength and the spring of power. We could not admit what we knew at some profound level to be the truth – that our mother was the stronger .... We kept our eyes fixed on the Man and pushed away the other incompatible knowledge of mad bad female strength, by its nature wicked, unclean, immodest, unchaste and worst of all unnatural.

This attitude, she continues,

> subsisted in the society around us: our obeisances to our males were repeated at every level. Women rear their girl children as they themselves were reared, to defer to males in their family ... to try to anticipate their every wish. These attitudes made enemies of men and women, and they might have spoken different languages for all the communication that seemed to take place between the sexes.... The legacy of such divides seemed to be a feeling of contempt on both sides, and suspicion, distrust and a certain amount of fear – of men for women and *vice versa* – fear of the unknown, if of nothing else (pp. 29–30).

In a society where male dominance is this marked, and gender dimorphism can be so oppositional, it is not surprising that the women authors pay special attention to the construction of masculinity and its varied class and sectarian formations. Moreover, the choices authors make in creating male characters often position their books politically in very revealing ways. When we compare, for example, the creation of so-called physical force nationalist IRA Provo men in two authors writing about the North, we find strikingly different strategies in the creation of the principal male characters. In Jennifer Johnston's *Shadows on Our Skin*, set in Derry, we find brutal and brutalizing creatures, whether they are old men or young. One of the two central women characters, the wife of an unemployed, drunken, violent, old republican layabout, encapsulates the position of the novel when she describes her husband thus:

> Why should anyone feel pity for you? You've never done a hand's turn in your life. Sit up above [in the pub] like Lord Muck with your stout and your betting slips telling us what a great hero you were. You say you're crippled. What about me? With you chained round my neck for life? Any pity I have in my heart is for myself and the fool I was.[30]

Salome, disappointed, turns harridan. The only male in the novel who escapes this kind of narrative dismissal is their young son, an aspiring poet, caught in the middle of the war inside and outside his home. Significantly, his sensitivity, so different from his male peers and family, is inculcated by his mother who tries to keep him in her company and away from boys and men: this sets him apart from, and attentively critical of, members of his own sex. In a revealing mistake, the publishers of the 1986 Fontana paperback version of the novel, reproduce on the cover 'Girl Studying' by C. Person.

When we contrast this bitter characterization of nationalist men, a characterization rendered intractable by the omniscience of the distancing third-person narration, with that of Mary Costello's *Titanic Town* we discover a very different picture. Here the fictionalized memoirs are located within a poor Catholic family of Belfast's Andersontown, and the IRA men are not just matey, generous, and (sometimes) competent, they are also willing to recognize and support (if also occasionally to use) their women in a quite reassuring fashion. With such men in charge – if only they could be in charge – justice might almost be attainable.[31] This is, however, a comic novel, one highly freighted with ironic displacement, a black humour mix of hilarious anecdote, caricatured characterization, and fictionalized history. Here, for example, is a rendering of the experience of teen-aged girls trying to go find 'male company' of an evening.

> A typical night out in Titanic Town. There were the parents to be persuaded. We would not be late, we would not drink, smoke or indulge in impure acts. We would not be set upon by gangs of rapists, bag-snatchers or drug-pushers. Nor would we get arrested, or involved in a riot or related incidents. We would not travel on a bus which would be hijacked. We would not place ourselves in the path of any bomb, bullet or simple incendiary device. We would not be induced to get into cars full of paramilitaries, especially not if they clapped hands over our mouths and placed black bags over our heads. We would not, in short, be assassinated. We would not be persuaded to give up our studies and run away to join the IRA. My parents between them thought of everything. Hilda's mother was merely anxious that we should remember to take an umbrella (p. 270).

No matter how inspired the humour of this Belfast version of parental fears, despair is at the heart of this story. As the novel's title suggests, Belfast is doomed to failure, 'the town that gave the world the Titanic, the ship would have been the highlight of our achievement. We did it arseways. Belfast holds the real secret of the sinking of the Titanic. It was the serial number on the ship; they say that if you held it up to a mirror it read: NO POPE HERE' (p. 25).

One of the novel's most developed, and least humorous sections (despite the menopause jokes), narrates the pathetic saga of the Peace Women's activism of 1976. With Annie's mother as the figure of Betty Williams, the novel figures the multiple pressures on the women from the warring factions and the manipulations by authorities (Catholic clergy and British rulers) that kill the initiative. The simplicity of the women who call for peace but not for social justice makes them easy dupes for the male leaders, a process that culminates in an internationally broadcast television 'photo-opportunity' which closes with one of the women asking the British secretary if he was pleased with them. 'Very pleased,' Mr. Brandywell pronounced, a contented growl, 'you've done very well indeed.' Switch to the viewers:

> The journalists heard it, the TV cameras picked it up, beamed it all over Andersontown, bounced it off Divis and Collin Mountains

until it came to rest like a damp mist over Bunbeg Gardens.... It would echo forever: *Very, very pleased. You've done very well indeed....* At that moment [Annie's] intuition told her that this would be the end, not the start of it. There would be no peace. There could be none (pp. 240–1).

This fictionalized retrospective of the 1970s was published in 1992. Thus, its final words, so nearly contemporary, are particularly bleak:

For there will be no surrender, fuck pope and queen both the same. Sons, sisters, fathers, daughters, husbands and brothers will not be grudged, though they go out to break their strength and die. We will not give an inch and shall not be moved, till the last drops of blood, orange and green, run down the street, through our four green fields, one of them in bondage, to mingle with the rivers of ceaseless rain, seep into the brown sucking bog and piss, peacefully at last, out into Belfast Lough, in the wake of the Titanic (p. 340).

Belfast fiction

Una Woods's *The Dark Hole Days* chooses an unusual approach among the books about, and from, Belfast: her central male character is a sympathetically presented loyalist paramilitary 'soldier'. As though to present the genealogy of shame and desire that motivates this kind of partisan, she creates 'Joe', a very young man who is unemployed, poor, the single child of a doting widow, a man who 'joins up' for reasons he elaborates on in his private diary, his opening words in the novella:

Out with Gerry and Sam getting some information for protection purposes. Learning how not to be selfish. Have learnt a lot since I met Gerry and Sam in the dole. There aren't enough people who care, Sam said. I was one. I was just messing around, playing billiards. I let others get on with it. Like the politicians. Can politicians protect us, Sam asked me. I said no (p. 1).

Sam's skillful recruiting of the young fantasist is enhanced by creating a sense of fellowship and shared purpose, a meaning for living: 'god you want to have seen them all tonight. I can't believe it's real. I think I'm dreaming or maybe watching a film, but then I realize it's me there with all the lads.... I always thought I would be something' (pp. 4, 6). This sense of purpose grows as he distances himself from 'ordinary life' and submerges his being in the cause. 'Sometimes I walk through the park and meet up with some of the old mates although I haven't much time for the idle chat these days. There's no meaning. Today I went out alone. I had a sense of power and even superiority' (p. 8). Not long into his new role, he fantasizes about his attractiveness to the pretty young clerk at the dole office, creating an ersatz sexual prowess out of his militarism. Delighted to be in the action, memorizing secret codes that remap the geography of Belfast according to loyalist strategies, he distances himself from his widowed mother ('It's a man's world, ma', p. 12) who nonetheless dances attendance on him, her only child and the centre of her life and love. Ironically, when Joe ends up under the floor boards of their home, hiding from retaliation after losing his nerve at a Catholic murder site, his mother gets him back, dependent, literally under her feet. The novella closes with Joe's desperate thoughts: 'What keeps me going? That I didn't kill the man, that it will be all over some day. I will walk out free. The police won't want me for whatever I was in, whoever was in it won't want me for opting out. And that girl from the dole loves me. She loves me.' Then, the realization of no exit: 'All thoughts stop with Sam' (p. 64).

With the exception of a women's romance novel by Niki Hill that puts a UDR man at the centre of female desire, most of the women's fictions dealing with the 'Sam' variety of militaristic machismo, loyalist or nationalist, do so by indirection and male absence.[32] We find this particularly in the elliptical approach of short stories. In Brenda Murphy's 'A Social Call', for example, the brutal beating of a wife trying to stop her IRA Provo husband leaving the flat with a gun for a 'punishment shooting' is narrated through the indirect discourse of a woman friend unable to shield her friend.[33] Similarly, when a woman engages in uninhibited if apolitical conversation with a British soldier in Fiona Barr's much anthologized 'The Wall Reader', she ends up with 'Tout' [informer, betrayer] written on her house, the very facelessness of the threat adding to its terror, and driving the woman and her family from Belfast into the Republic.[34] Even when the young soldiers-in-the-making are treated as completely feckless, as in Stella Mahon's 'On the Front Line', a small amount of violence can light the tinder of young male desire. While older neighbors laugh dismissively at 'our boul' Freddie', 'a general an' a half', up the road the riots have begun and 'two men lay dead, one with a bullet in his chest.'[35] This kind of male incompetence, which I would see as the narrative's displacement of women's fears, reaches one of its most derisive expressions in Mary Beckett's 'The Master and the Bombs'. Here a wife narrates – to an unnamed and possibly indifferent audience – the story of her schoolteacher husband's arrest when bombs are discovered in the school shed. 'You can take me away, Officer. I am entirely responsible', says the husband to his wife's astonishment. She assumes the husband is simply 'running away to prison' to escape their crowded and unhappy domestic life, and indeed, given the readiness of his ingenuous confession, she may be right. But what is striking about the story is the woman's assumption that he could not be involved in terrorism, that her own all-engrossing maternity offers a knowledge adequate to the terror of the times and place and the force of male desire. 'He was never out of the house long enough to belong to any illegal organization. Still, he decided to walk out on us so I'm going to pretend to respect his decision – I'm leaving it to him. He's the man, let him act like one.'[36]

Anne Devlin's book of short stories *The Way-Paver* offers a story remarkable both for its oblique but potent style and for the skill of its narrative focus on a woman's choice of violence after the 1969 events in working-class Catholic Andersontown. Unlike Joe and his cohort from *The Dark Hole Days*, who rename Belfast streets almost in the spirit of a cryptographic game, Finn repeats over and over the actual streets of West Belfast while under police interrogation – an obsessively accurate litany of stark landmarks under 'redevelopment ... the planners are our bombers now'.[37] To those who cannot understand her decision to join the 'cause', specifically her interrogators and her ex-lover (an English journalist), she says simply, 'Let's just say it was historical' (p. 117). But this example, and that of an IRA fighter in Briege Duffaud's *A Wreath Upon the Dead,* are unique in their portrayal of actual nationalist violence by women in fiction, although novelist Kate O'Riordan (another Irish émigrée to London) creates a terrifying Belfast matriarch who partners what is depicted as her son's pathological IRA terrorism in the novel *Involved.*[38] Most of the northern women's fiction is not preoccupied with women's violence but with the ways in which male violence is damaging to the lives of women and their children even when the characters support it owing to personal and tribal loyalty, proximate necessity, or a keen sense of the 'historical'. I turn now to novels that challenge in various ways the easy simplicities of oppositional gender and sectarianism.

Joan Lingard's *Sisters by Rite*

Joan Lingard's first Belfast novel for adults precedes the others discussed here by many years.[39] *The Lord on Our Side* was published in 1970, the second, and more successful, *Sisters by Rite*, a revision of the earlier book, in 1984. In both novels she puts at the centre a young girl growing up in the 1940s as a member of the Christian Science sect in the midst of Protestant working-class East Belfast, an autobiographical detail that works in the fiction both as a marker of marginality and as a location for extra-sectarian understanding. In the first book the girl lives entirely surrounded by Protestants so that her religion is seen as the odd or alien one. As her headmistress puts it in the mid-1940s: 'I prefer my girls to be normal. We can do well enough with Church of Ireland, Presbyterians and Methodists, without these odd sects. They tend to be quite narrow. Say what you like, they never do quite fit in' (p. 75). Needless to say, where Christian Science is odd and abnormal to the 'real' Protestants in the novel, Catholicism is treated as a pathology beyond toleration. But Catholicism and Catholics are only introduced tangentially, when a minor character, the homosexual son of a wealthy Christian Science matron, is converted to the religion through the offices of the family housekeeper. The form his Catholicism takes, perhaps all too predictably, is the choice of nationalist politics and his murder at the end of the novel by a demonic Orangeman is justified by the killer with the claim that the Lord is on his side. Placing these words in the final sentence of the novel suggests authorial judgment, yet the formulaic opposition Lingard creates here between Taig and Prod results in caricatures that do little to unpack the lived experiences of difference that fortify the hatreds.

Sisters by Rite, a much more complex novel, offers in 1984 a reprise of the earlier work, except that a triangular model of female friendship, instead of an individual girl's development, forms the moral and dramatic centre. Although the novel recounts again growing up in East Belfast in the 1940s, it does not follow the earlier novel's linear plotting from early childhood to adulthood. Instead, *Sisters* opens with a 1970 TV broadcast in a London home, where one of the friends is drawn back into her childhood neighborhood, and the reader into the viewer's childhood, as it flashes on the screen – that day's murder site from Northern Ireland. Drawing toward the screen 'as if [she] could move into the street with the camera' (p. 5), this narrative eye ('I') then recounts the story and explains its meaning. Herein lies the satisfaction of the novel and its weakness – the device of the adult narrator allows for a neatness of narrative and a comforting closure that solves the problem of 1970s Belfast with a 1940s personal accommodation.

The 'sisters' of the title are three unrelated girls who live as neighbors in a single block in East Belfast, in a time and place where different denominations might still cohabit, albeit uneasily. One, named Rosie, is a Protestant, Teresa is a Catholic, the third and mediating partner, Cora, a Christian Science girl whose home and family become the supposedly neutral terrain on which the traditional enemies can meet and eventually bond through a blood rite of sisterhood that lasts until ten years later when Cora and Rosie both fall in love with Teresa's brother. While their passion has nothing to do with politics, the effects of the passion cannot be separated from politics when the jealous Cora alerts Rosie's bigoted Orange uncle to Rosie's love of Catholic Gerard. The disaster that results suggests that no neutral places exist in the North wherein to lead a sectarian-free life.

What makes this novel so interesting is the way the author examines the construction of difference – class, gender and sect – in the lives of growing children instead of simply assuming the difference as she had in the earlier book. We follow the children through their differential educations and we watch as Cora, already attuned to the problems and possibilities of difference through her Christian Science upbringing, learns to question the orthodoxies she is being offered by the larger society. The marginalized religious belief becomes a tool whereby she can query and thus destabilize the rigid oppositional divisions afflicting the other children, just as the thoughtful Catholic boy Gerard uses his marginal position as Catholic to question the official historical constructions offered by the educational system. (The working-class Protestant Rosie does not have the same kind of marginality and never learns to read power relations with the kind of acumen the non-Protestants do.)

Like the earlier novel, the action hinges on violent religious conflict, but here the author uses the apolitical emotion of sexual jealousy as the catalyst that sets the vendetta in motion – one that has consequences that rip through Rosie's and Teresa's families over a generation and presumably beyond the end of the novel in 1970. Hatred in the form of religious bigotry circulates within the society, but it is a simple, rogue emotion that enables the clan warfare – an example of what Linda Anderson called 'the way all our "privacies" create the mutilating world.' It is not just religion that enshrines difference here, though; equally important is class difference. When Cora travels in 1970 through middle-class sections of Belfast, both Protestant and Catholic, she describes the tree-lined streets as 'area[s] that testified to law and order ... with no hint of menace,' reflecting 'professional and executive tastes ... well-kept gardens, well-kept houses, and well-kept lives, on the surface at least' (pp. 204, 210).

When Gerard becomes a doctor and thus crosses the class barrier, his family's history of religious war in the poor people's ghetto erupts into his new life, but it is significant that the violence occurs at his office in the Catholic Falls (Andersontown) area where he works, rather than the middle-class neighborhood in which he lives, this kind of horizontal class violence a familiar phenomenon.

Lingard's novels, then, are sensitive examinations of individual lives in a troubled society. But the exploration of the creation and perpetuation of religious bigotry is limited to settings of the 1940s and 1950s; the sudden shift to the time of the Troubles in 1970 does not attempt to show the now-grown characters in the complexity of their lives and struggles, or the lived experience of 1970 Belfast. For example, the novel simply offers, without conviction or explanation, the conversion to Catholicism of the Christian Science woman. Thus when the novel closes with a reforging of the friendship among the three main women after the brother of one has killed the uncle of another, it is an affirmation of the hope that historically-based difference marked in blood need be no barrier to strong, accepting human relationships. The ending feels too simple for the situation, almost sentimental despite the intelligence of the writing.

Linda Anderson's *To Stay Alive*

Linda Anderson's Belfast novel *To Stay Alive* (American title *We Can't All be Heroes, You know*), was published in 1985 a year after *Sisters by Rite*, but is set nine years later, in 1979, 11 years into the contemporary Troubles, and the text offers no relief from that inescapable present. Its avoidance of any deflecting humour, and its depictions of betrayal in all relationships in the novel, makes it the grittiest of the novels examined here. Once again the television camera 'makes' meaning but where the broadcast in Lingard's novel drew Cora back into her childhood neigborhood, the television functions very differently in Anderson's novel; here cynical Northerners have learned to use it to their own purposes, so seeing is definitely not believing and each group 'reads' through its own sectarian filter.

'What's all the commotion down the street, Marty?'
'It's just Canadian TV men. They're interviewing Mrs Hartley. You should see her! She's so delighted with herself, she's even taken out her curlers. The Brits ransacked her house during a raid, ripped up the floorboards, the lot. She's been keeping the damage

intact for four days. The whole Brit press has been given a conducted tour.'

Rosaleen laughed, visualizing the film that would result. An interview with a Brit officer, who would speak with the exquisite enunciation of an ex-Etonian of his men's courtesy and restraint .... Then there would be the cut to the havoc in the house, lovingly listed by the aggrieved woman. And all the Prods would watch and say: 'She did it herself. They'll go to any lengths to discredit the army' (p. 67).

The sympathies of this novel reside squarely with the poor Catholics of West Belfast; the author, herself a working-class Protestant, makes no attempt here to represent that experience. Like Lingard, Anderson also sets up a triad of characters whose personal struggles foreground the larger social milieu in which their kind struggle to stay alive. Grimly critical of the British army presence in Belfast, the novel moves the readers inside that presence, using the increasing disaffection and ultimate desertion of a young British soldier as a strategy for charting the atrocities of his superiors and colleagues. (One chapter even uses, somewhat unsuccessfully, the interior monologue of a sadistic British officer by way of showing the heart of darkness.) The other two main characters Dan and Rosaleen are a bright but poor young married Catholic couple, although Dan's middle-class background makes him an alien in the working-class world he chooses to inhabit in his domestic life with Rosaleen. Through their lives, Anderson explores how poverty acquires particular kinds of meaning and functions in a particular place. In this version of Catholic West Belfast, the unaware Protestant elite, the British army, and the local IRA Provos catch people like Dan and Rosaleen in a vise. While Anderson offers as back-drop to these abuses the animosity and prejudice of the Protestants, the novel treats the British, with their standing army, as the real enemy, and their ultimate weapon, sexual intimidation. For example, towards the end of the novel, when Dan has been lifted for interroga-tion and torture, his very body the signifier of helplessness, Rosaleen goes to a store on a deserted street where she is trapped by four British soldiers who sexually assault her and would have raped her had she not vomited in disgust on one of her assailants. Locking herself in her own home is no protection, though; at any time of the day or night, the army can legally enter and ravage her spaces. This particular form of humiliation is gendered as female, but the novel shows the equally grotesque male version of gendered humiliation when again and again Catholic men in West Belfast are forced to 'spreadeagle against the wall for frisking', the male body 'bent forward, rump jutting out like a female baboon inviting sexual entry' in front of the armed British soldiers (p. 169). This kind of ghastly experience of humiliation inflicted on the Catholic population in the most mundane of daily events serves as core and commentary in the novel; lest there be any doubt, the novel opens with a British paratrooper using Rosaleen's dog for target practice.

In such an environment even ability and promise can become a curse. Dan, a Catholic medical student, cannot refuse to help wounded Provos, especially since, as a poor man he has need of the money to support his family, and thus becomes compromised towards both factions, with no easy either/or judgments or decisions possible.

Rosaleen's fierce desire to stay alive in the face of so much death, despite her total sexual and social vulnerability in a city full of soldiers of all sorts (another kind of Belfast diversity), marks an heroic struggle against the false forms of heroism current in Belfast society. She would flee Northern Ireland if she could and if her husband Dan would, but Anderson refuses her readers any kind of closure in this 1985 novel which circles round and round the multiple ways that private relationships even among lovers are poisoned by the mutilating world. If Joan Lingard, a Protestant writer, explores differences among Protestants, Linda Anderson, a Protestant writer deeply sympathetic to the compromised situation of Northern Catholics, does the same among Catholics, and in both cases the murderous effect of difference within groups and among groups refuses any kind of solution other than self-exile.

Mary Beckett's *Give Them Stones*

Mary Beckett's 1987 novel *Give Them Stones* attempts the same kind of historical retrospective that Lingard's does but brings the portrait of Belfast society into the late-1980s when the British army is well established. Unlike Anderson's novel which relies on dialogue that gives it immediacy and power, Mary Beckett uses the device of a central musing consciousness that reconstructs and interprets events from the 1930s to the 1980s. Irish critic Eve Patten dismissed the novel as 'mere reportage'[40] as though the author and her character were transparently one, thereby ignoring the remarkable achievement of this creation, a simple, uneducated, poor Catholic (no resemblance to her author except in religious background) whose integrity and limited knowledge give the reader an unusual and relentless angle on Irish history. By temperament and choice a resister, Martha, bread-maker for the poor, offers a superb lens for examining the experience of outsider.

The novel begins in the 1980s with the now aging Martha deciding she will no longer support the IRA Provos in her district, no longer pay them their protection fee for acting as local police in her no-go area; she does this as an act of defiance against what she thinks of as gratu-itous cruelty when they double knee-cap a delinquent Catholic boy of the neighborhood against the side of her house. Martha is not unaware of the multiple oppressions of her group and of the respon-sibility of England and the loyalists in reproducing them. But against these groups she feels herself helpless to intervene whereas with the IRA Provos she feels the possibility of direct communication. As she says: 'I could do nothing about [the whole thing that was England]. It was all out of my reach but when the Provos took it on themselves to bring law and order to the district I got angry' (p. 141). But such indi-vidual acts of difference cannot be tolerated by a besieged paramilitary group whose effectiveness depends on absolute unity and support among 'their' people, so Martha's act of bravery costs her her home and her bread shop, both put to the torch in retaliation for her refusal.

It is in this dire situation that she needs to ask for temporary shelter from her sister, Mary Brigid, a woman who has managed to achieve professional independence and a well-heeled marriage and thus become a member of Belfast's middle class. Musing about Mary Brigid's position, Martha offers a very astute analysis of the occasion when diversity can be merely benign, when difference can be tolerated – a description reminiscent of the one I quoted above from Lingard. '[Mary Brigid] had a lovely house and garden and the district she lived in was quiet and content and green from the trees and the golf links. Everybody spoke to everybody else on the avenues and nobody seemed to mind who was Protestant and who was Catholic' says Martha. But then she adds that half a dozen houses were put up for sale when a new Catholic Church was built on a hill overlooking the place with the Angelus bell and the Mass bells ringing out every day over the district (p. 148). The cushion provided by security and wealth makes for different kinds of com-fortable interconnections among people, a cushion denied to those living at the limits as Martha and her family are. Near the end of the book Martha recounts a conversation she and her husband had about obtaining British compensation for the burning of their home, com-pensation that they obtain with help from the Sinn Fein advice centre.

The macabre contradiction here of the IRA Provos burning down the house that is rebuilt with the advice of the Sinn Fein, political wing of the IRA, is one that Martha and Dermot finally laugh at, recognizing that the powerless do not have the social maneuverability of her sister's middle-class family. 'It was all right for them,' she thinks, 'they never needed help. Nothing happened to them anyway in their nice house in their mixed district and if they wanted information they knew what to do and where to go. We didn't,' adds Martha, 'but we were getting a bit cuter' (p. 150). The novel ends with Martha planning a new bakery to replace the one burned down by the Provos. Although not entirely sanguine about its chances of surviving in the midst of war, she remains determined to give bread to people too long fed on stones. Her method of survival demands a clear-eyed analysis of the complex social relations and a fairly cynical decision to take advantage where one can in the fissures and contradictions among those relationships. Indeed by the end of the novel, on several occasions Martha and her husband, who agree on little else, agree that however much they disapprove of Provo violence, they perhaps ought to vote Sinn Fein, as they're 'the only people that scare the Brits'. But by then, even the independent Martha figures that she cannot 'be expected to be brave all the time', running a campaign all on her own in refusing to pay off her Provo 'protectors' (p. 150).

Who isn't invited to this novel? Again, it's the northern Protestants except as shadowy backdrop to the Catholic dramas. But within the latter group, Beckett achieves a rich 'heteroglossia' as the novel explores the various modes (and nodes) of Catholic resistance or complicity. For example, in its treatment of the events of 1968, the entire focus is on the contrary responses to the media depictions, the Catholic citizens loving the 'back-answers' Gerry Fitt and Bernadette Devlin were able to make on television to 'people we had never heard of before like Chichester Clarke.' Martha hopes for a united Ireland, the 'thought of the border's like a nail sticking up in my shoe', but her (Catholic) interlocutors perversely dismiss her concerns ('sure, we know nothing about them down there. A whole lot of them talk Irish, don't they? We wouldn't know what they're saying') or agree for the wrong reasons ('Aye, you're right there, love. Dublin's a lovely place') (pp. 117–18).

This complex and compassionate rendering of the northern situation is the more interesting when we learn that this author wrote the book as a deliberate intervention into the political situation, a writer's attempt to 'write' the wrongs in her former home from within the safe confines of her present Dublin location.[41]

Deirdre Madden's *Hidden Symptoms* and *One by One in the Darkness*

Deirdre Madden's 1986 Belfast novel *Hidden Symptoms* ostensibly moves its action away from the killing streets and into a world of two young writers from Queen's University. Almost immediately, however, the reader learns that one cannot escape those streets when the novel offers a grotesque plot twist that subverts the characters' ambitions and hopes, both because of their working-class locations and their Catholicism. Robert, a self-styled intellectual, believes he can move beyond his family's tribal religion and philistinism into a world of refined agnosticism where difference does not mean hate. But when he claims he is no longer a Catholic, Theresa, the other writer, mocks him with the challenge:

> Just tell me this: if you were found in the morning with a bullet in your head, what do you think the papers would call you? An agnostic? No, Robert, nobody, not even you is naive enough to think that. Of course you don't believe: but there's a big difference between faith and loyalty and if you think you can escape tribal loyalty in Belfast today you're betraying your people and fooling yourself (p. 46).

Theresa's cynicism is a result of her twin's torture and assassination two years earlier at the hands of undiscovered murderers, her brother an apolitical Catholic, a random victim. Like the situation in Woods's *The Dark Hole Days*, this kind of carefully calculated 'random' violence by loyalist paramilitaries takes us a long way beyond the symmetrical vengeances of Lingard's novels. Theresa is cast into absolute despair at Francis' death, yet she claims that 'the new Belfast [is] more acceptable than the city of her earliest memories, for the normality had always been forced, a prosperous facade over discrimination and injustice.' She elaborates: 'Ulster before 1969 had been sick but with hidden symptoms.... Belfast was now like a madman who tears his flesh, puts straw in his hair and screams gibberish' (pp. 14–15). Later the narrator, whose voice blends throughout with Theresa's, claims that 'the violence and political struggles had effected less change than was generally acknowledged; it had not altered Belfast's perception of itself' (p. 80).

Because both Robert and Theresa are writers who talk about the meanings and uses of art, the novel is as much an exploration of art as it is of Belfast politics. These are the people who, by their own lights, should be shapers of perception; that they feel so immobilized throughout the novel reveals the impasse of life in the Troubles. As Theresa says: 'It would be futile to look for [places] conceived in the memory, language and discourse of others ... because in the form she saw them they had never truly existed.' Of course the corollary of this is that, should she succeed in creating her own written discourse (as her author has), she might shift the perception of others, offer some original 'take' that could act as bridge among people.

Early in the novel the narrator has Theresa state her artistic purpose, and the rest of the novel centres Theresa's concerns. She tells Robert and their friend Kathy that she writes 'about subjectivity – and inarticulation – about life pushing you into a state where everything is melting until you're left with the absolute and you can find neither the words nor the images to express it.' (p. 28). The absolute for Theresa is the death of her twin and the impossibility of salvaging anything but evil from the event. In this way Belfast, the contaminated city and symbol of evil, becomes the site of the farthest reaches of human sanity and suffering. As she puts it:

> just as it would be impossible to find Francis now, no matter where in the city or the world one went, so also it would be impossible not to find somewhere the man who had killed him. That person was out there as surely as she was in bed in her room, and his invisible existence seemed to contaminate the whole world. She lay awake until morning, afraid to sleep in the darkness which contained him (p. 43).

Her way of handling this kind of terror is the acceptance of Catholic belief and practice.

Like Theresa, the writer Robert also stretches to find adequate articulation for his experience and the city's; he wonders what is worse, the 'claustrophobia of Belfast or the verbal deficiency which prevented him from describing it' (p. 77). But the very extremity of the place has its uses as it forces thoughtful people to consider the most difficult questions: the meaning of evil in human life, the experience and value of religious belief, questions of death and the afterlife. Like the murdered Francis, these fictional writers strain to think the unthinkable. This leaves them with no comfort or support against the void, and both experience an extreme sense of inescapable loneliness (p. 81).

Two artists struggling with questions of 'subjectivity' wonder about the use of art in such a universe, a situation that serves to raise the question beyond the limits of this novel. The argument persists throughout *Hidden Symptoms*, at one place Theresa arguing that art cannot, should not be 'obsessed with ... politics of the state of the world', at another that art must have social use, that the artist must have 'the guts to be partial'. One writes, she claims, even though nobody can understand anything more than 'one side, the side you happen to be on' (pp. 27, 101).

The bleakness of these lives is unrelieved, and no relief is offered at any point in the novel. If one is alert to the 'meaning' of the Belfast articulated here, human life is without any hope (except perhaps the transcendence beyond human life.) The novel closes with a final image of a mirror reflecting in distorted form the image of the viewer, a trope throughout the novel, and a comment on the problem of artistic articulation. In the final gesture of the novel, Theresa turns her back on the mirror 'with its cold, circular, distorted room, and looked around the real parlour in which she was standing ... Shivering, she crossed to the hearth, knelt down and tried to rekindle the dying fire' (p. 142). Little hope in the gesture, but still a deliberate and conscious choice to go on living despite this moral bleakness.

Of all the works discussed in this chapter, perhaps *Hidden Symptoms'* vision is the most despairing. The Belfast of Madden's novel is not presented as uniquely ghastly; it is just that the ghastliness of human life emerges in its clearest lineaments in a place where comfort and solace are depicted as chimeras. The close-in focus on these isolated young people creates an intense sense of claustrophobia.

In a second novel about the North, written a decade after *Hidden Symptoms,* Madden creates a more expansive world, even though, once again, a beloved, politically innocent, family member has been killed. Unlike the earlier novel set in Belfast, this one is set primarily in the rural North, with periodic forays into Belfast. The novel recounts two stories alternately, a narrative technique that opens up spaces in the novel as the reader moves back and forth between the eyes of innocence and those of tragic but courageous experience. The first story is the saga of a loving Catholic family with three daughters growing up during the 1960s and 1970s; the second, the story of a week in the 1990s when these three sisters meet at their family home two years after the murder of their father to hear the news that one of them has chosen to be a single mother.

The intractability of the northern situation is as unrelieved as that of Madden's earlier novel but a possibility this novel offers, balancing innocence and knowledge, makes room for individual decency and courageous resistance even in the places where public violence reigns. While it is clear that the sisters and their mother will never forgive the murder and the daily cruelties of an occupying army (to whom the Catholics are the enemies), it is also clear that the three daughters live by their father's life principle that all kinds of sectarian killing are senseless, that one can resist in one's private life the mutilating world, even if one cannot avoid being in the state where the 'war has gone into us'. After a funeral of one young IRA fighter, the father says to his daughters: 'Never forget what you saw today; and never let anybody try to tell you that is was anything other than a life wasted, and lives destroyed' (p. 105). This commitment to pacifism does not save him from murder, but he does manage to avoid the stalemate Linda Anderson depicts so effectively where 'public violence seeps in and deforms and creates what a man says to a woman in bed, for example, and the reverse situation, too'.

But it would be a mistake to think Madden's *Darkness* offers some kind of solution or closure. The fate of the victim may be ghastly, but it brings no comfort to Helen, the eldest sister and a defense lawyer of political murderers, to recognize that the fate of the perpetrator is dreadful, too (p. 52). When the reader focuses on the trajectory of the story tracing the 'gentle descent' of the sisters' childhoods through the carefully detailed human history of the Troubles, one experiences some hope in the transformative powers of the human spirit. When one reads the other story, of violent and senseless sectarian murder that lives alongside the first as though on a parallel channel, one is transported, with Helen, into a universe where 'the cold light of dead stars' lights 'the graceless immensity of a dark universe' (p. 180). Despite the family's love and mutual generosity, the expansion of the constricted eyes of childhood 'leaves Helen with a grief impossible to shed as 'one by one in the darkness, the sisters slept' (p. 181) – these the final words of the novel.

This book, the most recent of the ones examined in this chapter, is also the one most self-conscious about the presence of the camera as recorder and distorter of history and personal lives. Part of the education of the young sisters in the 1960s and 70s is learning 'not to make a noise while the news was on the radio or television', learning its importance because of the 'attention given to it not just by their parents, but by almost all the adults they know, who spent hours talking about what was happening, what might happen, and what ought to happen' (p. 94). Eventually such media representations not only mediate but actually stand in for the experience of otherness: 'They would see photographs of the Orange marches in the newspapers, or they would see reports on television, but they never, in all their childhood, actually saw an Orange march taking place....' (p. 75). Lingard's *Sisters by Rite* shows the TV carrying images of violence outward to a London viewer. In Madden's *Darkness*, the characters are actually forced to see themselves offered up as victims in the media, and by the media. When they watch 25-year-old tapes of the 1968 media representations of the emerging 'Troubles', they realize how the exposure has changed them utterly.

Most of the authors studied here avoid portraying the lives of northern Protestants. Many voices, many experiences of the North are inscribed in these fictional works, but the hierarchization referred to by David Lloyd places the moral centre of most women's fiction squarely amidst the Catholic poor, particularly, but not exclusively, among the women. This surely suggests that the 'normative ethical aim' of the works is a particular version of social justice.

Because so little has been published by northern women, each of these texts offers opportunities for rich explorations of diversity within this ethnicized group. There may be little exploration in this fiction of the bridge-building that might lead beyond the violence, but with their careful and unblinking representations, these texts create knowledge essential to a larger cultural understanding.

At this point I recall the heart-wrenching force of the Ann Zell lines at the beginning of this chapter: 'Before there were helicopters / there were dragonflies. / And will be, after.' The lyrical hope of the poetic voice offers a defiant rejection of the 'war that has gone into us'. The narrative voices and inscribed values of the northern women's fiction still carry a much more doubtful sense of an 'after'.

6

Traveling Back Home: the Blockbusters of Patricia Scanlan and Maeve Binchy

'And dance, dance
don't talk to me
about dance
you'll be dancing
that much,
they'll be seeing
sparks off your nipples ...
Mark my words.'
Rita Ann Higgins, 'I Want to Make Love to Kim Basinger.'[1]

What do women want? Presumably the authors who can sell them millions of books have some important insights into the matter. Women readers of popular fiction may be spendthrift with their emotions, but even the most hopeful realizes that buying a paperback will not transform her life. Still, the purchaser is buying more than a few hours of relaxation. To state the obvious, there are things in those best-selling books that matter to women readers. And in the last decade Irish authors have been busily adding to these popular and highly lucrative literary genres. How do these books (re)construct Irish culture? What do they suggest *Irish* women want? Are the Irish versions of women's blockbusters different from their cousins in other cultures? Do the books from the Republic resemble those from the North?

In the following pages I examine some of the critical approaches feminists have devised for understanding the appeal of fiction that appears to reinforce reactionary social paradigms, then explore these questions in the work of the Republic of Ireland's two most successful writers of women's blockbusters, Patricia Scanlan and Maeve Binchy.

Success here means number of sales and very few writers in the world have sold as many books as Maeve Binchy. This achievement might accord her a place in Cultural Studies but has not in Irish Studies where different genre, and gender, preoccupations have been dominant. It is my contention here that the success of popular fiction is too important to ignore.

In 1982 American critic Tania Modleski began her study of mass-produced fantasies for women by commenting that very few critics have taken Harlequin Romances, Gothic novels and soap operas seriously enough to study them in any detail.[2] By the 1990s, as a result of the explosion of work in feminist theory and Cultural Studies, many critics were studying women's mass market entertainments very seriously indeed. Some of the first feminist critics to make forays into the field, for example Americans Ann Snitow and Ann Douglas studying Harlequin pulp romance, dismissed it as soft core porn for women, dangerously reinscribing in palatable form men's patriarchal domination over women. Others such as Americans Lillian S. Robinson, Janice Radway, British Annette Kuhn, Christine Geraghty , Mairead Owen, and Canadian Angela Miles refused an analytical approach which defines women's experience in terms of men's.[3] These critics started from the premise that if millions of women, including often themselves, were enjoying 'mass culture' entertainments, they were probably involved in more complex cultural negotiations than the 'false consciousness' feminists seemed willing to grant. Radway, for example, argued that women are not just passive consumers but take an active role in interpreting pulp romance 'whose literary meaning is the result of a complex, temporarily evolving interaction between a fixed verbal structure and a socially situated reader' (pp. 54–5). Owen extends this analysis to the 'soft romances' of the Harlequin with their fairy tale structure and supine heroines, arguing that these novels offer the 'best solution' available to a disadvantaged sex class (women) living in 'an inimical world' where protection can only be insured via heterosexual marriage to a dominant male (p. 540).

All the feminist critics searching out more potent reasons than self-annihilation or escapism in women's reading or viewing habits are aware of problems in this work produced for the mass market. Few argue for their liberatory potential and all are aware that the 'consciousness industry', intent on financial profits, distorts the needs and desires of women consumers.[4] But as Lillian S. Robinson pointed out as early as 1978, a fully feminist reading of women's books must look at women as well as at books, and try to understand how this literature actually functions in society. As a literary person who remains frankly addicted to trashy fiction, I make no claim that this approach will reveal an underground and unexpected feminist literature. Rather, though no less ambitiously, I think it can tell us something about the materials women use to make their lives in our society (p. 205).

Taking seriously the idea that women choose their entertainments, often in the face of family derision or their own internalized inhibitions, in order to *use* them in their lives has prompted some feminist critics to attend carefully to the meanings of the textual pleasure women allow themselves. And yet relatively little attention has been given to the so-called 'romantic blockbuster', the 500–plus page 'women's novel'. One important exception is British critic Nicci Gerrard who starts her discussion with this generic description:

> big, for a start – not the kind of book you can comfortably carry around with you; more the kind you keep beside the bed. It is glossily packaged, frequently with embossed glittering jackets, displaying plunged cleavages and long legs ending in a stiletto heel. There is a hero (rich, grim, powerful and with concealed wells of tenderness beneath his manly chest); a heroine (beautiful, often poor-becoming rich, often an orphan or without family support); a huge amount of consumerism – clothes, objects and possessions are described in intricate detail; a fair sprinkling of misunderstanding and jealousy and melodrama.[5]

Gerrard's assumption that we will recognize the 'romantic block-buster' suggests a trans-cultural formula set by such British and American novelists as Jackie Collins, Barbara Taylor Bradford, Danielle Steele, or Jilly Cooper. And indeed, Irish novelist Patricia Scanlan's work admits its debt to such models with parodic intertextualities. The Irish novels of Deirdre Purcell and British-based Marian Keyes are not particularly marked in any distinctively local fashion, but many other Irish women writers are adapting international formulas to fit their own society and the expectations of Irish readers. Sometimes these changes are inconsequential, as for example in Rose Doyle's *Kimbay* where the heroine, owner of a beleaguered stud farm, rejects her aristocratic French fiancé for a local Irishman with good horse sense, or in Elizabeth O'Hara's *Singles* and Margaret Dolan's *Nessa* where the 'Irishness' is signified entirely by the heroine's red hair, ubiquitous marker of uncontainable female passion in Irish popular fiction. In other works, however, the plotting itself is much more intricately 'Irish'. While this is the case with Kathleen O'Connor's Glenbeg sagas of an extended family presided over by a sentimental-ized matriarch, it is obviously particularly true of historical romances that use the Irish myth or history to structure their plots as in Bríd Mahon's *Dervogilla*, Anne Chambers' *The Geraldine Conspiracy*, or Mary Ryan's *Whispers in the Wind*.[6] The last, which on one level might be described as a feminist and nationalist revision of David Lean's film *Ryan's Daughter*, has been shaped to the British and North American genre of the costume or 'Regency' historical romance, known in the trade as a 'bodice ripper'. For this local variant, Ryan uses the Anglo-Irish war of 1919–21 as setting and a 'Big House' Protestant Anglo-Irish landlord as hero. When the heroine commits her sexual transgression, she acts in a kind of unconscious swoon that could hardly count as a mortal sin at all. The novel ends with the death of not only the heroine's unacceptable husband but also of her guilty lover, whose heir she becomes. This conclusion – punishment for the unworthy men and independence for the heroine – is a powerful contemporary women's fantasy. But the resolution that banishes men from the center, leaving a group of women friends as the resolution (and solution) is far more apt to be a staple of Irish popular fiction than it is of any other western culture's contribution, an idiosyncrasy that might suggest important features of Irish society.

All these works come from the Republic. Only two blockbuster-type novels set in the North have been published. Mary A. Larkin's Cinderella-like *The Wasted Years* features the lives of Belfast women mill-workers in the 1930–40s, while Niki Hill's *Death Grows on You* is set in the contemporary 'Troubles' of Northern Ireland and offers a version of the 'Big House' novel with two warrior-heroes from the Unionist and Nationalist camps competing for the heroine's love. Hill's novel honours the Protestant military forces, which makes it an anomaly among women's war fiction from the North.[7]

Gerrard's use, and my own above, of the term 'blockbuster' suggests a specific genre of book, and when a critic invokes the term, as does Irish reviewer G.D. Ingoldby in the following review of Maeve Binchy's *Light a Penny Candle*,[8] the audience is assumed to recognize the genre as well: 'Whilst integrity is thin on the ground, there is nothing random about the writing of such formula blockbusters and life will be really unfair if the booksellers' Christmas returns for [*Light a Penny Candle*] aren't enormous.'[9] This contemptuous dismissal of author and book was made at the time of publication in 1982. While the publishers clearly market certain long novels as blockbuster hopefuls – those covers described by Gerrard – the term is actually a post-sales designation. The *American Heritage Dictionary* notes that a blockbuster is a 'film or book that sustains widespread popularity and achieves enormous sales.' Furthermore, Binchy's novel in no way resembles that formula invoked by Ingolby. Not that such a distinction would much impress this reviewer who tells us what Binchy's book 'means': 'a story written by a woman, for women, about women.... a cross between Enid Blyton and Claire Raynor' (p. 20).

This dismissal suggests Binchy's novel belongs in the 'trashy fiction' category evoked by Lillian S. Robinson. In a familiar pattern of social pejoration for phenomena associated with subordinated groups, mere mention of a 'story written by a woman, for women, about women' is sure to promote a cultural slide down among the women. But down among the women is not such a bad place for an author to reside. For one thing, women read more novels and, where they have access to money, buy more books than men. Maeve Binchy herself claims that even if most of her readers are women, she in no way feels that writing for such an audience is writing 'in and for a ghetto'.[10] As a writer whose titles *each* sell in the millions, she might well be pleased with her neighborhood.

In the following discussion I focus on Scanlan's and Binchy's novels instead of their audiences. Although I have collected a substantial amount of impressionistic evidence about these readers both in Ireland and abroad, I focus on textual constructions of women's worlds. I am not assuming thereby that the texts control their readers; obviously the texts will be constructed by their readers in different ways and my own readings are unavoidably partial and ideologically driven. My method here is to examine recurring elements in each of the writer's work in an attempt to see what kind of society is constructed within the fictional worlds of the novels, and to explore the values and behaviors being sold so successfully within these covers. But I set their work as well within contexts and practices of contemporary Irish society external to the novels as a way of trying to avoid a false binary division between text and lived experience.

It is not my intention to say how women ought to be disposing of their time and money; it seems more useful to understand what women are buying and how the purchases might signify in women's lives. Finally, then, this study is an exercise in cultural self-consciousness. To quote British critic Judith Williamson: 'We may feel we are free to slip in and out of "mass culture" in the form of movies, TV, magazines, or pulp fiction, but nowadays we know better than to imagine we can exist outside ideology.'[11]

Life in the package tour: traveling with Patricia Scanlan

When I sat down at a blank screen I always said a little prayer, 'Please, God, please inspire me.' He never failed. Thank you, God.

So reads the acknowledgment in Patricia Scanlan's second novel *Apartment 3B*.[12] In the acknowledgments to her third novel, she again thanks God, this time for directing her path. Whether these little prayers reveal an ingenuous self-confidence, a pious humility, a calculated playfulness, or some other attitude beyond my ken, Scanlan has certainly managed a magnificent reversal of the idea of female muse.[13] Of course she is not the first to claim divine inspiration for her text. What is original, however, is the use to which she has put her *imprimatur*; in her novels we find a distillation of materials from such sources as career women's self-help manuals, glamour magazines, lifestyle advertising copy, romance novels, sex blockbusters, women's newspaper columns, domestic novels and soap opera – a veritable compendium of women's entertainments, all set within braided narratives of female friendship usually shared by a redhead, a blonde, a brunette, all lower middle to middle class, all Catholic – as though this is the ethnic range of Ireland. Scanlan is unashamed of the derivative nature of her writing; indeed she celebrates it with self-conscious intertextualities as though to suggest that here are the makings of the good life for a young woman of the 1990s.

Whatever one might think of the ingredients, it is a recipe that works, as Scanlan herself puckishly reminds her readers in the following self-reference in her third novel when the figure of the female enemy, a staple in each of the novels, stormily considers the rejection of her novel *The Fire and The Fury*:

They had published some unknown civil servant who had written two blockbusters that had shot into the best-sellers' list and made her seriously rich and a media celebrity. It was galling. Barbara's novel had much more class than those two pathetic efforts! Well, the next one was due out soon and by the time Barbara got her hand on it, the author and publishers would be mightily sorry they had ever heard the name Barbara Jordan Murray![14]

Jo O'Donoghue, the editor at Poolbeg responsible for launching Scanlan's first novels, reports that Scanlan was 'immediately a huge popular and media success', with sales of 'about 60,000 of each title in Ireland' within the first year of publication while subsequent years saw the sale of hundreds of thousands.[15] These sales are prodigious for so small a population, and Bantam Doubleday Dell are now marketing the novels abroad even onto the pulp fiction shelves of my local supermarket on Vancouver Island. The publishers treat the books as consumer perishables, issuing them in cheap (by Irish standards) paperback form, the books offered in Ireland at the time of their first issue in large display packs placed prominently at the front of book-stores in a manner reminiscent of a cosmetic or junk food display. All the covers carry the same kind of expensively produced amateurish drawings, young, beautiful women's heads set in pseudo-photo frames, a code image to the knowledgeable woman reader looking for popular romance about resourceful heroines and happy endings having little in common with either the elegant, high culture look of a Virago paperback or the easy sexual turn-on described above by Nicci Gerrard. Jo O'Donoghue guessed that that the audience are women 'who do not otherwise read much', but Irish critic Ailbhe Smyth suggests that the reader profile is very broad and certainly a not insignificant part of an academic audience at University College Cork admitted to reading Scanlan when I informally polled them at a lecture I gave there on this topic in 1993.

The intertextualities of Scanlan's novels provide a convenient (if wooden) way of short circuiting the need for complex characteriza-tion or dialogue. With the use of familiar icons, Scanlan can summon up images known to any woman in the age of advertising, and can with these borrowings create the sensations of fantasy fulfilled. Here are characteristic examples from each of her first three novels, *Apartment 3B*, *City Girl*, and *Finishing Touches*:

That time he had seen her in that nothing of an emerald bikini, her skin tanned and glowing after a stopover in Santorini, her body far more curvy and sensual than [his wife's] could ever be, he had wanted her. (p. 42)

Devlin's aquamarine eyes sparkled with anticipation. After dressing in a light pale pink tracksuit she packed some clean lingerie, her shoes and a clutch bag into an elegant holdall and took a black and white Dior suit out of the mirrored wardrobe that stretched the width of her spacious apple green and white bedroom.[16]

David might be eleven years older than her, but he was the sexiest man she had ever met, with his piercing blue heavy-lidded eyes and that sensuous Welsh voice that she could listen to for ever, especially when he was whispering endearments to her during their lovemaking (p. 5).

The novels all revel in detailed recitations of designer clothing, package tour travel, upmarket apartments, stylish interior decorating, glamorous entertainments and people. But Scanlan mixes these fantasies with homely details of the simpler lives her main female characters 'transcend' but still cherish. Among these down-home elements is the careful delineation of family relations and friendships with all their familiar difficulties and comforts. A successful meshing of these different value systems would demand nothing less than social transformation and thus requires contortionate narrative strategies. For example, how is a city girl going to be able to juggle her career, her love relationship, and the needs of her Alzheimer-stricken mother who lives in the country? If a woman values her 'feminine duty', and Scanlan's heroines (and many women) do, the mother's need cannot be ignored. Scanlan's narrative solution to the problem in *Finishing Touches* is to have the woman return to the country, prove her filial worth and then have the mother die conveniently early before career and lover have disappeared under the weight of dirty laundry and 24-hour home service.

In this way, Scanlan touches experience that must be recognizable to many women readers struggling with family relations, but she uses a narrative shorthand to divide the negative qualities, for example, intransigent sibling jealousy, from the positive qualities, lodging the 'good' elements in one set of characters and the 'bad' in another. This device creates easy 'villain and friend' categories that smooth out the need to negotiate complex relationships and their narrative inscription. Friendship, too, is sketched in shorthand. Female 'best' friendship, the core value of the novels, can be described in this breathless way in *Finishing Touches*: '[Laura] was one of the best friends a girl could have and Aileen O'Shaughnessy was another. Just thinking of Aileen made Cassie laugh. She was mad as a hatter, even now, but a truer friend could not be found (p. 5).'

This reassuring triad of females friends (or friendly sisters-in-law) may be the emotional center of each of her novels but in every case the 'main girl' also has a male lover who is both highly desirable and obsessively devoted to the heroine. This last element is one Scanlan's novels share with the so-called pulp or 'soft romance' novels published by Harlequin. Tania Modleski observes in her study of this genre that male obsession with a woman, so contrary to most women's experience of long-term heterosexual relationships, is one of the methods women romance writers use for 'evening things up' between women and men.[17] It is also one of the most powerful stories within our culture, still often understood to be 'woman's destiny.'[18] In Scanlan's fictional world, the security of the male's affection (and steadfast lust) is presented as a trophy won through suffering and independent achievement on the part of the female protagonist, but once won it enables other freedoms for the woman. Far from being caught in a 'heterosexual romance' that precludes sexual or vocational fulfillment, Scanlan's novels ensure the attainment of all three. Indeed in this aspect of her work, Scanlan becomes very didactic. Hard work, self-sacrifice, and resourcefulness reap their just reward and there is more than a hint that any woman can achieve the triple success of faithful love, exciting sex and a good income as does *City Girl*'s Devlin, if only she has the right attitude and can exploit her 'inner resources' in the proper entrepreneurial way (p. 324). The narratives glance at the unexpected benisons of inheritance, insurance benefits or timely loans, but the emphasis remains firmly on autonomous achievement and self-fulfillment.

In concert with this emphasis we find libertarian values that explicitly laud pluralism and tolerance of difference. Although these take various forms, prominent among them is sexual liberation that defies the orthodox Catholic morality of Ireland and other traditional societies. Such matters as premarital sex, long-term sexual relationships outside of marriage, adulterous affairs and male homosexual relations are all treated as matter-of-fact concerns requiring personal ethical accommodation rather than an adherence to an external code of conduct. Given her large number of readers, it is possible that Scanlan's novels may have the effect of pushing social change out a little further than the majority wants to go, thus paving the way for their future travel. The question remains: what is the destination?

An excellent example of this progressive revisionism from *Finishing Touches* has Scanlan extolling religion class and Catholic moral teaching in a convent school in 1972: 'The teachers, too, now treated [the students] as adults. Class discussions were lively and challenging, particularly those in the religion class with Sister Eileen where they 'discussed ... love and sex and contraception and divorce, as they prepared to step out into the world to make their own choices and decisions' (p. 109).

While it seems preposterous that 'free choice' was being promulgated in Catholic convent schools in 1972, this detail is not entirely factitious, as educator Gráinne O'Flynn recounts in an analysis of girls' second level education in mid-twentieth-century Ireland. She argues that the official and relentlessly applied philosophy of docility for women was to some extent undercut by the encouragement of intellectual debate in religion classes.[19] To be sure, debate is one thing, actual 'free' choice affirmed in the matters of sexual behavior another. But what is interesting in the quoted passage is the way Scanlan rewrites history to accommodate a more liberal sexual ethos, one that must strike a responsive chord in many of her readers.

We find a similar kind of tolerance towards male homosexuality. Although a recurring motif, it appears most prominently in her first novel, *City Girl*, where one of the three central women, Caroline, discovers that her abusive husband is in fact a closeted gay. After the discovery Richard penitently offers to give her an annulment, suddenly willing to risk the shame that would ruin him in a society where, until 1993, male homosexuality was still officially a crime. But the three central friends, Caroline, Devlin and Maggie, agree that the only criminal thing about Richard's behavior was his dishonesty in hiding his sexual orientation from Caroline. As the narrative voice reflects: 'It was a hard world to live in, God knows, and a loving relationship was a precious gift no matter what gender you were' (p. 451).

This textual banishment of homophobia represents a revolutionary change of attitude for Ireland, a sign of resistance to its state- and church-ordered heterosexism. And given the package in which this paean to sexual pluralism is being delivered, it is possible that the message can have liberatory effects on the reader. But the ease of acceptance here is a powerful denial of the lived experience of gays and lesbians in Ireland: 'fear and prejudice is [sic] alive and well in Irish psyches and society, despite important legislative changes, unprecedented inclusion of lesbians and gay men in progressive social agendas, and increasing depictions of lesbians and gay men in art and culture.'[20] Richard's lover, for example, tells Caroline that, unlike Richard, he is not ashamed of his sexual orientation: 'I knew early in life I was homosexual. I didn't fight it. It's me, it's part of what I am and if people don't like it they can lump it.... A person's sexuality is his or her own business as long as it doesn't hurt anyone else' (p. 448).

Yet this is the same man who, on his first appearance in the novel, was on a heterosexual date with his longtime partner Richard, both of them pretending to be eligible ladies' men. Despite the explicit statement of bravery, the narrative implicitly suggests the impossibility of coming out of the closet if one wishes to be accepted in Irish middle-class society. While the narrative here employs what British critic Mark Finch calls 'liberal gay discourse', all of Scanlan's novels carefully avoid any use of the truly disruptive 'camp discourse of the modern gay movement' which cannot be accommodated within the confines of liberal tolerance.[21]

In fact tolerance can create a more insidious effect. As American sociologist Erving Goffman points out, tolerance keeps unequal power relations in place by offering conditional acceptance. Usually it is 'part of a bargain' which 'depends upon normals not being pressed past the point at which they can easily extend acceptance – or, at worst, uneasily extend it.'[22] The negative side of supposed tolerance of gays becomes evident when we consider Scanlan's chary treatment of lesbianism. Although tolerant mention is made of a lesbian couple who never appear in the narrative of *City Girl*, the author presents no lesbian characters in her novels. In Scanlan's fictional world, male homosexuality is just another one of the problem issues that can be managed by women (and women readers) so as to make the contradictions disappear. Lesbianism is far too disruptive a topic to be touched. Christine Geraghty, commenting on a similar use of tolerance towards gays and avoidance of lesbians in soap opera suggests the 'entry of a lesbian couple into this shared female world would be genuinely subversive, implying that lesbians are not separate from, indeed had things in common with, other women. The sexualisation of female friendship, however, through the presentation of a lesbian couple, could ... [call] into question the basis of the relationship between other women in the programme.'[23] And indeed we see this phenomenon named and displaced in the main narrative of *Finishing Touches*: 'You'd better stop hugging me. She'll think we're a couple of lezzers. You know her and her warped mind' (p. 41).

Another more or less taboo subject is abortion. I do not mean to suggest that unwanted pregnancy does not occur; most so-called women's issues occur in these novels. But with the single exception of a thoroughly feckless woman in *Finishing Touches*, none of the main women in the three novels under discussion here resorts to abortion. In fact, Devlin, heroine of *City Girl* (and Scanlan's fourth novel, *City Woman*), in London to have an abortion after her quasi-rape, walks out of the clinic at the last minute: 'What right did she have to deprive the child within her of the chance of ever witnessing a sunrise as beautiful and miraculous as she had just seen' (p. 111). With this sentimentalized evocation of the 'unborn child' ideology, Scanlan may well be speaking to the belief/experience of many of her Irish readers, but she is also erasing the experiences of the thousands of Irish women who do have English abortions every year and reinforcing the anti-choice culture. She also provides a powerful fantasy of escape for those women who do have abortions; with Devlin's luck and pluck, they might not have needed the abortion. Later, when Devlin discovers that she herself was adopted from an unwed mother, the anti-choice support intensifies. Yet even as she reads this scene of Devlin's decision, the reader, if she is attentive to the strictures of middle-class Catholic society, knows that Scanlan will have to dispose of this child 'honorably' if Devlin is to 'advance'.[24] A traffic accident performs the deed, leaving Devlin intact(a), and her way is clear for social success as a rich career city 'girl'.

What these examples illustrate is a very successful blending of the frank naming of contemporary women's problems with utopian solutions. Scanlan's narratives are full of touches reminiscent of feminist analysis ('The essay was entitled "The apostles' wives were the first deserted wives." Discuss.') Yet, the only self-identified feminist in her novels is a despicable character from *Finishing Touches* whose political consciousness, learned from *Cosmopolitan* magazine, doesn't reach beyond career ambition and the achievement of orgasm (p. 272).

Finally I would suggest that these novels are best described by what American critic Richard Dyer terms the use of utopianism in the entertainment industry of patriarchal capitalism. He argues that this industry does not seek simplistically to create false needs in its consumers as some Marxist critics have claimed; rather, it responds to 'real needs created by real inadequacies' albeit 'not the *only* needs and inadequacies of the society' [my emphasis].[25] Entertainment offers the 'image of "something better" to escape into, or something we want that our day-to-day lives don't provide' (p. 177). Yet – and this is the point at which Dyer's analysis is most fruitful – while utopian entertainment responds to real needs, it also defines and delimits what constitutes the legitimate needs of people in the society. In so doing it performs a very conservative function of reinforcing the status quo.

Consumers are not offered models for the reorganization of society as in classical utopian literature: instead, entertainment operates at the level of sensibility, allows us to experience how the utopia would feel. For example, Dyer claims that the exhaustion so endemic in modern society, due to alienated labor and the pressures of urban life, will be transformed in the vehicle of entertainment into a world where work and play are synonymous (pp. 183–4). In Devlin's effortless and fun management of the 'City Girl' health club, for example, exhaustion is replaced by energy that allows for the creation of affective living, honest relationships, and a sense of community.

I said earlier that Scanlan is aware of feminist ideas and concerns. Thus to Dyer's list of the inadequacies and scarcities in modern life can be added two categories from Scanlan's entertainments that particularly speak to women's lives and feminist awareness: male violence (physical, legal and economic) against women; and sexual and reproductive bondage. The utopian solution inscribed in Scanlan's novels is female autonomy, consisting of women's economic independence, female friendship, emotionally satisfying heterosexuality, and liberated motherhood. Her sensitivity to the problems of women's lives transformed by utopian solutions may very well account for the significant success of her books. And yet the kind of female paradise she offers mitigates against real liberation, based as it is on a consumer-oriented, individualistic pursuit of money and pleasure among rags-to-riches career women. The following description of the eponymous 'City Girl' health club serves as an emblem for the utopian paradise, providing one can obliterate one's class consciousness:

> The relaxing ambiance exuded a subtle air of wealth, tinged with unmistakable sophistication. It was the perfect place for a busy business woman or rich wife to relax with friends ... the rooftop swimming pool, Jacuzzis and saunas ... intimate restaurants ... attractive Spanish-tiled shopping mall ... wildly expensive goods ... a small library where the weary city girl could relax over the daily newspapers, or read a few chapters of the last on the best sellers list. If she wished she could take a linguaphone course while having a pedicure, or perhaps, dictate a business letter while having her manicure, to a top class secretary who would have it ready for her departure (pp. 364–5).

In the title to this discussion of Scanlan's novels, I evoke the package tour, the plane trip that takes the consumer to an exotic and distant place, a superficial view of the host culture, perhaps, but one full of ready-made pleasures. A recent novel, similar cast of characters and plots, carries the title *Foreign Affairs*.[26] Such packaging is, of course, class-marked; the rich do not need to rely on such conveniences. Scanlan's characters regularly undertake such journeys and her readers are invited to do likewise. In the inscription of oppositional meanings and self-conscious intertextualities, Scanlan's novels appear to offer rich possibilities for exploring cultural identities. But on closer scrutiny, all that energy is reabsorbed and reified and we become witnesses to the spectacle of a commodified society. One imagines that most of the voyages taken by Scanlan's readers are not to private city clubs but on public city busses.

Back home in Maeve Binchy's village

'She taught me something about the world of women.'

'Now I understand better what my Irish mother means when she talks about Ireland.'

'Her plots and characters are predictable, but never simplistic. Plain but riveting.'

'She's got huge heart in her writing – sympathy towards women and men, children and old people.'

'You could extract morals from her books to teach your kids. "Beauty isn't everything, but it helps." "Men are nice to have, but women better learn to depend on themselves."'

'You find justice in her books. That's why women like them. Women like things that seem fair.'

'Back in the 1950s everything was safer. I like to revisit the period.'

'I didn't know she was an Irish writer.'

Of the representative quotations above which I gathered from Maeve Binchy readers in Canada and the United States, the most surprising is the last. With the exception of her volume of short stories *Victoria Line/Central Line*, a London novel, *Silver Wedding*, and Dublin-based *Evening Class* and *Tara Road*, all of Maeve Binchy's novels have as their primary setting small Irish villages drawn with precise local detail.[27] And yet the thing her readers and reviewers often comment on is how universal her subjects seem, how familiar the situations and problems. There is something about the fictional world she creates that feels like returning to the home we once had (or wish we had?) But who is this 'we'?

Maeve Binchy's audience defies easy generalization. It is so vast that one needs to be wary of assuming who those readers are. She informed me in an interview that each of her novels now sell approximately two million copies in Britain and North America; furthermore, all are translated into several foreign languages, and are bestsellers in such places as Israel and Finland.[28] Certainly reviews of her work appear everywhere from *The Honest Ulsterman* to *The New York Times Book Review*. The novels' first appearance in expensive hardback, sold in fine bookstores, or as book-of- the-month-club selections, suggests one kind of market. Their reemergence in paper covers in airport terminals among the novels of Robert Ludlum, Danielle Steele, Stephen King, and Michael Crichton may suggest another, although both audiences fit the stereotype of 'middlebrow' cultural consumers.[29] And yet their next manifestation as dog-eared paper-backs in secondhand bookstores, where I first found her work, perhaps suggests still another audience. Only recently have her books appeared among the pulp novels of the supermarkets where Patricia Scanlan's now lodge, although the covers of the earliest novels had the sentimentalized, poorly drawn pictures of the pulp market. But the hardbacks are now adorned with elegant graphics and illustrations. Which takes us back to the question of 'whose home', and by extension, whose idea of 'justice' and 'fairness', those values evoked by the readers quoted above.

One of the homes where all her novels resided was Barbara Bush's White House. The then-Presidential wife, who named Maeve Binchy as her favorite writer to Oprah Winfrey on American television, reported that although she had grown up as a Presbyterian in New England, her own childhood felt just the same as the Irish experience inscribed in the novels. This kind of reader recognition and identification the author attributes to the 1940s and 1950s settings. 'We were all the same in those days. Now we're all different.'[30] Maeve Binchy explains further that she is trying to 'bring out the normal human predicaments and put imaginary characters around them and see how they work themselves out.' As she says, 'there's a first dance in every country; there's a girl who makes a fool of herself over a fella; some-body is having a child when she shouldn't have a child; there's a marriage that's very bitter. These are readily identifiable emotions.'[31]

The situations are familiar, although one might question whether the emotional and social responses are so predictably homogeneous. She deploys a huge cast of characters in each of her books, so the canvas of emotional life is very wide. But how valid is the claim, supported by her readers quoted here, that 'what [she] writes is representative of a whole generation?' The novels largely avoid depicting what Irish sociologist Ursula Barry claims are the three most long-standing and continuing Irish problems: extreme poverty, mass emigration and the unresolved effects of Partition to which we might add in the late 1990s the effects on women of economic globalization.[32] Instead, the narrative attention focuses primarily on home and family life in a spectrum of people from the lower middle class to the professional middle class; characters who were able to attend university in that period, for example those in *Circle of Friends*, *Echoes*, and *The Glass Lake*[33] were part of a privileged elite in a country where even at the beginning of the more prosperous 1960s only one in seven students succeeded in earning their 'Leaving Certificate' (high school diploma).[34]

But while the narrative interest is on the middle class, the author's own background, the distinctions among the classes, and the consequences of those distinctions, are precisely delineated in all of her works. For example, in *Light a Penny Candle* the narrative voice functions as the village choral voice in this set of class differentiations which describes a daughter of the central Irish family, shopowners of the village of Kilgarret, as 'too respectable to go to the local dance, where messenger boys and maids went....but not well born enough for the tennis parties and supper parties of the people in the big houses' whose children came home from Dublin boarding schools trailing lacrosse sticks and blazers. Another village girl, Berna, 'as a doctor's daughter, could have been their social equal ... but for all their gentility, it was known that her father had a problem with the drink. It was well hidden, but well known at the same time. So Berna missed her chance. Sweet little thing – such a pity about her father' (pp. 42–3).

Where the author uses an upper-class character as one of the central characters, for example Eve Malone of *Circle of Friends* or Leo(nora) Murphy in *The Copper Beech*, she cannot participate in that class's privilege because of some family flaw which makes her an outsider.[35] Characters from the (economically) lower orders are treated generously if they share the community values of the middle class, but her narratives often turn on disruptions resulting from cross-class intercourse.

An interesting example of this, and a further illustration of the meaning of 'home' in these novels occurs in *The Copper Beech* where, for the first time, a member of the traveling people, Ireland's traditional ethnic minority, plays a significant if marginal role. Leo Murphy's family maid had controlled Leo by threats of evil 'tinkers' who might kidnap naughty children. In a characteristically generous revision of such bigotry (Maeve Binchy usually dwells on such failures only among the more privileged), the novel shows Leo later outgrowing the unreasonable fear and even envying the 'marvelous free lifestyle of people who had no rules or no laws to tie them down' (p. 245). This sentiment seems almost gratuitous in its infusion of liberal benevolence, until later in the novel, when Leo's mother, involved in a love match with a young traveling man, kills him and indirectly herself, events that function to teach her daughter the meaning of 'no rules or no laws to tie them down'. Of course the traveling people would have their own rules; but nowhere in the novels is there any attempt to explore the mores of such excluded classes or castes. Instead, in this case, the travelers, outside the law, are thereby dangerous. In other words, the author writes about the historical past of her own class-marked childhood, and writes it as she might have known it as an especially alert child. This is a period of which she says she has perfect recall, because it was a 'time of such heightened expectation and great charge for me'.[36]

But the exclusions – which can also be described as erasures – make for reassuring simplicities. The imaginative creation of a coherent community, what British critic Raymond Williams called a 'knowable community', is a kind of writing Maeve Binchy shares with another very popular Irish women writer, Alice Taylor, who provides narrative bromides of the old, gold village days.[37] The idealised hope of safety in sameness (albeit one that also has room for eccentrics) reconstitutes the past in nostalgic, homogenizing terms. And yet the nostalgia for community which manifests itself in the impulse for a unified social world has positive as well as negative implications.[38] In the following pages, I will explore briefly the idea of the nostalgic community that Maeve Binchy creates, then suggest ways in which her use of the past often transcends the impulse for marketable nostalgia in unflinching social analysis and in explorations of the pre-history of second-wave feminism.

Maeve Binchy's seven Irish village novels have similar constructions.[39] She moves her characters about the village where they intersect continually in their daily lives. The intertwined narratives are chronological, often covering more than a decade, but the plot progression resembles 'people bytes'[40] rather than extended diegesis; each movement forward in time centers on a character or small group of characters for a few pages then ends abruptly with an implicit promise of 'to be continued'. The staccato, open-ended effect of this organization makes for a swift pace in long novels and allows for multiple 'takes' on a single event or character. These 'takes' coalesce into a communal and coherent view among the discerning characters, a village ethos by which to understand and finally judge the worth of people. The layered plotting also provides Maeve Binchy with a flexible vehicle for light-handed but acerbic social analysis. The abrupt shifts allow the narrative voice to establish its position while avoiding the appearance of extended polemic. In *Echoes*, for example, a generous local teacher helps the doctor's son, home from boarding school, with his lessons during the holiday. In a complex little negotiation, Maeve Binchy allows her readers to appreciate the teacher's intelligence, generosity and social acumen without particularly abusing the boy nor facilely solving the problem of class and gender inequity. This exchange closes the narrative byte:

'So, College Boy,' she said to David, 'let's get on with the hedge school before the gentry come down from Dublin and catch us with our love for books!'

'You're great, Miss O'Hara,' said David admiringly. 'Wasn't it a pity you weren't a man, you could have been a priest and taught us properly' (p. 46).

I referred above to the existence of 'rules and laws that tie people down'. One of the major tasks of each novel is to establish what these would be in a given community (and they are nearly interchangeable among the novels despite the time shifts) then to clarify which among the communal rules are worthy of respect. These strictures or customs do not center on individual aggrandizement, as in the work of Patricia Scanlan; instead they characteristically protect the group which in turn supposedly enhances life possibilities for individual members of the group. A certain muting of centrifugal, individualistic energies is thus required of people. If they cannot abide this, like Gerry Doyle and Caroline Nolan in *Echoes* or Richard Hayes and Miriam Murphy in *The Copper Beech*, they pay a heavy price. Or, if they are *too* tolerant of difference, as is the hermit nun in *The Glass Lake*, then too they can become a danger to community and thus require expulsion. If, however, they can put those energies to work within the community, they are rewarded. This kind of 'justice' resembles wish fulfillment for her readers rather than an accurate social mimesis, although the *experience* of mimesis is the implicit promise of Maeve Binchy's fiction.

The novels abound with examples of this process of reincorporation into the community. A representative example of this process occurs at the end of *Echoes* where both Clare and her estranged husband David are dragooned by wise elders into attending a funeral they both wish to avoid. Both are exhorted to keep secret the unmentionable behaviors in their past, to carry on after the damage, to cement their place in the community through attendance at a communal ritual:

> 'There's going to be talk if you don't go.'
> 'That's nonsense, the church will be full, the whole of Castlebay will be there.'
> 'And you should be there.'
> 'But there are a lot of things I can't explain.'
> 'And there's no need why you should explain, just come up to the church with me now, David, it's a small thing to do, but it's a big thing if you don't do it' (p. 549).

Discretion, patience and community spirit, so unlike the heroic 'silence, cunning and exile' canonized in James Joyce's *A Portrait of the Artist as a Young Man*, can, and often do, result in keeping secret and thus containing in a positive way outlaw events that might have destroyed worthy characters were the secrets broadcast. And in protecting its worthy denizens, this triad of virtues also protects the stability of the community. Despite the bland face and simple rhythms of daily life, such acts as murder, abortion, wife battering, drunkenness, adultery, madness and suicide occur as staple events in these novels. The ability to protect or divulge such secrets and the right to be protected mark the morally worthy characters, as for example at the end of *Light a Penny Candle* when characters omit evidence at the inquest examining the death of Elizabeth's battering husband, thus allowing her manslaughter of Henry to go undetected. In this way, Maeve Binchy protects worthy individuals *and* the social fabric.

If one postulates community as an ideal, then the distinctions between insider and outsider, and what constitutes each to the dominant viewer, become the overriding consideration. In these novels, the point of judgment remains firmly within the village or that community structure (neighborhood or evening class) that functions as a village. So, for example, in *Firefly Summer* when Patrick O'Neill, a rich American, thinks he can come 'home' to the Irish village his father left as a poor man, the entire novel centers on the error of his assumption, the price of his misreading, and his eventual expulsion from the community. Even homegrown characters might face expulsion; many are killed off by their author, and all must earn their right of place in the community's moral universe. Privileged social class does not signify moral worth; in fact, in every novel Maeve Binchy creates situations that disqualify the privileged from the ranks of the morally intelligent, while emphasizing the discernment and generosity of characters whose own more mixed or troubled background teaches them compassion or egalitarianism. To borrow an insight from Charlotte Brunsdon's analysis of soap opera, a genre to which these novels bear a structural resemblance, the question the Binchy reader ideally asks is not 'What will happen next?' but 'What kind of person is this?'[41] What this suggests, and I believe it explains a great deal about the appeal of Maeve Binchy's novels, is that the reader is expected to be competent in recognizing the generic possibilities of the village saga-novel, and the ways the discerning members of the group construct and enforce a moral consensus about the conduct of personal life.

My criticism here about problems of nostalgic reconstruction does not give adequate attention to what I consider the great achievement in Maeve Binchy's novels: the author's ability to create narratives that indirectly provide shrewd social commentary as well as the accurate charting of historical changes in Irish women's lives since the 1940s. The novels abound with examples, but I will focus here on only one, the treatment of married women's economic position in the family.

Light a Penny Candle, Maeve Binchy's first village novel, is also the one set earliest in time, beginning in the early 1940s. Unlike the vast majority of novels about women by women, this novel shows men and women working together in a family business, a partnership that gives the woman considerable power within the family. As the young London visitor, Elizabeth, remarks:

> The other girls [in the Catholic school] were from farms near Kilgarret, or else their parents had small businesses in the town. It was all so different from home. Hardly anyone's father went out to work at a place and then came home from it in the evening (p. 47).

The women do not wonder where the men are, what they're up to. They are always there on the periphery of the woman character's (and woman reader's) eye and if they do have other interests, pleasures and social groupings, they cannot stray very far without detection and retribution. This functions as a pretty effective means of social control. In the marital partnership of the central O'Connor family, the wife's contributions to the family/village economy are presented as more important than her husband's because her culturally constructed skills of femininity – sensitivity and perception – combine with strength of character and business acumen, a combination that equips her specially well to negotiate a village life that does not separate public and private spheres.

In historical time, the social value of this model of marital partnership was eroded after World War II. In an examination of this change Irish educator Gráinne O'Flynn describes the development of what she calls the 'suburban microcosm' which was embedded in the 1937 Irish Constitution then ratified in the wider social sphere in a way that limited all women to a separate domestic sphere. She explains the psychological background as follows:

> Our fathers had clerical jobs and were in many cases the first generation of their own families to have had these kinds of jobs. Each one, consciously or unconsciously, wanted to maintain and increase his standing as a middle-class respectable citizen. The desire encompassed family life as well as work life. A family in which, for instance, a wife worked would have been regarded as one which was economically insecure' (p. 89).

The corollary to the women-in-the-home ideology was the women-in-the-workplace-earning-pin-money belief, convenient for keeping women's wages low.

Maeve Binchy's novels chart this large historical change, and calibrate the differences in particular situations with remarkable accuracy. Ten-year-old Benny, for example, wonders in 1949 why her mother does not help her father in the family business:

> 'Couldn't you keep the books, Mother?' Benny suggested suddenly.
> 'No, no, I'd not be able to.'
> 'But if it's as simple as Father says ... '
> 'She'd be well able to but your mother has to be here, this is our home, she runs it for you and me, Benny.'
> 'Patsy [the maid] could run it. Then you wouldn't have to pay Sean [the new assistant].'
> 'Nonsense, Benny,' her father said.
> But she wasn't to be stopped. 'Why not? ... It would be something for Mother to do all day.'
> They both laughed.

'Isn't it great to be a child?' said her father.

'To think that the day isn't full already,' agreed her mother.

Benny knew very well that her mother's day was far from full. She thought it might be nice for Mother to be involved in the shop, but obviously they weren't going to listen to her (p. 18).

The situation is again analyzed in *Echoes* and again the child of the family provides the implicit commentary. In this case set in 1950, the family is quite poor, and the child is older and more self-consciously subversive, so instead of the disarming ingenuousness of the previous episode we find this knowing irony:

'Your parents don't take much part in things, do they?' [asked the doctor's son] enviously.

'They work too hard,' Gerry said. 'It was always like that. It's a dog's life, and Mam hates the work but what else is there?'

'What would she prefer to be doing?'

'Arranging flowers on a hall table in a house like yours.' Gerry laughed. 'But isn't that what every woman would want?' (p. 62)

Of course that wasn't what every woman wanted. In the 1952 of *The Glass Lake*, Helen McMahon longed to join her husband in his pharmacy, just so as to have something to do, but their daughter, hardly older than Benny,

realised that for people such as they were it would have been unsuitable for Father to have let [Mother] work there. Only people like Mrs Hanley, who was a widow and ran the drapery, or Mona Fitz, who was the postmistress because she wasn't married, or Mrs Dillon whose husband was a drunk, worked in businesses. It was the way things were in Lough Glass, and everywhere' (p. 11).

This she knew even though her mother gave her advice few middle-class women were giving in those days, to have a career 'so that you'll always be able to choose, so that you won't have to do things because there's nothing else to do' (p. 41).

This concern about women needing economic independence, a career of their own, recurs in *Firefly Summer* when the mother decides to take a part-time clerical job to earn the necessary spare cash that cannot be provided from the family pub, less prosperous than the 'Gentlemen's Outfitters' owned by Benny's family in *Circle* or the

McMahon pharmacy in *Glass Lake*. Again, the analysis is put into the mouth of a child, but in this novel the time is 1962 and in the new economic climate the acquisition of cash enhances the woman's position, even if she works to buy school clothes for her children.

In *The Copper Beech* we discover in the 1970 setting that five couples have formed egalitarian economic partnerships. But here for the first time one feels that the multiple resolutions to the encroachments of modern urbanization and village isolation produce too glib a conclusion; the final picture of blissful harmony in the village of Shancarrig rings a truly false nostalgic note against the grim depiction of middle-class life in Dublin where the total division of public and private in Richard Hayes's life appears not as a generalized social phenomenon but as a personal predicament caused by his earlier sexual misbehaviors.

The Lilac Bus, set in the 1980s, offers a representation of a family pub in which male-female partnership takes yet another shape with 'poor Kate ... on her own while the husband drank at one end of the bar with his own little circle' (p. 157). The daughter of this family, one of Binchy's strong, life-enhancing characters, is asked by her friend if she would work outside the home after marriage. Celia Ryan answers: 'Bloody sure I would. Catch me giving up a job to cook meals and clean a house for a man. Anyway everyone has to nowadays. How would you have any life at all if you didn't?' (p. 199).

In the most recent novels, set in 1990s Dublin (*Evening Class* and *Tara Road*) the varied characters function as an intentional community, all worthy 'villagers'. In this, as in their pat solutions to life's many problems, the novels disappoint, but their depictions of women's extra-domestic labor are as astute as ever, with such labor a necessity in the contemporary society.

Maeve Binchy's focus on women's work and their strength, flexibility and resourcefulness reveals a subtext of feminist analysis and an exploration of the prehistory of second-wave feminism in Ireland. In 1961 only 5 per cent of married Irish women worked outside the home, whereas in 1994 almost half of the female labor force was made up of married, separated or divorced women, even though Article 41.2:1–2 of the Irish Constitution still equates 'woman' with 'wife and mother'.[42] Given this disjunction between official policy and lived realities, the reader understands the function of Celia Ryan's adamant assertion above about the need for female self-sufficiency even within marriage.

Like Patricia Scanlan, Maeve Binchy focuses on female friendship and support as a fundamental precondition for women's independence, although, like Scanlan, Binchy avoids lesbianism except in *Tara Road* where a completely peripheral couple live together openly and apparently effortlessly, this being 'the 1980s and not the Dark Ages' (p. 61). But Maeve Binchy's short stories, not included in this discussion, move into contemporary plots which foreground very challenging feminist struggles like free choice in abortion, a stance that has more meaning when one realizes that her brother, William Binchy, was a leader of the successful anti-choice constitutional amendment crusade of the early 1980s.[43] Thus, I would argue that, unlike Patricia Scanlan whose novels borrow from other cultures to ring changes according to market conditions, Maeve Binchy quietly challenges her readers to struggle with at least some of the potent realities of Irish women's lives. Her vision of communalism is, to be sure, another fictionalized construct and by no means unproblematic for women, the focal caregivers. But its appeal to women readers, Irish and foreign, is, I would assert, not merely one of escapism. A brief comparison of her best-selling novel *Circle of Friends* with the successful 1995 film made of the novel can tease out those elements which make these Irish books so potent for women living some version (however modernized) of the traditional heterosexual gender roles of mother, wife, daughter, sister, friend and community builder.

The novel ends with the protagonist Benny refusing to be paired up with the attractive but unreliable hero, Jack, whereas the screenwriter, Andrew Davis, requires it of the plot. Furthermore, the movie eliminates all the strong older women characters (nuns and single business women) whose activities are a central and enabling part of the younger women's stories. In effect, this means that the screenplay revision of the book erases a strong women's culture from the script, inscribing instead the heterosexual love story *precisely* as the solution that the novel rejects. This narrowing of focus makes the film more akin to a Harlequin romance than a Binchy village-saga. These changes are not mitigated by the film's decision that Benny will be both a wife *and* a writer, a change worthy of Patricia Scanlan, albeit parallel to Maeve Binchy's own life.[44] Hollywoodizing the novel erases those Irish elements that one assumes are important to Binchy's readers: an astute sense of the actual conditions of (some) women's lives, and the foregrounding of powerful, compassionate women who, in concert with at least a few compatible men, are capable of building cohesive family and community despite systemic barriers that distort or limit women's possibilities.

In the novel, Benny makes a choice for the city and its greater opportunities for women, essentially a refusal of the village life, if not the village ethos. The film, on the other hand, works hard to create a sense of the desirability of the picturesque village and its geographic surroundings (the filming took place in Kilkenny instead of the outskirts of Dublin as demanded by the plot). The filmscript may assert the awfulness of a marriage of convenience in a stultifying little village, but the camera returns again and again to an idyllic Irish countryside in the summer. The film's closing frames offer a warm wash of rural beauty as metonym for the heterosexual climax of virginal Benny and the recaptured Jack.

To return to my earlier trope: travel. Patricia Scanlan borrows foreign goods to take her women readers on larky 'foreign' affairs before bringing them 'home', via supportive female friendship, to ideal marriages. Maeve Binchy offers her readers the chance to imagine a better 'home' than the one they inhabit. One might see here the novels' primary *uses* for women readers.

7
Feminist Fiction

> This silence has been
> A sore thing, grievous even.
> At times it seemed
> Nothing would restrain
> Its fury and flame.
> Banked down, smouldering
> Might it now shower
> Someday on the innocent
> Rockets of power,
> Catherine-wheel fragments?
>
> Maeve Kelly, 'Feminist III'[1]

> 'About
> the witch in the bushes,'
> it said,
> 'Watch her,
> she never sleeps.'
>
> Rita Ann Higgins, 'Witch in the Bushes'[2]

Defining the Genre

Relatively few women in Ireland – including some of the ones I discuss in this chapter – would choose to have their work labeled 'feminist'. The word has become so politically over-determined, so loaded with negative implication by non- and anti-feminist sources, that the term itself is a threat. Which of course, in its positive sense, it should be. Feminism, which would dismantle and re-vision, or at the very least question existing social, emotional and economic structures that are damaging to women, can hardly be comforting to those men or women who either support (and perhaps survive owing to) the status quo, or at least see accommodation as preferable to painful change. But even writers sympathetic to feminist political theory and practice are often wary of the notion of feminist art. When the British journalist Nicci Gerrard interviewed over 50 anglophone women writers in the late 1980s, she found that

> writer after writer makes an explicit separation between being a feminist and being a feminist author – until it comes as a great relief to come across Angela Carter describing herself as 'a feminist writer because I'm a feminist in everything else and one can't compartmentalize these things in one's life'.[3]

It is not difficult to understand why an artist might be chary of an ambiguous and misleading label. Furthermore, any rich work of art has heterogeneous meanings. As the American critic Rita Felski remarks, 'it should not be necessary to point out that a consideration of the current social significance of feminist literature does not imply that its meanings can be limited to or exhausted by this social function. It is a defining characteristic of texts as such, as recorded forms of communication which outlive the original conditions of their production, that they will constantly be subject to new interpretations that neither their authors nor their original readers could have anticipated.'[4]

An author's rejection of a false formulaic is one thing; fear of being cast as the delinquent woman another. Mary Dorcey, an 'out' lesbian poet and fiction writer in the Republic, declares:

> just the label 'feminist' on its own may threaten as much as the label 'lesbian'. I think many women in Ireland have a deep fear within this virulently misogynist literary culture of being considered feminist writers or of being seen to identify in any political way with their own sex.[5]

Given differing theoretical and personal orientations, one needs to attempt a precise definition of the term 'feminist fiction', a task that considers possible audience reception and social effect as much as formal device. While I maintain that feminist fiction is art, not polemic, I do not intend in saying this to recuperate feminist fiction as art at the expense of its political aspect. In the present cultural context of Ireland, and indeed in many other countries of the world where the influence of women's movements exists, we find a focus on gender, sexuality, ethnicity and class with their interconnecting effects on women's lives. One finds in both positive and negative reviews, an explicit recognition of this focus. Several of the writers whose fiction I mention below have indicated clearly that they are writing feminist fiction; that is, that they understand that art does have political consequences and that a self-conscious political focus will, ideally, engender particular kinds of social effects. The novel I shall examine closely at the end of this chapter, *Necessary Treasons*,[6] is an unusual example of this phenomenon as it reveals not just a feminist ideology in its orientation but actually narrates personal and political events of the Irish women's movement. The text grows out of that movement and nourishes it in its turn.

To think about feminist fiction we need to go back a few paces and to reassert what has often been argued: feminist fiction is not the same as 'fiction by women', for example that of Iris Murdoch (whose Irishness would probably surprise most of her readers). Murdoch was more likely to foreground the experience and perspective of male characters than of female ones and gave little emphasis to the problematics of gender in *The Red and the Green*, her novel of the Easter Rising.[7] Nor is feminist fiction synonymous with the category 'women's fiction' although it is contained within it. Yet many critics and reviewers use the term women's fiction as though it were self-evident and all inclusive in its meaning. The term 'women's fiction' then is used to suggest any book by a woman that (some) women might like to read. This has the positive effect of helping women find 'their' books, but has the negative effect of marking women's fiction as 'other', allowing men's fiction to stand as the unmarked standard. Yet for many people, even some feminist critics, the term women's fiction simply designates the so-called popular women's fiction genres like Harlequin or Mills and Boone 'soft' romances, shopping and sex blockbusters, or family and village sagas of the sort discussed in Chapter 5. There now exist enough of these sorts of women's novels to constitute a category in the Irish context; that is, in the last few years a fairly significant number of shopping-and-sex blockbusters, 'soft' romances, and family saga novels have appeared by Irish women for Irish (and other) audiences. But if we designate the novels of such writers as Patricia Scanlan, Mary Ryan, Deirdre Purcell, Kathleen O'Connor, Maeve Binchy or Marian Keyes as 'women's novels', what will feminist publishers eager to reach a more 'intellectual' audience call the difficult, elegantly crafted novels of such Irish writers as Kate O'Brien, Elizabeth Bowen or Janet McNeill? The director of Virago, the British publisher who reissued the novels of all three of these women, deflects the definitional problem by describing Virago publications as comprising 'things in books which are central to women's experience'.[8]

The British critic Rosalind Coward has attempted to sort out these definitional ambiguities in two important articles in which she distinguishes 'feminist fiction' from her portmanteau category, usefully named 'women-centred fiction'.[9] In the group of 'women-centered' fictions she includes everything from the male-authored *Pamela* and *Clarissa* to Mills and Boon romances to Virago-published 'classics' by women. But she then undercuts her own inclusiveness, or perhaps deliberately reveals the imprecision of the term, by limiting the 'multi-faceted phenomenon' to a 'type of narrative which corresponds to existing (and therefore problematic) ways of defining women through their sexual personhood'. This she means to designate 'knowledge or understanding' that is focused exclusively on sexual experience – love, marriage, divorce or just sexual encounters' (pp. 44, 47). While such a generalization accurately denotes the subject of many women-centered novels, there are a number of Irish women's novels that foreground mother-child, sibling, friend and community relations rather than a concern with 'sexual personhood' that still would not qualify as 'feminist fiction'.

Fiction writers from Ireland, South and North, who write about 'things that are central to women's lives' could include this partial list: Mary Beckett, Emma Cooke, Ita Daly, Anne Devlin, Polly Devlin, Anne Enright, Kathleen Ferguson, Jennifer Johnston, Molly Keane (M.J. Farrell), Susan Knight, Mary Lavin, Mary Leland, Deirdre Madden, Kitty Manning, Frances Molloy, Mary Morrissy, Melissa Murphy, Janet McNeill, Val Mulkerns, Dorothy Nelson, Edna O'Brien, Kate Cruise O'Brien, Eithne Strong, Dolores Walshe.[10] It could also include, of course, some of the works by Irish male writers like William Trevor, Brian Moore, Roddy Doyle, and John McGahern. But as this extremely heterogeneous list makes clear, the attempt to make precise the terms 'women's fiction' and 'women-centred fiction', deliberately chosen for their useful inclusivity, proves unfruitful. The terms gesture almost as much towards the assumed gender of audience as towards the works' contents, although we discover the predictable irony that women-centered books by men, for example those I've just mentioned, have mixed-gender audiences whereas women-centered books by women generally have only female audiences.

But if these terms remain imprecise, I would argue that the same cannot be said of feminist fiction which characteristically exhibits at the very least an inscribed political awareness and sometimes even a discernible ideological framework that marks it as socially progressive, or as writing that inscribes a journey 'going from here to somewhere else'.[11]

A useful illustration of what I mean by political awareness can be found in a review of Kitty Manning's novel *The Between People*. This review is written by Linda Anderson, a Northern Irish writer whose second novel, *Cuckoo*, I would characterize as a feminist novel.[12] Anderson criticizes Manning's treatment of Kate, the protagonist, and of Harriet, her mother, stating: 'There is something reactionary about presenting this sort of stoical long-suffering woman in an unexplored, *de facto* way. If we do not see the process and the motivation behind [Harriet's] decisions, it is easy to lose sight of the fact that Harriet could have made other choices. The absence of that sense of other possibilities contributes to the largely dispiriting mood of this book. I think it is important to writers to explore, subvert or discard stereotypes, not merely to recycle them.'[13] I should state the obvious here: Linda Anderson is surely not calling for fictional depictions of Amazonian triumphs or utopian transformation; in fact I can hardly think of work more dispiriting, to use her word, than her representations of the intractable civil war of Northern Ireland in her novels *To Stay Alive* and *Cuckoo*.[14] Instead it is her emphasis on the need to 'explore, subvert or discard stereotypes' that marks the politically motivated novelist, that suggests a vision, perhaps even a program, motivating the writer.

Fiction, then, may be termed 'feminist' if it treats gender as a social construction that specifically disadvantages women; that recognizes, however implicitly, that what has been constructed may at least be questioned, could be transgressed, and might be reconstructed; and that uses narrative as a tool in this project. What these terms suggest further is that the personal or isolated consciousness of the characters and the microstructures of their personal histories will be embedded within the larger social context that shapes, and is shaped in turn, by the characters. While the narrative may attend to the individual consciousness of a central character, the work will explore the personal and collective forces that shape consciousness. As the category 'woman' does not exist apart from other 'positions', these forces will necessarily be explored at gender's intersections with race, class, ethnicity, sexual orientation, nationality, religion – the overarching ideological frameworks and the material institutions that shape individuals' lives.[15] Finally, one must add that this definition does not merely gesture towards abstractions: feminist fiction, which inscribes such political analysis in narrative, is a part of the cultural life of the women's liberation movement and has helped to create that social revolution both in our century and in the last.

Thus far I have attempted only a very general definition of feminist fiction. I do not assume, nor could anyone defend, the idea that there is a single kind of feminist fiction, any more than there is a single kind of feminist theory and practice. Similarly, under this general designation of feminist fiction one finds many different literary forms, as feminist authors have been extremely inventive in adapting existing genres. Feminist fairy and folk tale, fable, science fiction, utopian and dystopian visions, fantasy, historical fiction, the detective novel, confessional realism, *Bildungsroman*, postmodern metafiction, all of these have served as vehicles for feminist writers and all of these genres have been published by Irish women.

But to locate this generalized discussion of genre in Ireland, one needs first perhaps to wonder if conservative Ireland, South and North, might be particularly problematic places for feminist thought and art. Gerardine Meaney gives historical background useful to this question in her pamphlet *Sex and Nation*: 'Women [in postcolonial conditions and here specifically the Republic of Ireland] become the guarantors of their men's status, bearers of national honour and the scapegoats of national identity, ... the territory over which power is exercised.'[16] Because of the fragility of the postcolonial state, it is difficult for its citizens, even the subordinated ones, to challenge the new orthodoxies. Meaney elaborates on the cultural consequences for women of political colonization: 'the Irish woman reading Irish writing finds in it only a profound silence, her own silence' because the 'exclusion of women was constitutive of Irish literature as it was constitutive of the Irish Republic' (p. 17). If this is the situation in the politically stable South, the situation in Northern Ireland is even worse, argues Edna Longley, with its physically violent 'patriarchies like Unionism, Catholicism, Protestantism, Nationalism.'[17]

As Ailbhe Smyth puts it in her introduction to the anthology *Wildish Things* which includes women's writings from South and North: 'it is not easy to write yourself up from under the closely meshed layers of the facts of femininity and Irishness.' What is required, she says, are not just 'imaginative transfiguration[s]' which may empower [Irish women] but 'foundations of truthfulness and passionate authenticity on which to build a future.'[18] In the same introduction she also makes an assertion useful to the question of defining feminist writing in Ireland: 'Women who write and who go on writing are by definition survivors. Women who refuse, in and through their writing, to accept the so-called truths imposed upon them, are by definition subversive' (p. 14).

This focus on the refusal and subversion of received orthodoxy, to say nothing of an appeal to extra-textual 'truthfulness and authenticity', assumes conscious political decision, a usual precondition of feminist writing. But the Irish critic Janet Madden-Simpson, in her introduction to an anthology of pre-1960 Irish women's writing, broadens the definition; she makes the bold claim that 'most Irish female writing [is] feminist.' She goes on to state that even a 'reading of the women who facilely transmitted the orthodox attitudes about women's place and women's function reveals that they were as intimately aware of the difficulties of being a woman [in Ireland] as were writers who approached their subjects from a more crusading and analytical angle.'[19] While this is an astute observation about the achievement of publication for women writing themselves 'up from under', it is in the late 1990s too all-inclusive a definition to be useful.

In the next section I offer examples from different genres of 'women's fiction' that can be read as feminist within the Irish context. The selection includes works that span a spectrum from the easily accessible 'popular' fiction of Maeve Binchy to the most arcane, a historiographic dystopia by Eilís Ní Dhuibne.

Reading through a feminist lens

In the mid-1980s I began collecting every work of fiction and poetry by Irish women I could discover, an undertaking that took a great deal of effort as these were not on university curricula or in critical studies. On one such foray, I asked in a Dublin used books store for help from a young clerk. He piled dozens on the counter, then produced from a corner a book which he handed me nervously. 'This might offend you,' he explained, 'it's about abortion. Would you want to read such a thing?' I did and so discovered the psychological novels of Emma Cooke. At that time I did not know she was a respectable middle-class wife and devout Catholic mother of nine from the conservative west of Ireland, nor that she was a writer who would deny being a feminist, nor that Emma Cooke was a *nom de plume* (a useful strategy for inscribing the contradictions within a split subject). Instead, in her

novels, *A Single Sensation* and *Eve's Apple*, I discovered distinctly feminist representations of the experiences of unwanted pregnancy and
abortion: 'I struggle [says the unmarried, unpartnered Jessica in *A
Single Sensation*] to talk in a companionable way, to forget the thing
inside me, growing in the warm wetness, weighing me down, dragging
my soul – for want of a word – towards a false centre.'[20] In this novel,
Jessica moves with grief but no guilt toward the decision to abort. In
Eve's Apple, the 42-year-old married woman pregnant by a lover has
his baby and goes mad. But there are deceptively bald statements
about the fictional representations of rich and subtle psychic
processes, and the ways these are shaped by, and against, their social
surroundings.

At the beginning of *Eve's Apple* we meet Angel King, who is still
fulminating about sexual double standards in the most predictable,
nonsubversive way, merely stating facts:

> 'If you can't be good, be careful,' [my stepmother] used to say to my
> father whenever he was going off on one of his rare sprees. Of
> course men can get away with anything. Creeping off to their
> conferences, and fishing trips, getting up to all kinds of tricks and
> no repercussions. Not that it means I have any excuse for my lack
> of clear-headedness, my abandoning of years of skepticism. I have
> always accepted the rules inflicted by my state in life, otherwise so
> much of it would seem superfluous....[21]

By the end of the novel Angel is cooking herself and her baby to
death. Her friend Geraldine, who as her husband's lover, is also her
enemy, comes to visit.

> 'This room is boiling hot,' [Geraldine] said. But that's the way I
> want it. I refused to let her open a window. 'Here's [the baby],' I
> said, and pulled down the blanket an inch so that she could see.
> There you lay, my little honey, looking good enough to eat. [At this
> point the devastated visitor runs for help and the novel ends with
> what in the context I read as a horrifying paragraph.] 'I'm still here,
> waiting for her to come back, and you to wake up. I don't mind in
> the least. While I wait I can feel myself growing stronger and
> stronger, strong enough to be the mother of all mankind (p. 166).

Both of these books were written and published in the time of the
great abortion debate in the early 1980s, a debate that continues even

though – or because – the Republic added an amendment to their Constitution in 1983 that guaranteed the right to the life of the fetus, thus enshrining the long-standing legal and *de facto* prohibition against abortion. Emma Cooke wanted, she says, to reposition at the center of the debate the pregnant woman who had been erased or fetishized in a discourse dominated by men.[22] As such, the novel becomes an emblem of its time, with the political and social turmoil manifesting itself in the madness of Angel at the eye of the storm.

Another subversive treatment of the Catholic prohibition against abortion and women's myriad responses to it was published in the same period in what might at first appear an unlikely source, Maeve Binchy's enormously successful blockbuster *Light a Penny Candle*.[23] Again the character is a married, middle-aged mother, but this time one living in the 1940s. Pregnant at the age of 40, and already mother of six, Eileen O'Connor takes matters into her own hands and conscience:

> Eileen's period resumed before she had told anyone of its delay. For four evenings she had had very hot baths and a glass of gin. It was just a relaxing thing to do after a day's work. She didn't even think she would worry Father Kenny by telling him about it in confession. It wasn't a sin or anything, it was just something women did to get their bodies back to normal when they were a bit overstrained (p. 42).

While Maeve Binchy's novels and short stories are more likely to show people's generous if painful accommodations to an intransigent social order than to imagine a different order, her work is replete with examples of shrewd feminist and class analysis. In a short story set in the 1980s, Binchy creates a character that gives one face at least to the horrifying statistics of Irish women going to England for abortion.[24] But she also shows how women enable their own continuing oppression when the woman, named May, decides to protect her lover Andy from the knowledge of her pregnancy and her abortion. Her decision to protect him allows him, and, indirectly, his wife, to maintain a dishonest but complacent sense of morality. Her English roommate (named Hell) at the London nursing room insists on confronting her partner with the news and the consequences of her unwanted pregnancy, while May instead spends her time mourning the fact that Andy, in her absence, would be 'going home to his wife [and four children] because there would be no one to cook him something exciting and go to bed with him in his little manager's flat.' The story ends with the observation that 'May didn't think Hell had got it right about telling all about the abortion. Andy might be against that sort of thing. He was very moral in his own way, was Andy.'[25] Despite the light touch, this is an astute analysis of the social dishonesties and female complicity necessary for the maintenance of a total ban on abortion.

Other fictional forms sometimes offer more inventive and challenging feminist visions, as for example the brilliant experiments of Eilís Ní Dhuibhne in revisionist folk tale (*The Inland Ice and Other Stories*) or historiographic metafiction (*The Bray House*).[26] The latter reproduces in the form of archaeo-anthropological reports, scholarly 'readings' of dysfunctional, urban family life in an Ireland of the 1980s from the viewpoint of an indefinite time in the future when Ireland is buried under layers of radioactive dust, owing to a nuclear 'accident'. In one of the most imaginative explorations in Irish fiction of the artificiality of gender construction, Ní Dhuibhne parallels this self-conscious narrative of traditional gender roles in contemporary Irish life to a Swedish narrative of the future. In the latter, Ní Dhuibhne's anthropologist exhibits a hyper-masculinized gender within a female body, a complicated layering that reveals how unnatural and damaging hierarchical gender is, and how necessary to the maintenance of unequal power relations between, and within, the sexes.

Or, again from the same author, a fable in the title story of the collection *Eating Women is Not Recommended* which inscribes the damage done to female-female relations in a patriarchal order. Here the analysis of menstrual blood shame – the opening words of the story are, appropriately enough 'Bloody hell' – turns the protagonist Lennie into a tigress whose 'low undergrowl' reduces the female manager in her pinstriped suit to a crumpled heap on the floor:

> You reproached me in public for having blood on my pants. Do you walk up to men who have blood stains on their collars and reproach them? Do you attack children who have cuts on their knees?... No, you do not. But you harass me because my blood is different, isn't it? It's women's blood. It's menstrual blood. In this shop, this capitalist, exploiting shop, where they sell fruit from South Africa, where they pay women less than a pound an hour, where even the managers are dupes, where the clothes are cheaper than anywhere in town because they're made by slave labourers, menstruating women are tabooed.[27]

The strategy of humour in this politicized diatribe does not deflect the deeper social satire; indeed the didacticism would sink the story were it not for the lightener. The entirely predictable result of Lennie's outburst is her arrest for breaching the peace. The woman manager may be routed, but the real danger, a patriarchal, capitalistic state and culture enforced by a real policeman, carries on in 'matter of fact tones' (p. 141).

The female *Bildungsroman*, a rich genre in contemporary Ireland, both North and South, offers widely divergent narratives of gender relations that need to be placed under a feminist lens if one is to understand the pathos of their systemic reach. We discover that relations between women are, if anything, as deeply damaged as those between men and women. And mother-daughter relations are especially vulnerable. This passage from Moya Roddy's *The Long Way Home*, for example, turns on the young daughter's need for her mother's courage and the mother's inability to meet her daughter's demand because of her isolation and emotional, social, and economic dependencies. The novel represents well the ways such power makes tyrants even of well-meaning men, destroying relations between mothers/daughters, husbands/wives, fathers/sons, fathers/daughters, brothers and sisters:

'Daddy doesn't give you enough money either. You're always saying, "How can I feed them on the money you give me?" Mr. Burns gives all his money to Mrs. Burns and she gives him money. Loretta told me.'

Mrs. Nowd gripped Jo by the shoulders. 'I hope you don't go repeating things between me and yer daddy to that Loretta Burns?'

'Well, it's true.'

'I don't care. That's all Dublin people want to do is gossip. We keep ourselves to ourselves and so should you. They'll only talk behind yer back. That Loretta is too cute for you,'

'She's my friend.'

'And if she's your friend, how come you're into me crying all the time? You should listen to yer mammy.'

It was on the tip of Jo's tongue to say nobody listened to her but she needed her mammy to like her now.

'Mammy?'

'What now?'

'Why don't you stand up to him?'

For a moment Jo held her mammy's eyes. Just let her say she will

and I'll help. Go on, mammy.
    Mrs. Nowd's eyes dropped.
    'Don't ask questions. You'll know all about that soon enough.'[28]

This promise of future knowledge that will trap the girl 'soon enough' hangs like a cloud over a great many women's novels in Ireland and its ubiquitous presence sometimes has the effect of naturalizing the threat. This is not the case in Moya Roddy's novel which ends with the coming-of-age and independence of the young protagonist. But the vague hope of a different set of possibilities for a feisty-enough youngster offers little real vision about that 'somewhere else' where women and men might engage differently. This one finds in feminist fiction.

'From here to somewhere else'

In her discussion of feminism as a transformational politic, the American poet and critic bell hooks argues that feminists' struggle to end patriarchal domination should be of primary importance to women and men globally not because it is the foundation of all other oppressive structures but because it is 'that form of domination we are most likely to encounter in an ongoing way in everyday life'. Sexism, unlike other forms of domination, 'directly shapes and determines relations of power in our private lives, in familiar social spaces, in that most intimate context – home – in that most intimate sphere of relations – family'. Yet even though family relations 'may be, and most often are, informed by acceptance of a politic of domination, they are simultaneously relations of care and connection'. This convergence of contradictory impulses 'provides a practical setting for feminist critique, resistance, and transformation'.[29]

    Although hooks limits her focus here to political praxis, it might usefully be applied to those art forms intent on social reform, in this case, feminist fiction. Any creative writer attempting to challenge oppressive gender relations by means of her work has to be extremely sensitive to the actual conditions of women's lives if she is to speak successfully to a local audience or interest a foreign one. Feminism is the politics most grounded in everyday life – what the British critic Maggie Humm calls 'the politics of representation'; likewise feminist fiction, with its intermingling of the contradictory aspects of personal history, daily experiences, family time and the impinging social contexts, is an art of representation. But not the representation of traditional realism. Instead, as Maggie Humm explains, feminist writers, like the cuckoo, 'lay texts of similar hue and size but which hatch into a very different politics.' This Humm calls 'border crossing' and she suggests in this term the crossing of traditional genres, the changing of language, the breaking of traditional images – all strategies of response to the misrepresentation of women in literature and to the 'urgent threat of patriarchal closure.'[30]

This aesthetics of the border is a most challenging one: creating the experience of actual existence while attempting to rupture it. One strategy for manufacturing this kind of creative dissonance uses border crossings between countries and cultures as its narrative structure. We find this in Mary Rose Callaghan's *The Awkward Girl* which self-consciously positions women's lives against men's in both Ireland and the United States.

Callaghan has created a protagonist who is a version of the classic castrated woman, the silly creature who always messes up, whose endless disasters form her identity.[31] One of her many ridiculous failures is her adoption as a university student of imported feminism, a 'Simone duh Beaver and Satyr' act, spiced up with a dash of Maoism. Callaghan displays this pretentiousness at one point by putting Sally Ann into conversation with a former schoolmate whose own class background forces her out of high school, into a service job. The self-centered callowness of the young middle-class feminist is a powerful indictment of the unthinking importation of foreign ideologies. And yet this awkward girl whose life is the orb around which the novel circles is only one consciousness in the novel and arguably one no more central that than of Sister Rita, her teacher-mentor. In the novel's 13 sections, more akin to short stories than to chapters, Mary Rose Callaghan emerges as a remarkably adroit story-teller as she creates the consciousness of different people and the connectedness of a variety of lives – nuns, working-class women and men, privileged Irish artists or would-be artists and critics, bourgeois housewives, male academics, lesbian mothers, lawyers and doctors. The composite portrait of Dubliners and Americans in the end support the feminist and class perceptions of the bumbling Sally Ann, whose final vindication, and biggest disaster, comes in the supreme irony of death-in-childbirth, the age-old leveler of women, treated here as a kind of tragicomedy. As even this brief summary should indicate, the novel suffers somewhat from the need for self-conscious protection, via irony, of its own pieties. And yet in its structural use of interlinked multiple narratives, it explores the ways consciousness grows within the communal life and charts the subversions and retrenchments of contemporary Irish society.

Mary Rose Callaghan reveals more than a little unease when she narrates feminism; she dares to give her protagonist this line: 'Ireland would make a feminist out of a stone. It's an absolute patriarchy', then undercuts it with the facetious intensifier: 'I'm dead serious' (p. 175). In the rest of the chapter Sally Ann relates incidents of male chauvinism in such graphically obvious terms that the reader is allowed to see it as more of the eternally adolescent Sally Ann's narrative distortion. No such awkwardness is evident in the work of another feminist writer, Mary Dorcey.

I earlier spoke of the damage done to mother-daughter relations within male-dominated society. The dynamic of lesbian relationships, within which women move their emotional, social (and sometimes economic) centers away from hegemonic male control, should result in a safer position for lesbians. But of course it does not. Instead, the image/practice of women-identified women can set in motion the machinery whereby heterosexism is protected. Mary Dorcey's lesbian fiction gives convincing representation to my bald declaration. In one of her stories, for example, two women dancing in a country inn, momentarily forgetful of their surroundings as erotically connected lovers tend to be, are suddenly in mortal danger:

> I open my eyes. The music has stopped. Behind you I see a man standing; his eyes riveted to our bodies, his jaw dropped wide as though it had been punched.... You return to consciousness and walk from the floor. I follow, my skin suddenly cold. I want as quickly as possible to be gone from the spotlight. I have remembered where we are: a Friday night country dance, surrounded by drunken males who have never before seen two women dance in each others' arms. All about the room they are standing still, watching. As we cross the empty space to our table no one moves.[32]

In the terrifying moments that follow, the two women plot and effect their escape. Their greatest danger lies not in that well-lighted public place, but in the exterior darkness, no-woman's land. 'Under all the theatrics lies the clear threat that if we dare to leave, they can follow, and once outside, alone in the dark, they will have no need for these elaborate games' (p. 57).

But the remarkable element of Mary Dorcey's fiction is not in this delineation of the outlaw status and resulting danger of lesbian life; it is in her ability to narrate the ways in which rich, complex lives can be created within this occupied territory. In effect, she redraws the emotional and social map of our time. Not all readers credit her with this achievement. For example, in a review of the story Irish poet and critic Janet Shepperson argues that while

> the atmosphere of menace where the two women find themselves surrounded by hostile men at a disco is convincingly drawn ... [but] the analysis of the relationship is too drawn-out, as if the writer were determined to convey every nuance of her narrator's thoughts, second thoughts, and even third thoughts, surely an indulgence which writers of the short story can ill afford.[33]

In my own reading, the achievement of the story is precisely that 'A Country Dance' does not end with the escape which would be a stunning but ideologically simple conclusion. Instead it opens out into the sexual union of the two women which, despite its temporary pleasures, will bring its own difficulties and the need for ethical decisions about the betrayal of other lovers, the repelling of further dangers, the possible return to the 'hard-won pleasures of realism and self-sufficiency' (p. 52). The final, indeterminate moments of the story show the women's temporary repossession of the dark, the untamable if fleeting zone of the erotic: 'For a little longer night holds us beyond the grasp of speech. I lean and blow out the candle' (p. 63). This is not just another love story, although it is that, too. It is a step out onto a 'visionary terrain' where a whole new kind of order might be created.[34]

In preparing to write this book I have read over 200 novels and collections of short stories by Irish women. Reading with a feminist lens, I am struck by the fictional naturalization in recent years of the presence of the women's movement(s) in Ireland. Given the not undeserved bad press the Republic of Ireland receives abroad in progressive publications, particularly in matters reproductive, this presence is too important to be ignored, as is the astonishing fact that the conservative Republic of Ireland elected in 1990 the only woman president in the world who made her political/legal career in feminist and human rights litigation. In other words, despite the well-entrenched traditional structures – cultural, religious, legal and emotional – that support male hegemony, we find a number of women writers offering not just feminist characters, but feminist organizations, feminist spaces, feminist practices, informal and formal sisterhoods, as though these were quite a natural way of living even if the need for feminism points to an ongoing personal and social struggle rather than an achieved state. By the late 1990s the daughters of second-wave feminist mothers have moved to centre stage, as in Katy Hayes's collection of stories, *Forecourt*.[35] This, while not unique to Ireland, is genuinely new in literature and marks a revolution in Irish literature. The theme of this phenomenon might well be, to borrow a title from feminist writer Evelyn Conlon, 'my head is opening'.[36]

To offer a few examples: we find in a Dorcey short story a single mother of two children who realizes that there are other ways of living, other roads going 'from here to somewhere else' when she listens to a women's call-in, consciousness-raising program on Irish daily radio.[37] Or in Mary O'Donnell's *The Light-Makers*,[38] where a woman photographer, devastated by her husband's desertion and her own infertility, chooses to go to a psychotherapist at the Dublin Women's Centre, as though this service were a normal channel through which to rediscover health. En route to her appointment she stops off to view a women's art show, an event so well established that even a feminist critic concerned to celebrate new female talent will use critical standards that distinguish among the good, the mediocre and the appalling. In Evelyn Conlon's *Stars in the Daytime*, the contemporary presence of women's political activity is simply a given.[39] When Rose, whose story it is, becomes upset about witnessing a wife-battering, she decides 'to attend a political meeting'. She finds two posters and, choosing one, begins on a trajectory that leads first to a marriage with a communist, then a British divorce. 'If she had gone to the other one she would have been saved a lot of trouble' (pp. 130–1). Some years later, when Rose is single and pregnant, the reader learns what the other option might have offered when her ex-roommate, now a 'busy feminist', is called in by doctor and parents to help the 'deranged' Rose. Dymphna arrives with 'great noise and a bosomly confidence':

> 'Sure sign something's really gone wrong when you're calling on us. You must have fucked up badly if it's time to call in the women.
> 'Jesus, [thinks Rose] she didn't get that confidence rubbing up and down men's legs (p. 160).

It is precisely this note of confidence, this certainty about the reality and value of feminist practice that sounds such an original note in Irish writing and life, even if it is offered in this tempering context:

Dymphna had become a busy feminist, she had spoken from the back of trucks and had even been asked to represent Ireland at an international conference. 'But that's not Ireland', the Irish said, 'that's only the women,' Dymphna bellowed in at Rose. They laughed (p. 160).

A very pertinent illustration of this change, from the Irish publishing world, is the success of the Attic Press, now part of the Cork University Press. This press, which has published so many of the titles that appear in this book, has been one of Ireland's largest publishers. When an American scholar asked Ailbhe Smyth, then an editorial director at Attic, is it 'a contradiction that a radical, feminist press exists in Ireland?', Ailbhe Smyth's response was:

I know what foreigners mean but they're being very foreign. Many people outside of Ireland have no understanding of how incredibly active and dynamic the women's movement has been in this country since 1970. Attic ... is an absolutely inevitable growth of what has been happening in this country for the last 30 years. [Feminist] publishing is part of that total context, not the perceived, stereotypical image of Ireland.... Ireland is a Catholic country ... a conservative country ... [but] it's also other things. It's also the country that elected Mary Robinson. Mary Robinson didn't spring out of a vacuum.[40]

Maeve Kelly's *Necessary Treasons*

One also finds the opposite of feminist celebration, the inscription of explicit attacks on feminism, which is, of course, another way of charting its existence.[41] Resistance to feminism, put into tension with some women's growing belief in the necessity of feminist action in Ireland, forms the core of Maeve Kelly's *Necessary Treasons*. This novel offers the country's most sustained narrative attempt to understand the psychosocial history of the development of feminist consciousness in an Irish setting as well as one of the most complex explorations of the reasons why Irish women should not yet celebrate 'liberation'. But it sets these contemporary phenomena in a counterpointing parallel with those of an earlier historical period of monumental importance in Irish history, the final defeat of Gaelic Ireland by the British in 1691.

Reviewers of this novel have neglected entirely this historical parallel, tending to read the book as though it were exclusively a contemporary narrative of personal development in one of the four central characters, a young teacher named Eve Gleeson who near the beginning of the novel becomes engaged to a middle-aged Limerick doctor, Hugh Creagh. From this position, and almost by chance, Eve gets drawn into the movement to establish a shelter for battered women in the city, and in the course of the novel evolves into a feminist who breaks off her engagement to the unreconstructable male chauvinist.

If one reads this text as another novel of awakening, as did the *Times Literary Supplement* reviewer, one might fault the novel for being a 'dubiously polemical novel' set in an 'ancestral home by the pounding sea', with some 'lurid reality of domestic violence' thrown in as incidental color.[42] But such a reading erases the real interest of the novel, to say nothing of its basic facts, which is not so much concerned with Eve, as with representing changes in consciousness under the violent experiences of colonization, England's colonization of Ireland, men's of women and children.

Both the historical times of the novel use Limerick and its environs as setting. The seventeenth-century narrative is created entirely through a set of eight family letters and transplanters' documents, which, unbeknownst to Hugh Creagh, have been passed down over the centuries to the Creagh daughter in each generation named Honora after the author of most of the letters. These papers, created as a kind of historiographic exercise by Maeve Kelly, force us (and Hugh) to confront in very personal terms the extraordinary losses and, in some cases, the choice of 'necessary treasons' by those Irish dispossessed of their land, language and fundamental human rights after their defeat by King William of England. In the course of the novel Hugh is allowed access to the letters by his elder sister, Honora, who wants to amuse him in his visits to the ancestral home where she and her three sisters still live. He becomes obsessed with the letters, realizing that here he is being given a privileged entry into the experience and ambiguous meaning of supposedly familiar 'history'. The papers offer a very cryptic record of the Jacobite-Irish challenge to British hegemony in the period of 1685–1688, and of the Irish defeat followed by transplantation and destruction of families, execution of rebels, and the loss of cultural, legal and material possessions during the following years. Here, despite the brevity of the papers, Kelly nonetheless manages to create a whole set of dramatic Irish characters who respond in various ways to the events: violent attempts at revenge, intransigent and principled refusals to accommodate, opportunistic (or, under a different light, sane) rejection of Irish faith and language as a means of survival, tribal loyalties or treacheries, redefinitions of tribe. How to interpret the behaviors? How to formulate an ethical response to suffering on such a scale? How to use the knowledge gained from this historical encounter in other historical situations? This is Hugh's struggle and his is perhaps the most intriguing characterization of the novel. For in Kelly's treatment – and the implied *caveat* here reaches beyond the novel – Hugh will finally be unable to understand history except in accordance with his own desires and needs. Significantly, he gives up his historical searches when, in the course of the novel, he is elected city councilor (p. 233).

What Hugh longs for is the continuation and refurbishment of his family genealogy. He wants a son, hence his need to marry, and he wants a political career of the sort his nineteenth-century male relatives were able to create when they had repossessed the land and home they had lost two centuries earlier. But in order to achieve this he is willing to colonize his young fiancée (his 'little lamb', his 'poor mouse', p. 84) and resolutely dismisses her own growing concern for battered women and women's rights. A characteristic response to her discussing her work in this movement is 'Are you talking about this women's rights thing? We should be talking about human rights. We all want the same thing. Peace and justice.... Of course there are no rights without responsibilities. Feminists and women's libbers should remember that' (p. 85). Resentful of Eve's demands and her sense of outrage at women's dangers and the men's resistant responses, Hugh finally even resents the demands from the past made by the martyred Honora whom he encounters through her letters as though still alive. Hugh complains to his friend Adrian: 'Damn women and their complaints. They make you feel pain in spite of yourself' (p. 193). Rather than respond to that pain, he deflects it. Excusing his male ancestor who refused to help Honora and her family, then ingratiated himself with the conquerors as a means of survival (a case of a 'necessary treason'), Hugh salves his own conscience, and the historical nightmare, by deciding the victim, Honora, deserved her fate: the execution of her sons, the death of her husband, the loss of the family possessions, her own mutilation and death. He manages this response by reshaping her character in the anachronistic model that he finds most threatening:

> Very likely this Honora was a tough woman, well able to fight for herself – maybe, for all he knew, a seventeenth-century feminist. If that were the case, she was courting trouble and she certainly got what she

deserved. Some women did not know when the time to stay quiet had
arrived. Eleanor could never keep her mouth shut' (p. 161).

This unexpected shift in Hugh's thoughts to Eleanor, his sister-in-
law and one of the other main characters, opens another whole
narrative of tragic loss and ultimate accommodation. This one specifically explores women's maternal 'destiny' and the ways this role puts
women into positions of dependency. Eleanor, as a young medical
student, had become pregnant by Hugh's brother. Forced to give up
her own career plans, she demanded understanding and help from her
lover, also a medical student but one who could continue his studies
while Eleanor stayed home with their child. His response when he did
the 'noble thing' (p. 218) and married her was violence, divorce and
eventual abduction of their child. Alone, she returns to medical
school, then as a doctor in Limerick eventually creates a special clinic
for battered women. At the time of the novel, 17 years after these
events, she is a determinedly single woman.

Much of young Eve's education comes initially from Eleanor, whose
pungent and cynical observations open Eve's eyes to the meaning of
social constructs she had never thought to question. A characteristic
offering goes like this:

> And don't give me history. History is crap. Men invented history
> and God at the same time because they were too lazy to draw the
> water and hew the wood and the hunting was poor, and they had
> to have some excuse for their idle ways or the missus wouldn't let
> them leap into the hay with her (p. 60).

Eleanor functions as feminist analyst within the novel, a role that
teeters occasionally on the brink of bald didacticism but which is
always played out in narrative dramatizations. Speaking of women
'falling in love', she observes the woman loses herself in her lover.

> For such a sacrifice there has to be a reckoning.... Disillusion, the
> sad undeniable truth of the man's frailty, the mourning for the
> death of her own self. Then comes the desperate, despairing urge to
> rediscover self .... Divided and torn, not just by husband or lover
> but by the children who have come from their union, she has to be
> reborn while still giving birth. Her life is an endless contradiction.
> Mocked for her passivity, abused for her aggression, she embodies
> everyone's failures and guilts....

She ends this impassioned assertion with the statement, 'only one thing is certain: women are the skivvies of the world' (p. 189).

The young Eve, despite initial resistance to this uncomfortable, didactic and verbally aggressive presence, is nevertheless drawn to Eleanor because she admires her courage and frankness, and because Eleanor's presence reminds Eve of the mistake she is making in her engagement to Hugh. And yet despite Eleanor's apparent independence she once again falls in love, this time with Hugh's friend Adrian, who is a writer of Irish-language poetry. Almost a *topos* in Irish women's writing, the male poet has had an erotic appeal difficult to resist and fierce Eleanor ends up sitting at Adrian's feet (p. 200), marrying him (p. 216) and having a child at the age of 40 (p. 239), thus affording him the opportunity of composing a poem, like Coleridge and Yeats, on the birth of the child. ('New life. There was surely something new to be said about that and the mother, the vessel. He looked with interest at her, conscious of the irony of it. That would make a poem' (p. 239). The novel ends abruptly at this point, with Adrian walking through the hospital corridor glimpsing reclining mothers with their bundles of pale pinks, baby blues. 'Everything was very well organized. He felt enormously contented' (p. 240).

This ominous ending reminds the reader of the prevailing winds. Just in case the point needs underlining, the novel's penultimate page chronicles the simultaneous events of Eleanor's labor and the stabbing of Miranda Connors, a woman whom the shelter workers, including Eve, had attempted to protect after her husband's multiple beatings. And near the end of the novel, Ann, the inspiration and practical leader of the women's shelter movement in Limerick, dies of a cavalierly misdiagnosed and thus untreated cancer. A bleak closure, or, to put it differently, an inscription of the status quo challenged, perhaps, but still intact.

Given this grim picture, how accurate was my assertion at the beginning of this chapter that this novel, which grows out of the Irish women's movement, nourishes that movement in its turn? Could it, like the North American and British feminist novels of the 1980s examined by Gayle Greene, be described with such words as 'defeated and inturned', full of 'division', 'disillusion', 'dismember', 'dissever', 'dismantle', 'disremember'? Worse, would it be accurate to say that like feminist writing abroad, Kelly's feminist novel (or my own criticism) 'can no longer claim to be activism, since most of it is barely comprehensible?'[43] My own writing others will judge. But in the case of *Necessary Treasons*, one finds a narrative performance of the ways

gender as a social construct can be damaging, and how personal trans-
formations and collective resistance can challenge those constructs. In
this way, Maeve Kelly's art is functioning obliquely but self-
consciously as a political tool.

Once in the early 1980s I heard the American author May Sarton
declare that someone should publish the novel of the women's collective bookstore. To my knowledge, no one has. But in *Necessary
Treasons* we find the novel of the women's refuge movement. Unlikely
as it sounds, the novel enacts the rationale of the movement, its
historical development, discussions of political strategies and barriers,
analyses of the patterns of problems among the refuge clientele, and
the embattled but effective female collectivity that makes the institution possible.[44] Moreover the novel inscribes at its center a young
woman who will carry on the work after the death of the founder, and
the end of the novel. Despite its starkness (and because of it), the
narrative might aid in the social transformation feminist writers hope
their work can effect.

As a way of illustrating this assertion, I offer this anecdotal evidence.
In my researches about the subject and author of this novel, I decided
to visit the Limerick women's refuge. Unlike shelters, called Transition
Houses in my own country, whose locations are kept secret as a way
of protecting the threatened women and children, the Limerick Adapt
House is purposely made known to all citizens. This I discovered as,
suitcase in hand, I searched out its location. With grave and uneasy
concern, people I questioned for directions sent me on my way. The
place I was searching for had this description in the novel: 'crammed
with mothers and children, including one infant of two weeks and
one of seven weeks, the building was only temporary accommodation'. As the city councilors to whom the women appealed for better
quarters were 'shocked at the mud being thrown at the good name of
the city', it was unlikely that a permanent site would be obtained
(p. 177). Yet when I arrived at the shelter of the 1990s what I discovered was a massive, beautifully appointed, renovated school. Its very
existence, of course, surrounded by its high fence, signals the continuing violence against women and children. But the solidity of its
imposing structure also declares the success of the attempt of women,
in this case led by the author herself, to name the phenomenon and
find ways of alleviating the suffering.

This may be an unusual icon of women's efforts to effect social
change, just as *Necessary Treasons* is an idiosyncratic creation within
Irish culture in its use of explicit feminist analysis and the inscription

of political engagement as a strategy for structuring a novel. But if it is a radical example of engaged art, the novel forms part of a developing artistic world that reveals what Mary Dorcey has named 'this second Ireland, this concealed Ireland, this Ireland which up to now has been silenced by emigration.'[45] Irish scholar and artist Angela Bourke offers a crucial insight into this kind of artistic practice when she claims 'we have urgent need of stories in Ireland at the moment, as our society comes to terms with painful memories.... The old narratives will no longer serve.... More and more, as silenced voices speak, the need for different kinds of language is being acknowledged.'[46]

The poem at the start of this book celebrates the 'unleashing' of women's words – the 'torrents of speech' with which women are exploring old territories and carving out new shapes for the 'pool'. If we listen with new ears, we can hear how this floodtide of women's narratives is changing Ireland. In a culture where words and their makers matter, the effects of such creative expression will be deep and lasting.

Notes

1 Introduction

1. Jo Slade, 'Waterfall', *The Vigilant One* (Galway: Salmon Poetry, 1994), p. 21.
2. Works that address the issue of women's changing status are cited within the following chapters as specific subjects become pertinent. One can find useful summaries of general changes in the Republic in Ailbhe Smyth, 'States of Change', *Feminist Review* 50 (Summer, 1995): 25–43, and Gemma Hussey, 'Women and Life in Ireland', *Ireland Today: Anatomy of a Changing State* (London: Penguin Books, 1995), pp. 417–44. Important works from the 1980s, like *Crane Bag* (Special Issue: *Images of Irish Women*, ed. Christina Nulty, 4:1 (1980); Eiléan Ní Chuilleanáin, ed., *Irish Women: Image and Achievement* (Dublin: Arlen House, 1985); Ailbhe Smyth, *Women's Rights In Ireland* (Dublin: Irish Council for Civil Liberties, Ward River Press, 1983); Ursula Barry, *Lifting the Lid: Handbook of Facts and Information on Ireland* (Dublin: Attic Press, 1986); Jenny Beale, *Women in Ireland: Voices of Change* (Dublin: Gill and Macmillan, 1986); Eileen Evason, *Against the Grain: the Contemporary Women's Movement in Northern Ireland* (Dublin: Attic Press, 1991); Ruth Hooley, ed., *The Female Line: Northern Irish Women Writers* (Belfast: Northern Ireland Women's Rights Movement, 1985) have achieved nearly historical status because the changes have been so rapid that even works written a decade ago may be dated. One needs to consult a variety of recent sources, including journals devoted to the topic of gender and Irish women: *Irish Journal of Feminist Studies* and *Women's Studies Review* (National University of Ireland, Galway); special issues or regular features in such journals as *Women's Studies International Forum, Feminist Review, Writing Women, Graph, Krino, HU/ The Honest Ulsterman, Journal of Women's History, Canadian Journal of Irish Studies, Feminist Studies, The Colby Quarterly, Canadian Women's Studies/Cahiers des femmes*. Most useful might be such texts as Ailbhe Smyth, ed., *Irish Women's Studies Reader* (Dublin: Attic, 1993), Anne Byrne and Madeleine Leonard, eds, *Women and Irish Society: a Sociological Reader* (Dublin: Beyond the Pale Publications, 1997).
3. Julia O'Faolain, *Women in the Wall* (London: Faber & Faber, 1975, rpt. London: Virago, 1985) and *The Judas Cloth* (London: Sinclair-Stevenson, 1992); Dolores Walshe, *Where the Trees Weep* (Dublin: Wolfhound, 1992).
4. This study examines only fiction written in English. Very little fiction has been published in Irish although some is available in dual-language translation. See 'Beleaguered but determined: Irish Women Writers in Irish', Mary N. Harris, *Feminist Review* 51 (Autumn 1995): 26–40.
5. For a study of major women poets writing today, see Patricia Boyle Haberstroh, *Women Creating Women: Contemporary Irish Women Poets* (Syracuse, NY: Syracuse University Press, 1996; Dublin: Attic Press, 1996).
6. Ann Owen Weekes, *Irish Women Writers: an Uncharted Tradition* (Lexington, Kentucky: The University Press of Kentucky, 1990). Page

references are cited in the text.

7. Mary O'Donnell, *Virgin and the Boy* (Dublin: Poolbeg, 1996), pp. 14–15. Other page references are cited in the text.

8. Mary Dorcey, 'The Spaces between the Words', *The Women's Review of Books*, 8:3 (December 1990): 22. Page numbers are cited in the text.

9. Edna O'Brien, *Mother Ireland* (London: Weidenfeld and Nicolson, 1976; rpt. London: Penguin, 1978), p. 87.

10. In this case, a 14-year-old raped girl was denied permission to leave Ireland for the purpose of obtaining an abortion in England because of the prohibitions built into the Irish Constitution in 1983, as a result of a Republic-wide referendum. For a feminist discussion of this ruling and its aftermath, see Ailbhe Smyth, ed., *The Abortion Papers* (Dublin: Attic Press, 1992).

11. Ailbhe Smyth, 'Introduction', *Wildish Things: an Anthology of New Irish Women's Writing* (Dublin: Attic Press, 1989), p. 8.

12. See, for example, Eilís Ní Dhuibhne, ed. 'Introduction', *Voices on the Wind: Women Poets of the Celtic Twilight* (Dublin: New Island Books, 1995) and Ann Ulry Colman, *A Dictionary of Nineteenth Century Irish Women Poets* (Galway: Kennys Bookshop, 1996). To discover a rich harvest of studies on Irish women's lives and works, see the *Irish Journal of Feminist Studies* for lists of the graduate theses being produced on feminist topics within Women's Studies Programs in Irish universities.

13. Eavan Boland, *Object Lessons: the Life of the Woman and the Poet in Our Time* (London: Carcanet Press, Ltd., 1995; rpt. London: Vintage, 1996), p. 254.

14. Katie Donovan, *Irish Women Writers: Marginalized by Whom?* (Dublin: The Raven Arts Press, 1988), p. 7. Other page references are cited in the text.

15. John Boland, 'And Let's Not Forget the Men', the *Irish Times*, Saturday, 28 June 1997:8.

16. Emma Donoghue, 'Noises from Woodsheds: Tales of Irish Lesbians 1886–1989', Ide O'Carroll and Eoin Collins (eds), in *Lesbian and Gay Visions of Ireland: Towards the Twenty-First Century* (London: Cassell, 1995), p. 159.

17. Medbh McGuckian, 'Birds and Their Masters', *Irish University Review* 23:1 (Spring/Summer 1993): pp. 29–30.

18. Maeve Kelly, 'Making a Space', Unpublished speech delivered at the Women Writers Circle, Fourth International Interdisciplinary Congress on Women, Hunter College, New York, July 1990, p.2.

19. Frances Molloy, *No Mate for the Magpie* (London: Virago Press, 1985), p. 170.

20. Nuala O'Faolain, *Are You Somebody? The Life and Times of Nuala O'Faolain* (Dublin: New Island Books, 1996), p. 77.

21. Caroline Walsh, ed., *Virgins and Hyacinths: an Attic Press Book of Fiction* (Dublin: Attic Press, 1993), p. 6.

22. Poet and novelist Juanita Casey might be considered an exception to the silence of Traveler women, and she is often claimed as an Irish writer because her Traveler mother, who died at Casey's birth in England, was Irish. She was raised by a 'settled' English family, but in her adult life followed the Romany pattern of her biological parents' lives. (Freda Brown Jackson, 'Juanita Casey', *Dictionary of Literary Biography*, Detroit: Bruccoli

Clark Book, 1983). Casey's *Horse of Selene*, partially set in Ireland, is a beautiful rendering of the excitements and possibilities of the liminal life between 'civilization' and solitary freedom. (Portlaoise, Ireland: The Dolmen Press, 1971.)

23. Maeve Kelly, 'Orange Horses' in *Orange Horses* (Belfast: The Blackstaff Press, 1990); Clare Boylan, *Black Baby* (New York: Doubleday, 1989); Ronit Lentin, *Night Train to Mother* (Dublin: Attic Press, 1989) and *Songs on the Death of Children* (Dublin: Poolbeg, 1996).

2 Authorship, the forbidden country

1. Mary Dorcey, *Moving into the Space Cleared by Our Mothers* (Galway: Salmon Press, 1991), p. 26.
2. Anne Le Marquand Hartigan, *Clearing the Space: a Why of Writing* (Knockeven, Co. Clare, 1996), p. 14.
3. Nuala O'Faolain, 'Irish Women and Writing in Modern Ireland', *Irish Women: Images and Achievements,* ed. Eiléan Ní Chuilleanáin (Dublin: Arlen Press: 1985), p. 130. Other page references are cited in the text.
4. Nuala O'Faolain has subsequently disavowed these statements and, in her remarkable memoir *Are You Somebody? The Life and Times of Nuala O'Faolain* (Dublin: New Island Books, 1996) talks of freeing herself from internalized sexism. Yet even so, when she discusses the dozens of writers she admires, she still includes only four women among them.
5. Eiléan Ní Chuilleanáin, 'Woman as Writer: the Social Matrix', *Crane Bag* 4:1 (1980): 101, 105.
6. Luce Irigarary, *Speculum of the Other Woman* (Ithaca: Cornell University Press, 1985), p. 135. While some feminist and poststructuralist critics may fault Irigarary for using dichotomous divisions in her thought (e.g., monolithic discourse and fluid female opposition), the term 'economy of the same' is not an inaccurate way to describe the historical situation in the Republic of Ireland in the twentieth century, although I myself am uneasy about her homology between female sexuality and women's language. For further discussions of these problems see Rita Felski, *Beyond Feminist Aesthetics: Feminist Literature and Social Change* (Cambridge: Harvard University Press, 1989).
7. Luce Irigaray, 'Power of Discourse', *This Sex Which is Not One*, trans. Catherine Porter (Ithaca: Cornell University Press, 1985), p. 76. Other page references are cited in the text.
8. Molly Hite, *The Other Side of the Story* (Ithaca: Cornell University Press, 1989), pp. 144–5.
9. A valuable book length study of one possible tradition is Ann Owen Weekes's *Irish Women Writers: an Uncharted Tradition* (Lexington: University of Kentucky Press, 1990). Page references are cited in the text.
10. Ailbhe Smyth, 'Ireland', *Bloomsbury Guide to Women's Literature,* ed., Claire Buck (London: Bloomsbury, 1992), p. 37.
11. Ailbhe Smyth, Lecture, University of Victoria, Canada, 3 March 1992.
12. Ann Owen Weekes, *Unveiling Treasures: the Attic Guide to the Published Works of Irish Women Literary Writers* (Dublin: Attic, 1993).

13. Eavan Boland, *A Kind of Scar: the Woman Poet in a National Tradition* (Dublin: Attic Press, 1989), p. 8. Page references are cited in the text.
14. Eavan Boland, Lecture, Conference of the International Association of Anglo-Irish Studies, Trinity College Dublin, 13 July 1992.
15. 'An Interview with Eavan Boland' by Jody Allen Randolph, *Irish University Review* 23:1 (Spring/Summer 1993): 130. Pertinent to my argument here, this interview is published in an issue wholly devoted to the work of Eavan Boland, who is the only woman poet so honoured up to that time in the seventeen issues dedicated to individual Irish writers. Fiction writer Mary Lavin is the other woman thus featured.
16. Both these terms are problematic. There is obviously no single essence of Irish, but I am using here the poet's own conflicted designation. I use the term 'femininity' to refer to the social constructions made of female biological sex, although I realize a danger exists in continuing to use a word that reenforces the politically disadvantageous, traditional and *lived* opposition between 'masculine/feminine' in the 'ruling social/linguistic order'. (Toril Moi, 'Feminist, Female, Feminine', *The Feminist Reader: Essays in Gender and the Politics of Literary Criticism*, ed. Catherine Belsey and Jane Moore (London: Macmillan, 1989), pp. 126–32. Eavan Boland has very sophisticated explorations of these issues in her poetry and prose essays.
17. Mary O'Donnell, In Her Own Image – an Assertion that Myths are made by Men, by the Poet in Transition', *Irish University Review* 32(1):40. Other page references are cited in the text.
18. Eve Patten, 'Women and Fiction: 1985–1990', *Krino* 8–9 (1990): 2,7.
19. Mary Leland, *Approaching Priests* (London: Sinclair-Stevenson Ltd, 1991), p. 237. Other page references are cited in the text.
20. This is a topic discussed by a number of novelist-critics, for example Carolyn G. Heilbrun, *Writing a Woman's Life* (New York: Norton, 1988) and Margaret Atwood, 'The Curse of Eve – Or What I Learned in School', *Second Words: Selected Critical Prose* (Boston: Beacon, 1982), pp. 215–28.
21. Two fine examples of letter or journal novels by Irish women are Mary Dorcey, *Biography of Desire* (Dublin: Poolbeg, 1997) and Ita Daly, *Unholy Ghosts* (London: Bloomsbury, 1996).
22. Interview with the author, Dublin, 1 July 1992.
23. Mary Beckett, 'A Literary Woman', in *A Literary Woman* (London: Bloomsbury, 1990), p. 127.
24. Gayle Greene, *Changing the Story: Feminist Fiction and the Tradition* (Bloomington: Indiana University Press, 1991), p. 189. She quotes here from Nancy Miller's 'Arachnologies: the Woman, the Text and the Critic', *The Poetics of Gender,* ed. Nancy Miller (New York: Columbia University Press, 1986), p. 271.
25. Briege Duffaud, *A Wreath Upon the Dead* (Dublin: Poolbeg, 1993).
26. Greene, *Changing the Story*, p. 189. She borrows the term from Steven G. Kellman, 'The Fiction of Self-Begetting', *Modern Language Notes* 91 (December 1976) 1243–56.
27. In my use of the term 'social reality' I borrow from American philosopher Sandra Lee Bartky who defines the term thus: 'the ensemble of formal and informal relationships with other people in which we are now enmeshed or in which we are likely to become enmeshed, together with the attitudes,

values, types of communication, and conventions which accompany such relationships. "Social reality" is the social life-world, the social environment as it is present to my consciousness.' *Femininity and Domination: Studies in the Phenomenology of Oppression* (London: Routledge, 1990), p. 121.

28. Jennifer Johnston, *The Christmas Tree* (London: Hamish Hamilton, 1981). Page references are cited in the text.

29. Maeve Kelly, *Florrie's Girls* (London: Michael Joseph, 1989). Page references are cited in the text.

30. Maeve Kelly describes her satisfaction in the book's ability to provoke such extremes of criticism as this suggests the book is touching important nerves. Interview with the author, 3 July 1992, Inishmore, Aran Islands, Ireland.

31. Clairr O'Connor, *Belonging* (Dublin: Attic Press, 1991). Page references are cited in the text.

32. Clairr O'Connor, *When You Need Them* (Galway: Salmon Publishing, 1989). O'Connor's second novel, *Love in Another Room* (Dublin: Marino Books, 1995) does not attempt the challenging metafictional devices that her first does, but has a polished skill that will probably ensure it a better critical reception.

33. Jennifer Johnston speaks of her own desire for literary immortality ('making an impression') after realizing that having children 'wasn't much of a stab at immortality'. Michael Kenneally, 'Q. and A.', *Irish Literary Supplement* 3:2 (Fall 1984): 25.

34. Gayle Greene describes this kind of narrative time, 'very common in contemporary women's fiction' as the 'structure of circular return, wherein episodes set in the past are alternated with episodes in the present ... enabling a circling back over material which allows repetition with revision'. *Changing the Story*, p. 14.

35. Marianne Hirsch, *The Mother-Daughter Plot: Narrative, Psychoanalysis, Feminism* (Bloomington: Indiana University Press, 1989), p. 129.

36. Lynn Sukenick, 'Feeling and Reason in Doris Lessing's Fiction' *Contemporary Literature* 14(4):519, quoted in Adrienne Rich, *Of Woman Born: Motherhood as Experience and Institution*, Tenth Anniversary Edition (New York: W.W. Norton, 1986), p. 235.

37. Christine St. Peter, 'Jennifer Johnston's Irish Troubles: a Feminist-Materialist Reading', *Gender in Irish Writing*, ed. Toni O'Brien Johnson and David Cairns (Buckingham: Open University Press, 1991), p. 124.

38. Weekes, *Irish Women Writers*, p. 206. She does, however, offer a valuable political reading that this relationship 'suggests the orphaned situation of women in Ireland' (210).

39. Luce Irigarary, 'And the One Doesn't Stir Without the Other', *Signs* 7:1 (Winter 1981): 67.

40. The dynamic of Deirdre's relationship to her father, as of Constance Keating's to hers, resembles that of nineteenth-century women writers discussed in Sandra M. Gilbert and Susan Gubar's *The Madwoman in the Attic* (New Haven: Yale University Press, 1979), Chapter 1. Margaret Atwood states the dynamic in more pithy terms in *The Handmaid's Tale* when she deconstructs Freud's 'penis envy' as the 'Pen is envy.' (Toronto: McClelland and Stewart, 1985), p. 174.

41. For thorough discussions of these matters, particularly the 1992 'X-case',

from feminist perspectives, see *The Abortion Papers: Ireland*, ed. Ailbhe Symth (Dublin: Attic Press, 1992).

42. Adrienne Rich, *Of Woman Born*, p. 237.
43. See note 34.
44. Maggie Humm, *Border Traffic: Strategies of Contemporary Women Writers* (Manchester: University of Manchester Press, 1991).
45. Interview with the author, Inishmore, Aran Islands, Ireland, 2 July 1992.
46. Maeve Kelly and Leland Bardwell, both novelists/poets in their 60s, describe themselves as 'always having been a writer' by which they meant that writing had been an intrinsic part of their childhoods, a 'natural' part of their lives. Leland Bardwell recalls her surprise when aspiring writers in writing workshops she offers speak of the 'decision to become' writers. Interviews with the authors, 2 July 1992; 20 November 1993.
47. For a history of this work see Maeve Kelly's 'Background and Context' in *Seeking a Refuge from Violence: the Adapt [House] Experience* (Dublin: Policy Research Centre, 1992), pp. 1–13. See also my discussion of her novel *Necessary Treasons* in Chapter 7.
48. Virginia Woolf, *A Room of One's Own* (1929. Reprint. New York: Harcourt, Brace and World, 1957). Page references are cited in the text.
49. *Cherry Ames, Student Nurse*, written by Helen Wells, was first published in 1943 (New York: Grosset and Dunlap) then later published in Britain (London: World Distributors, 1956). This enormously successful book was followed by a series of Cherry Ames nurse novels, some written by Julie Tatham.
50. These and the following quotations Maeve Kelly made in a speech delivered at the Women Writers Circle of the Fourth International Interdisciplinary Congress on Women at Hunter College, New York, 1990. I am indebted to Sylvia Bowerbank for the text of this speech and to Maeve Kelly for permission to quote from it.
51. These stories appear in her two volumes of short stories *A Life of Her Own* (Dublin: Poolbeg, 1976) and *Orange Horses* (London: Michael Joseph, 1990).

3 Women writing exile

1. Roz Cowman, *The Goose Herd* (Galway: Salmon Publishing, 1989), p. 36.
2. Mary O'Malley, *Where the Rocks Float* (Dublin: Salmon Poetry, 1993), p. 29.
3. Eavan Boland, *Outside History* (Manchester: Carcanet Press Limited, 1990), p. 41.
4. Historical accounts of women's emigration remain relatively rare, although a number of studies have appeared in recent years. For an important historiographical and sociological summary and bibliography, see Ann Rossiter, 'Bringing the Margins into the Centre: a Review of Aspects of Irish Women's Emigration from a British Perspective' in *Irish Women's Studies Reader*, ed. Ailbhe Smyth (Dublin: Attic Press, 1993), pp. 177–202. See also the following not included in the Rossiter bibliography: Grace Neville, '"She Never Then After That Forgot Him": Irishwomen and Emigration to the United States in Irish Folklore' in *Mid-America: an*

Historical Review 74:3 (October 1992); Report from Ireland's National and Social Council, *The Economic and Social Implications of Emigration*, no. 90 (Dublin: Stationary Office, 1991); Suellen Hoy, 'The Journey Out: The Recruitment and Emigration of Irish Religious Women to the United States, 1812–1914' in *Journal of Women's History* 6:4/7:1 (Winter/Spring 1995): 64–98; Suellen Hoy and Margaret MacCurtain, *From Dublin to New Orleans: the Journey of Nora and Alice* (Dublin: Attic Press, 1994). Page reference are cited in the text.

5. Maureen Murphy, 'The Fionnuala Factor: Irish Sibling Emigration at the Turn of the Century', *Gender and Sexuality in Modern Ireland*, eds Anthony Bradley and Maryann Gialanella Valiulis (Amherst: University of Massachusetts Press, 1997), pp. 85–101.

6. Hasia R. Diner, *Erin's Daughters in America* (Baltimore: Johns Hopkins University Press, 1983); Janet A. Nolan, *Ourselves Alone: Women's Emigration from Ireland, 1885–1920* (Lexington: University of Kentucky Press, 1989); Donald Akenson, *The Irish Diaspora: a Primer* (Toronto; P. D. Meaney, 1994).

7. Diner explains this assumed freedom from emotional pain – itself a questionable idea – with what appears to be a surprisingly uncritical acceptance of traditional Irish mother-blaming. In her account, mothers were responsible for the low esteem of daughters, as well as for the unusually high incidence of male schizophrenia in Ireland, a result, it seems, of suffocation by their mothers. She leaves undeveloped the problem of patriarchal/ economic exigencies, as for example the possible connections between mental illness and the sexual repression that enabled male inheritance in a colonized society. Hasia R. Diner, *Erin's Daughters in America*, pp. 19–22.

8. Mary Daly, *Women and Poverty* (Dublin: Attic Press, 1989), p. 9.

9. Mary Lennon, Marie McAdam, *Across the Water: Irish Women's Lives in Britain* (London: Virago, 1988); Ide O'Carroll, *Models for Movers: Irish Women's Emigration to America* (Dublin: Attic Press 1988); Sheelagh Conway, *The Faraway Hills Are Green: Voices of Irish Women in Canada* (Toronto: The Women's Press, 1992). Page references are cited in the text.

10. Edna O'Brien, *Mother Ireland* (London: Weidenfeld and Nicolson, 1976), pp. 11, 23, 24, 32.

11. David Seidel, *Exile and the Narrative Imagination* (New Haven: Yale University Press, 1986).

12. Ailbhe Smyth, 'Introduction', *Wildish Things: an Anthology of New Irish Women's Writing* (Dublin: Attic Press, 1986), p. 8.

13. O'Carroll, *Models for Movers,* p. 99.

14. Mary Dorcey, 'The Spaces Between the Words', *Women's Review of Books* 8: 3 (December 1990): 22.

15. Anne Enright, *The Wig My Father Wore* (London: Jonathan Cape, 1995), pp. 1, 56–7.

16. Frances Molloy, *No Mate for the Magpie* (London: Virago 1985). Page references are cited in the text.

17. Joan Lingard, *Sisters by Rite* (New York: St. Martin's Pres,s 1984). Page references are cited in the text.

18. Linda Anderson, *To Stay Alive* (London: The Bodley Head, 1985). In the United States this was published under the title *We Can't All Be Heroes, You*

Know (New York: Ticknor and Fields, 1985). Page references are cited in the text.

19. Kathleen Ferguson, *The Maid's Tale* (Dublin: Torc, 1994). Here the point of maturity is not chronological 'adulthood' but advanced middle age.
20. Mary Costello, *Titanic Town* (London: Methuen, 1992).
21. Edna O'Brien, *A Pagan Place* (London: Weidenfeld and Nicolson, 1970); *The Country Girls* (London: Hutchinson, 1960); *The Lonely Girl* (London: Jonathan Cape, 1962).
22. Leland Bardwell, *Girl on a Bicycle* (Dublin: The Irish Writers' Co-operative, 1977). Page references are cited in the text.
23. Jane Mitchell, *Different Lives* (Dublin: Poolbeg 1996).
24. Moya Roddy, *The Long Way Home* (Dublin: Attic Press, 1992).Page references are cited in the text.
25. Aisling Maguire. *Breaking Out* (Belfast: The Blackstaff Press, 1996).
26. Eithne Strong, *The Love Riddle* (Dublin: Attic Press, 1993). Page references are cited in the text.
27. Edna O'Brien, *Girls in Their Married Bliss* (London: Jonathan Cape, 1964); *The High Road* (London: Weidenfeld and Nicolson, 1988).
28. Ita Daly, *Dangerous Fictions* (London: Bloomsbury, 1989).
29. Julia O'Faolain, *The Irish Signorina* (New York: Viking Press, 1984).
30. Margaret Mulvihill, *Low Overheads* (London: Pandora, 1987).
31. Leland Bardwell, *That London Winter* (Dublin: Co-op Books, 1981). She has also written of a man's self-exile in *The House* (Dingle Co: Brandon Books, 1984).
32. Mary Rose Callaghan, *The Awkward Girl* (Dublin: Attic Press, 1984); *Emigrant Dreams* (Dublin: Poolbeg, 1996).
33. Dolores Walshe, *Moon Mad* (Dublin: Wolfhound Press, 1993).
34. Deirdre Madden, *Remembering Light and Stone* (London: Faber and Faber, 1992).
35. Kitty Manning, *The Between People* (Dublin: Attic Press, 1990).
36. Polly Devlin, *Dora* (London: Chatto and Windus Ltd, 1990).
37. Linda Anderson, *Cuckoo* (Co. Dingle: Brandon, 1988).
38. Evelyn Conlon, *My Head is Opening* (Dublin: Attic Press, 1987). Page references are cited in the text.
39. Mary Dorcey, *A Noise from the Woodshed* (London: Onlywomen Press, 1989). Page references are cited in the text.
40. Helen Lucy Burke, *A Season for Mothers* (Dublin: Poolbeg, 1980).
41. Rita Kelly, *The Whispering Arch and Other Stories* (Dublin: Arlen House, 1986).
42. Ita Daly, *The Lady with the Red Shoes* (Dublin: Poolbeg, 1980).
43. Angela Bourke, *By Salt Water* (Dublin: New Island Books, 1996).
44. Briege Duffaud, *Nothing Like Beirut* (Dublin: Poolbeg, 1994).
45. Evelyn Conlon, *Stars in the Daytime* (Dublin: Attic Press, 1987). Page references are cited in the text.
46. Leland Bardwell, *There We Have Been* (Dublin: Attic Press, 1989).
47. This term was coined by Steven G. Kellman in 'The Fiction of Self-Begetting', *Modern Language Notes* 91 (December 1976), 1245.
48. See Chapter 2 for a discussion of these novels.
49. Mary Leland, *The Killeen* (London: Hamish Hamilton, 1985).

50. Anne Devlin, *The Way-Paver* (London: Faber and Faber, 1986).
51. See Chapter 4 for a discussion of this novel.
52. Kate O'Riordan, *Involved* (London: Flamingo, 1995).
53. Fiona Barr, 'The Wall Reader,' in *The Wall Reader* (Dublin: Arlen House Ltd, 1979).
54. Jennifer Johnston, *Shadows on our Skin* (London: Hamish Hamilton, 1977); *The Railway Station Man* (London: Hamish Hamilton, 1984).
55. Jane Urquhart, *Away* (Toronto: McClelland and Stewart, 1993).
56. Moy McCrory, *Bleeding Sinners* (London: Methuen, 1988).
57. Maude Casey, *Over The Water* (London: Macmillan, 1987).
58. Fiona Farrell, *The Skinny Louie Book* (Auckland: Penguin Books, 1992).
59. Leland Bardwell, 'The Dove of Peace' in *Different Kinds of Love* (Dublin: Attic Press, 1987).
60. Emma Cooke, *Wedlocked* (Dublin: Poolbeg, 1984).
61. Harriet O'Carroll, 'The Day of the Christening' in *Territories of the Voice: Contemporary Stories by Irish Women*, ed. Louise DeSalvo, Kathleen Walsh D'Arcy, Katherine Hogan (London: Virago Press, 1990).
62. Maeve Kelly, 'Orange Horses', *Orange Horses* (London: Michael Joseph, 1990).
63. Jennifer Johnston, *The Invisible Worm* (London: Sinclair-Stevenson, 1991).
64. Frances Molloy, *Women Are the Scourge of the Earth* (Belfast: The White Row Press, 1998).
65. Eilís Ní Dhuibhne, 'Midwife to the Fairies' in *Territories of the Voice*.
66. Dorothy Nelson, *In Night's City* (Dublin: Wolfhound Press, 1982) and *Tar and Feathers* (Dublin: Wolfhound Press, 1987).
67. Lia Mills, *Another Alice* (Dublin: Poolbeg, 1996).
68. Edna O'Brien, *Down By the River* (London: Weidenfeld and Nicolson, 1996).
69. Richard Kearney, 'Migrant Minds', *Across the Frontiers*, ed. Richard Kearney (Dublin: Wolfhound Press, 1988): pp. 185–204.
70. Evelyn Conlon, 'Millions Like Us', *Graph* 5 (1988):4. Conlon is referring to another book edited by Richard Kearney, *The Irish Mind* (Dublin: Wolfhound, 1985). In an analogous example of this kind of gender-'neutral' approach, we find that in *Gender in Irish Writing* only one of the eight articles, my own on Jennifer Johnston, actually deals with the work of a woman author.
71. Stuart Hall, 'Cultural Identity and Diaspora,' in *Colonial Discourse and Post-Colonial Theory*, ed. Patrick Williams and Laura Chrisman, (London: Harvester Wheatsheaf, 1993), p. 402.
72. Clare Boylan, *Holy Pictures* (London: Hamish Hamilton, 1983); *Home Rule,* (London: Hamish Hamilton, 1992).
73. Clare Boylan, interview with the author, Dublin, 6 November 1993.
74. In 'Petrifying Time: Incest Narratives by Irish Women', in *Contemporary Irish Fictions: Themes, Tropes, Theories*, ed. Liam Harte and Michael Parker (London: Macmillan, 1999), I have discussed both Nelson's and O'Brien's novels in detail.
75. See Chapter 4 for a discussion of the work of some of these northern writers.
76. Linda Hutcheon, 'Circling the Downspout of Empire: Post-colonialism and

Postmodernism', *Ariel* 20:4, 1989, reprinted in *The Post-Colonial Studies Reader*, ed. Bill Ashcroft, Gareth Griffiths and Helen Tiffin (London: Routledge, 1995), pp. 130–5.

77. Victor Luftig (ed.), 'Frances Molloy: In Memoriam', *Irish Literary Supplement*, Fall, 1993:39. Other page references cited in the text.

78. For a discussion of these aspects of their work, see Patricia Boyle Haberstroh, *Women Creating Women: Contemporary Irish Women Poets* (Syracuse, New York: Syracuse University Press, 1996.

79. Leland Bardwell. Interview with the author, Ballinful, Co. Sligo, 22 June 1995. One can also find useful mini-biographies in Ann Owen Weekes, *Unveiling Treasures*, pp. 23–5, and in Caroline Walsh, 'Happy to be back from Killinarden', the *Irish Times* (2 November 1984): 13.

80. Leland Bardwell, interview with the author, Ballinful, Co. Sligo, 30 November 1993.

81. Bardwell, p. 160. In her story 'Nesting', Angela Bourke gives the foreign (or young Irish) reader an idea of why the call of the increasingly rare corn-crake has such resonance. *By Salt Water* (Dublin: New Island Books, 1996), pp. 131–6.

82. Bardwell reports that many people wanted her to write a sequel to this novel. While she refused to do this, she says that her novel *That London Winter* (Dublin: Co-op Books, 1981) does offer a 1959 chapter in the life of a Julie-like character. Interview, 30 November 1993.

83. Strong, p. 18. In her recent collection of selected poems, the 72–year-old poet still uses this description as her way of living and knowing: 'As for me, I am always jigsaw / ... Given head, [shapes] can rush, become a tumult / which must thresh its arbitrary course. / When it settles, I can go around – / it takes much time – fitting convex to concave, / create design. It takes much time.' Eithne Strong, 'Curves', *Spatial Nosing: New and Selected Poems* (Dublin: Salmon Poetry, 1993), p. 131.

84. See, for example, Mieke Bal, *Narratology: Introduction to the Theory of Narrative* (Toronto: University of Toronto Press, 1985), Chapters 3, 5.

85. Penn Reade is drawn on the model of Jonathan Hanaghan, teacher and analyst of Strong's husband, Rupert Strong. Interview with the author, Monkstown, Co. Dublin, 4 July 1995.

86. The reader of this novel can find fictionalized sequels of this experiment in Strong's collection of short stories, *Patterns* (Dublin: Poolbeg, 1981).

87. Interview with the author, 4 July 1995; Eithne Strong, *Flesh, the Greatest Sin*, 1980 rpt (Dublin: Attic Press, 1993).

88. 'An Interview with Eithne Strong' by Nancy Means Wright and Dennis Hannan, *Irish Literary Supplement*, Spring 1994: 13.

89. Dorcey, 'The Spaces Between the Words', *Women's Review of Books* 8:3 (December 1990): 22. Other page references are cited in the text.

90. Evelyn Coulon, 'Home – What Home', *My Head is Opening* (Dublin: Attic Press, 1987).

91. A similar situation is depicted in Emma Donoghue's story 'Going Back' , *Alternative Loves: Irish Gay and Lesbian Stories*, ed. David Marcus (Dublin: Martello Books, 1994), pp. 208–21.

92. Dorcey, 'Nights', p. 189. Dorcey describes this use of voice in her fiction as 'a person talking, addressing itself aloud to a listener. And it is this

assumption of a listener that is all-important. I think women probably have fewer inner monologues than men because we talk to each other so much more. We share our thoughts and feelings to such an extent that the characteristic voice for a woman is the speaking voice.' (Dorcey, 'Spaces,' p. 24).

93. According to Irish scholar Ide O'Carroll, Ireland does offer at least potentially, a 'good situation for lesbians' as it is a small nation where 'people know people's people' and its history of colonization makes Ireland especially able to connect with and accept other oppressed groups. (Ide O'Carroll, 'A Lesbian Vision of Ireland', Speech at the American Conference of Irish Studies/Canadian Association of Irish Studies at Queen's University Belfast (July 1995).

94. Mary Dorcey, 'Interview with Mary Dorcey', *Lesbian and Gay Visions of Ireland*. p. 43.

95. John McGahern, *Banned in Ireland*, ed. Julia Carlson (Athens: University of Georgia Press, 1990), p. 64.

4 Returning from the 'Ghost Place': recomposing history

1. Eiléan Ní Chuilleanáin, *The Brazen Serpent* (County Meath: The Gallery Press, 1994), p. 16.

2. Eavan Boland, *In a Time of Violence* (Manchester: Carcanet, 1994), p. 43.

3. Carolyn Steedman, 'Culture, Cultural Studies, and Historians', *Cultural Studies*, ed. Lawrence Grossberg, Cary Nelson and Paula A. Treichler (New York: Routledge, 1992), pp. 613–14.

4. Paula Meehan, 'Ard Fheis', *The Man Who Was Marked by Winter* (County Meath: Gallery Press, 1991), p. 21.

5. Declan Kiberd, 'The War Against the Past', *The Uses of the Past: Essays on Irish Culture*, ed. Audrey S. Eyler and Robert F. Garrett (Newark: University of Delaware Press, 1988), pp. 24, 28–9. Page references cited in the text.

6. R.F. Foster, *Modern Ireland: 1600–1972* (New York: Viking, 1988), p. ix.

7. Margaret Ward, *The Missing Sex: Putting Women into Irish History* (Dublin: Attic Press, 1991), p.3; Maria Luddy and Cliona Murphy, 'Cherchez la femme': the Elusive Woman in Irish History, *Women Surviving: Studies in Irish Women's History in the 19th and 20th Centuries* (Dublin: Poolbeg Press, 1990), p. 7.

8. Edna Longley, *From Cathleen to Anorexia: the Breakdown of Irelands* (Dublin: Attic Press, 1990), p. 4. Reprinted in *The Living Stream: Literature and Revisionism in Ireland* (Newcastle upon Tyne: Bloodaxe Books, 1994). Page references are cited in the text.

9. See, for example, Gerardine Meaney, *Sex and Nation: Women in Irish Culture and Politics* (Dublin: Attic Press, 1991). Page references are cited in the text.

10. Homi K. Bhabha, 'Introduction: Narrating the Nation', *Nation and Narration* (London: Routledge, 1990), pp. 1–3. Other page references are cited in the text.

11. Julia O'Faolain, *No Country for Young Men* (Middlesex: Penguin, 1980). Page references are cited in the text.

12. Kathleen O'Farrell, *The Fiddler of Kilbroney* (Co. Kerry: Brandon, 1994). This

novel reimagines events of the rebellion of 1798.

13. Anthony Roche, 'The Ante-Room as Drama', in *Ordinary People Dancing: Essays on Kate O'Brien,* ed. Eibhear Walshe (Cork: Cork University Press, 1993), p. 87.

14. George Lukács, *The Historical Novel* (London: Merlin Press, 1962); Avrom Fleishman, *The Historical Novel: Walter Scott to Virginia Woolf* (Baltimore: Johns Hopkins, 1971). Page references are cited in the text.

15. James M. Cahalan, *Great Hatred, Little Room: the Irish Historical Novel* (Syracuse: Syracuse University Press, 1971). Page references are cited in the text.

16. Iris Murdoch, *The Red and the Green,* (London: Viking, 1965). Eilís Dillon, *Across the Bitter Sea* (London: Hodder and Stoughton, 1973) and *Blood Relations* (London: Hodder and Stoughton, 1977).

17. Leah Watson, *Taking Back History: Irish Women's Fiction 1928–1988,* Ph. D. diss. University of Saskatchewan, 1991, p. 143. Other page references are cited in the text.

18. For a discussion of these activities, see Margaret Ward, *Unmanageable Revolutionaries: Women and Irish Nationalism* (London: Pluto Press, 1983), pp. 107–18.

19. Julia O'Faolain, *The Judas Cloth* (London: Sinclair-Stevenson Ltd, 1992); *Women in the Wall* (London: Virago, 1973).

20. Edna O'Brien, *The High Road* (London: Weidenfeld and Nicolson, 1988), p. 14. Other page references are cited in the text.

21. Jennifer Johnston, *Fool's Sanctuary* (London: Hamish Hamilton, 1987). Page references are cited in the text.

22. Jennifer Johnston, *The Old Jest* (London: Hamish Hamilton, 1979). For a consideration of these questions in her first eight novels, see my article 'Jennifer Johnston's Irish Troubles', *Gender in Irish Writing,* ed. Toni O'Brien Johnson and David Cairns (Milton Keynes: Open University Press, 1991), pp. 112–27.

23. Mary Leland, *The Killeen* (London: Hamish Hamilton, 1985). Page references are cited in the text.

24. Mary Leland, interview with the author, 24 November 1994, Blackrock, Co. Cork.

25. This description of Mary MacSwiney comes from Margaret Ward's *Unmanageable Revolutionaries,* p. 224.

26. R.F. Foster, pp. 547–50. It is worth noting here that a number of important Irish politicians in the Fine Gael party that had accepted the Treaty flirted with fascism at this time in the 'Blue Shirts' movement, as did a number of artists, including W.B. Yeats.

27. One sees this particularly clearly in her treatment of the idea of the Big House in Chapter 5 of *Approaching Priests.*

28. Sighle Bhreathnach-Lynch, 'Landscape, Space, and Gender: Their Role in the Construction of Female Identify in Newly-Independent Ireland', *Canadian Woman Studies Les cahiers des femmes* 17:3, (Summer/Autumn 1997): 28.

29. This offers an excellent barometer of different kinds of reader response; I found these pages fascinating with their focus on the lives of a nun and a 'ruined woman' while Irish reviewer John Dunne comments that he found

them to be 'as dull as anything I've read this year'. 'Canon Fodder' *Books Ireland*, 96, September 1985: 142.

30. Terence Brown, *Ireland: a Social and Cultural History 1922–1985* (London: Fontana Paperbacks, 1981), pp. 59, 63.

31. R.F. Foster reports that only 17.6% of the Irish could still speak any Irish by 1911. For a discussion of this policy of Gaelicization see Foster, pp. 518–19, and Brown, Chapter 2.

32. Catherine Ward, 'Land and Landscape in Novels by McLaverty, Kiely and Leland', *Eire-Ireland* 23:3 (Fall 1988): 77–8.

33. Aoife Feeney, 'Wallowing in Overwriting', *Irish Literary Supplement*, 4:2 (Fall 1985) :50.

34. Although important feminist and socialist women continued their struggles in the emerging state, they were effectively subordinated, even silenced, by the demands of nationalism. A growing number of texts discusses this phenomenon, among them the following: Cliona Murphy, *The Women's Suffrage Movement and Irish Society in the Early Twentieth Century* (Brighton: Harvester Wheatsheaf, 1989); Rosemary Cullen Owens, *Smashing Times: A History of the Irish Suffrage Movement* (Dublin: Attic Press, 1984); Leah Levenson and Jerry H. Natterstad, *Hanna Sheehy-Skeffington: Irish Feminist* (Syracuse: Syracuse University Press, 1986); Maria Luddy and Cliona Murphy, *Women Surviving*; Margaret Ward, '"Suffrage First – Above All Else!" An Account of the Irish Suffrage Movement', *Irish Women's Studies Reader*, ed. Ailbhe Smyth (Dublin: Attic Press, 1993); Margaret Ward, 'Nationalism, Pacifism, Internationalism: Louie Bennett, Hanna Sheehy-Skeffington, and the Problems of "Defining Feminism"', *Gender and Sexuality in Modern Ireland*, Bradley and Valiulis, pp. 60–84; *Feminist Review* (Special Irish Issue) 50 (1995); Dana Hearne, 'The Irish Citizen 1914–1916: Nationalism, Feminism, and Militarism' and Maryann Gialanella Valiulis, 'Defining Their Role in the New State: Irishwomen's Protest Against the Juries Act of 1927', *Canadian Journal of Irish Studies*, 18:1 (July 1992); Mary E. Daly, 'Women in the Irish Free State, 1929–39: the Interaction between Economics and Ideology' and Maryann Gialanella Valiulis, 'Power, Gender, and Identity in the Irish free State', *Journal of Women's History* 6:4/7:1 (Winter/Spring 1995) :99–116, 117–136.

35. Ward, *Unmanageable Revolutionaries*, pp. 237–8.

36. A woman named McKenna Napoli did accompany de Valera on his American tour. I am grateful to Jennifer Fitzgerald for this information.

37. Aisling Foster, *Safe in the Kitchen* (London: Hamish Hamilton, 1993), pp. 345–6. Other page references are cited in the text.

38. Mary Robinson, 'Women in the Law in Ireland', *Irish Women's Studies Reader*, p. 100. This is a transcription of her plenary speech delivered at the 3rd International Interdisciplinary Congress on Women in Dublin, July, 1987, then published in *Women's Studies International Forum*, 11:4 (1988): 351–4.

39. Meaney, *Sex and Nation*, p. 7.

40. Useful discussions of these mythic and historical intertextualities occur in: Ann Weekes, 'Diarmuid and Gráinne Again: Julia O'Faolain's *No Country for Young Men*', *Éire-Ireland* 21:1 (Spring, 1986) :89–102; in Leah Watson, 'No Country for Women', *Taking Back History: Irish Women's Fiction*

1928–1988, Dissertation, University of Saskatchewan, 1991; and in James M. Cahalan 'Forging a Tradition: Emily Lawless and the Irish Literary Canon', *Colby Quarterly,* 27:1 (March, 1991) :27–49. Jennifer Fitzgerald reminds me of others, namely the use of 'Owen' and 'Owen Roe [O'Neill]' and 'O'Malley' to evoke great Irish political family dynasties of the seventeenth century.

41. This is a reference to the secret Noraid Fund provided by sympathetic Irish-Americans willing to buy arms for the nationalists. I am indebted to Jo Murphy-Lawless for this identification.
42. O'Faolain, p. 155. This description of women as receptacles of men's excretions recalls Germaine Greer's famous dictum in *The Female Eunuch* (London: Paladin, 1971), p. 254.
43. Briege Duffaud, *A Wreath Upon the Dead* (Dublin: Poolbeg, 1993). Page references are cited in the text.
44. Colm Tóibín, *Bad Blood: a Walk Along the Irish Border* (1987. Reprint London: Vintage, 1994), pp. 183–4.
45. Philippa Gregory, 'Historical Present', *Sunday Times,* 3 October 1993: 6, 12.
46. Interview with the author, 19 July 1994, Laballe, France.
47. Duffaud, p. 359. The author, who moved away from Northern Ireland in 1962, returned home to participate in the Civil Rights marches. Interview with the author.
48. Interview with the author.

5 'The war that has gone into us': troubles from the North

1. Medbh McGuckian, 'The War Ending', in *Marconi's Cottage* (Loughcrew, Co. Meath: the Gallery Press, 1991), p. 82.
2. Ruth Carr, formerly Ruth Hooley, 'Parity', *Women and Irish Politics,* Special Issue of *The Canadian Journal of Irish Studies,* ed. Christine St. Peter and Ron Marken, 18: 1 (July 1992): 111. Also *There is a House* (County Donegal: Summer Palace Press, 1999).
3. Ann Zell, 'Nature Programme', in *Word of Mouth,* ed. R. Carr, G. Tobin, S. Wheeler and A. Zell (Belfast: The Blackstaff Press, 1996), p. 45.
4. Eilish Rooney, 'Political Division, Practical Alliance: Problems for Women in Conflict', *Journal of Women's History,* 6: 4/7: 1 (Winter/Spring 1995): 42. Other page references are cited in the text.
5. Elizabeth Shannon, *I am of Ireland: Women of the North Speak Out* (Boston: Little Brown and Company, 1989), p. 5. Other page references are cited in the text.
6. David Lloyd, 'Nationalisms Against the State: Towards a Critique of the Anti-Nationalist Prejudice', in *Gender and Colonialism,* ed. Timothy P. Foley, Lionel Pilkington, Sean Ryder and Elizabeth Tilley (Galway: Galway University Press, 1995), p. 265. Page references are cited in the text.
7. This term quoted from Cathy Harkin by Monica McWilliams in her article 'Struggling for Peace and Justice: Reflections on Women's Activism in Northern Ireland', *Journal of Women's History* 6:4/7: 34.
8. Two remarkable exceptions to this rule occurred recently: one in the creation of the Northern Ireland Women's Coalition in 1996 whereby

women gained access to the table of the 'Peace Process' that resulted in the 'Good Friday Agreement' of 1998; the other in the support for funding to women's centres across sectarian lines in Belfast. For discussions of these initiatives, see: Nell McCafferty, 'A Women's Party Outwits the System in Northern Ireland', 1996 (rpt: *Canadian Woman Studies/Les cahiers des femmes* 17: 3 (Summer/Fall 1997): 64–7; and Begoña Aretxaga, *Shattering Silence: Women, Nationalism, and Political Subjectivity in Northern Ireland* (Princeton, NJ: Princeton UP, 1997.) Page references are cited in the text.

9. There are, however, publications to mark various initiatives women have taken as, for example, in the newspaper *Women's News*, or a report of a conference of republican nationalist women involved in the campaign for 'national self-determination', held in West Belfast, 12 March 1994. A record of that conference appears in *Women's Agenda for Peace: Conference Report* (Derry: A Clár na mBan Publication, 1994). I am grateful to Marie Quiery for this report.

10. For an example of this concept in action, see Eileen Evason's study of the contemporary women's movement in Northern Ireland, *Against the Grain* (Dublin: Attic Press, 1991).

11. Edna Longley, *Women, Criticism and Ireland, Special Issue of Krino: the Review*, ed. Eve Patten, 15 (Spring 1994): 7.

12. For discussions of women's theatre in the North see Maria R. DiCenzo, 'Charabanc Theatre Company: Placing Women Center-Stage in Northern Ireland', *Theatre Journal* 45 (1993): 175–84, Carol Martin, 'Charabanc Theatre Company: "Quare" Women "Sleggin" and "Geggin" the Standards of Northern Ireland by "Tappin" the People', *The Drama Review* 31:2 (Summer 1987): 88–99. Among the few dramatic texts published are Christina Reid's *The Belle of Belfast City* (London: Methuen Drama, 1989), and Anne Devlin's *After Easter* (London: Faber and Faber, 1994).

13. *The Female Line: Northern Irish Women Writers*, ed. Ruth Hooley [now Ruth Carr] (Belfast: Northern Ireland Women's Rights Movement, 1985); *Wildish Things*, ed. Ailbhe Smyth (Dublin: Attic Press, 1989); *Writing Women* 11 n.d.: 3/12: 1, ed. Linda Anderson, Andrea Badenoch, Cynthia Fuller, Debbie Taylor, with *Irish Supplement*, ed. Ailbhe Smyth, pp. 61–110; *Pillars of the House: an Anthology of Verse by Irish Women from 1690 to the Present*, ed. A.A. Kelly (Dublin: Wolfhound, 1988).

14. Patricia Boyle Haberstroh gathers together the evidence of how 'women are severely underrepresented in contemporary [Irish poetry] anthologies' in her 'Introduction' to *Women Creating Women: Contemporary Irish Women Poets* (Syracuse: Syracuse University Press, 1996), pp. 2–17.

15. Nell McCafferty *Peggy Deery: a Derry Family at War* (Dublin: Attic Press, 1988); Rosemary Sales, *Women Divided: Gender, Religion and Politics in Northern Ireland* (London: Routledge, 1997); Eileen Fairweather, Roisín McDonough, and Melanie McFadyean, *Only the Rivers Run Free: Northern Ireland: The Women's War* (London: Pluto Press, 1984); Mary Ferris, Anna McGonigle, Patricia McKeown, Theresa Moriarty, Marie Mulholland, *Women's Voices: an Oral History of Northern Women's Health (1900–1990)*. The reference to a northern story of prostitution occurs in Fairweather, pp. 5–15. For an important memoir of a prostitute's life in the Republic, see June Levine and Lyn Madden, *Lyn: a Story of Prostitution* (Dublin: Attic

Press, 1987).

16. Polly Devlin, *All of Us There* (Belfast: Blackstaff, 1983), p. 12. Other page references are cited in the text.

17. Bernadette Devlin, *The Price of My Soul* (New York: Alfred A. Knopf, 1969), p. vii.

18. Mary Costello, *Titanic Town* (London: Methuen, 1992), p. I. Other page references are cited in the text.

19. Caroline Blackwood, *Great Granny Webster* (Boston: G.K. Hall and Co., 1979); Polly Devlin, *Dora or The Shifts of the Heart* (London: Chatto and Windus Ltd, 1990); Kitty Manning, *The Between People* (Dublin: Attic Press, 1990); Kathleen Ferguson, *The Maid's Tale* (Dublin: Torc, 1994); Deirdre Madden, *The Birds of the Innocent Wood* (London: Faber and Faber, 1988); *Remembering Light and Stone* (London: Faber and Faber, 1992); *Nothing is Black* (London: Faber and Faber, 1994); Kathleen Coyle, *A Flock of Birds* (rpt. 1930: Dublin: Wolfhound Press, 1995); Anne Crone, *Bridie Steen* (London: William Heinemann Ltd, 1949).

20. Ann Owen Weekes, *Unveiling Treasures*, p. 16.

21. Brian McIlroy, 'When the Ulster Protestant and Unionist Looks: Spectatorship in (Northern) Irish Cinema', *Irish University Review* 26: 1 (Spring/Summer 1996): 154.

22. 'Ireland: Island of Diversity', Joint Meeting in Belfast of the American Conference of Irish Studies, the Canadian Association of Irish Studies, and the Queen's University Centre for Irish Studies, 26 June–1 July 1995.

23. Victor Luftig, 'Frances Molloy: In Memoriam', *Irish Literary Supplement,* p. 39. See Chapter 3 for a discussion of this article and of Molloy's *No Mate for the Magpie.*

24. Una Woods, 'The Dark Hole Days', in *The Dark Hole Days* (Belfast: Blackstaff Press, 1984), p. 3. Other page references are cited in the text.

25. The term 'loyalist' refers to the most radically unionist of the Protestants, including groups that use paramilitary violence in their struggle to remain within the United Kingdom.

26. Joan Lingard, *Sisters by Rite* (New York: St. Martin's Press, 1984); Linda Anderson, *To Stay Alive* (London: Bodley Head, 1984); Mary Beckett, *Give Them Stones* (New York: William Morrow, 1987); Deirdre Madden, *Hidden Symptoms* (New York: the Atlantic Monthly Press, 1986); Deirdre Madden, *One by One in the Darkness* (London: Faber and Faber, 1996). Page references are cited in the text.

27. Paul Bew and Gordon Gillespie, *Northern Ireland: a Chronology of the Troubles 1968–1993* (Dublin: Gill and Macmillan, 1993), p. 12.

28. Mary A. Larkin, *The Wasted Years* (London: Judy Piatkus, 1992), reprinted three times by Warner Books.

29. Margaret Ward and Marie-Thérèse McGivern, 'Images of Women in Northern Ireland', in *The Crane Bag* 4: 1 (1980): 66.

30. Jennifer Johnston, *Shadows on Our Skin* (London: Hamish Hamilton, 1977), p. 136. Other page references are cited in the text.

31. The most sympathetic treatment of an IRA character in women's fiction appears at the greatest distance from their primary action – in the novel of an Irish emigrant to London. In her novel, *House of Splendid Isolation,* Edna O'Brien's IRA Provo is superbly disciplined and effective, a man who even

cleans the house he commandeers. Edna O'Brien, *House of Splendid Isolation* (London: Weidenfeld and Nicolson, 1994).

32. The Ulster Defence Regiment (UDR) is a regular regiment of the British Army recruited in Northern Ireland and entirely Protestant, thus considered another enemy force by nationalists. Niki Hill, *Death Grows on You* (London: Michael Joseph, 1990). See Chapter 6 for a brief discussion of this novel.

33. Brenda Murphy, 'A Social Call' in *The Hurt World: Short Stories of the Troubles*, ed. Michael Parker (Belfast: the Blackstaff Press, 1995), pp. 270–3. Murphy's critical 'take' on this man's violence needs to be seen in the context of her own history as an IRA prisoner in the Armagh prison's 'dirty protest' in the 1980s. My thanks to Michael Parker for helping make this connection. See also Begoña Aretaxaga's *Shattering Silence*, pp. 139–41.

34. Fiona Barr, 'The Wall Reader', in *The Wall Reader* (Dublin: Arlen House, 1979).

35. Stella Mahon, 'On the Front Line', *Sisters* (Belfast: The Blackstaff Press, 1980), pp. 81, 84.

36. Mary Beckett, 'The Master and the Bombs', in *A Belfast Woman* (Dublin: Poolbeg, 1980), pp. *77*, 75.

37. Anne Devlin, 'Naming the Names', in *The Way-Paver* (London: Faber and Faber, 1986), p. 118. Other page references are cited in the text.

38. Kate O'Riordan, *Involved* (London: HarperCollins Publishers, 1995).

39. Joan Lingard also began publishing in 1970 a series for young adults on the 'Troubles' in Belfast. This series, centred on the cross-sectarian friendship, then love, and marriage of Protestant Sadie and Catholic Kevin, has been adopted into school curricula around the English-speaking world, particularly the first of the series, *The Twelfth Day of July* (New York: Thomas Nelson Inc, 1970). Interview with the author, Edinburgh, Scotland, 17 July 1993.

40. Eve Patten, 'Women and Fiction', *Krino*, 8/9 (1990): 2.

41. Interview with the author, Templeogue, Co. Dublin, 1 July 1992.

6 Travelling back home: the blockbusters of Patricia Scanlan and Maeve Binchy

1. Rita Ann Higgins, *Philomena's Revenge* (Galway: Salmon Publishing, 1992), p. 87.

2. Tania Modleski, *Loving with a Vengeance: Mass-Produced Fantasies for Women* (Hamden, Conn.: Archon Books, 1982), p. 11.

3. Lillian S. Robinson, 'On Reading Trash', in *Sex, Class and Culture* (Bloomington: Indiana University Press, 1978); Janice Radway, 'Women Read the Romance: The Interaction of Text and Context', *FS/Feminist Studies* 9:1 (Spring, 1983) and *Reading the Romance: Women, Patriarchy and Popular Literature* (Chapel Hill: University of North Carolina Press, 1984); Annette Kuhn, *Women's Pictures: Feminism and Cinema* (London: Routledge and Kegan Paul, 1982); Christine Geraghty, *Women and Soap Opera: a Study of Prime Time Soaps* (Cambridge: Polity Press, 1991); Mairead Owen, 'Reinventing Romance: Reading Popular Romantic Fiction',

Women's Studies International Forum 20:4 (Fall 1997); Angela Miles, 'Confessions of a Harlequin Reader: Romance and the Myth of Male Mothers' *The Hysterical Male: New Feminist Theory*, ed. Arthur and Marilouise Kroker (Montreal: New World Perspectives, 1991.)

4. This term was created by Hans Magnus Enzensberger, *The Consciousness Industry: On Literature, Politics and the Media* (New York: Seabury, 1974.)

5. Nicci Gerard, *Into the Mainstream: How Feminism Has Changed Women's Writing* (London: Pandora, 1989), p. 131.

6. Rose Doyle, *Kimbay* (Dublin: Town House in association with Macmillan, London: 1994); Elizabeth O'Hara *Singles* (Dublin: Basement Press, 1994); Margaret Dolan, *Nessa* (Dublin: Poolbeg, 1994); Bríd Mahon, *Dervogilla* (Dublin: Poolbeg, 1994); Anne Chambers, *The Geraldine Conspiracy* (Dublin: Marino Books, 1995); Mary Ryan, *Whispers in the Wind* (Dublin: Attic Press, 1990.)

7. Mary Larkin, *The Wasted Years* (London: Warner Books, 1993); Nikki Hill *Death Grows on You* (London: Michael Joseph, 1990).

8. Maeve Binchy, *Light a Penny Candle* (London: Century, 1982). Page references are cited in the text.

9. G.D. Ingoldby, 'Wiping a Waxed Floor with Men', *Fortnight* (Belfast) 191 (February 1983), 20.

10. Maeve Binchy, Interview with the author, Vancouver, 4 October 1992.

11. Judith Williamson, 'Woman as an Island: Femininity and Colonization', *Studies in Entertainment: Critical Approaches to Mass Culture*, ed. Tania Modleski (Bloomington: Indiana University Press, 1986), p. 100.

12. Patricia Scanlan, *Apartment 3B* (Dublin: Poolbeg, 1991). Page references are cited in the text.

13. Ailbhe Smyth suggests that Scanlan's semi-ironic dedication has the effect of requiring that the audience read the book as 'literature'. Personal correspondence with the author.

14. Patricia Scanlan, *Finishing Touches* (Dublin: Poolbeg, 1992), p. 560. Other page references are cited in the text.

15. Jo O'Donoghue, Letter to the author, 16 November 1992.

16. Patricia Scanlan, *City Girl* (Dublin: Poolbeg, 1990), pp. 2–3. Other page references are cited in the text.

17. Modleski, *Loving with a Vengeance*, p. 16.

18. For a discussion of the heterosexual romance as 'women's destiny' see Rachel Blau de Plessis, *Writing Beyond the Ending* (Bloomington: Indiana University Press, 1985), p. 15.

19. Gráinne O'Flynn, 'Our Age of Innocence', in *Girls Don't Do Honours*, ed. Mary Cullen (Dublin: Women's Education Bureau, 1987), p. 87.

20. Geraldine Moane, 'Lesbian Politics and Community', *Women and Irish Society: a Sociological Reader*, ed. Anne Byrne and Madeleine Leonard (Belfast: Beyond the Pale Publications, 1997), p. 431.

21. Mark Finch, 'Sex and Address in *Dynasty*', *Screen*, 27:6 (Nov/Dec. 1986): 33.

22. Erving Goffman, *Stigma: Notes on the Management of Spoiled Identity* (Englewood Cliffs, NJ: Prentice-Hall Inc, 1963), pp. 120–1.

23. Geraghty, *Women and Soap Opera*, p. 158.

24. The main character of *Apartment 3B* chooses to become pregnant out of wedlock but her lover is the acknowledged father and the heroine is

already moving to Majorca.

25. Richard Dyer, 'Entertainment and Utopia', *Movie*, 24 (Spring 1977), republished in *Genre: the Musical: a Reader*, ed. Rick Altman (London: Routledge and Kegan Paul, 1981), p. 184. Other page references are cited in the text.

26. Patricia Scanlan, *Foreign Affairs* (Dublin: Poolbeg, 1994). She has published two subsequent novels, *Promises,* (Dublin: Poolbeg, 1996); *Mirror, Mirror* (Dublin: Poolbeg, 1997).

27. Maeve Binchy, *Victoria Line/Central Line* (London: Coronet, 1987); *Silver Wedding* (London: Century, 1988); *Evening Class* (Boston: Little Brown, 1996); *Tara Road* (London: Orion Books Ltd, 1998).

28. Interview with the author, Vancouver, 4 October 1992.

29. For a discussion of the gender implications of the terms mass and middlebrow culture, see Janice Radway, 'Mail-Order Culture and its Critics: the Book-of-the-Month Club, Commodification and Consumption, and the Problem of Cultural Authority' in *Cultural Studies*, ed. Lawrence Grossberg, Cary Nelson and Paula Treichler (London: Routledge, 1992), pp. 512–26.

30. Interview, 4 October 1992.

31. Francine Cunningham, 'Maeve in full flow in Dalkey', *Irish Times*, Thursday, 4 October 1990: 8.

32. Ursula Barry, 'Women In Ireland', *Women's Studies International Forum*, 11: 4 (1987): 317–19. For a useful discussion of globalization issue as it affects Irish women, see Ethel Crowley, 'Making a Difference? Female Employment and Multinationals in the Republic of Ireland', *Women and Irish Society*, ed. Anne Byrne and Madeleine Leonard (Belfast: Beyond the Pale Publications, 1997), pp. 81–96.

33. Maeve Binchy, *Circle of Friends* (London: Century Hutchinson, Ltd, 1991) *Echoes* (London: Century Publishing Ltd, 1985), and *The Glass Lake* (London: Orion Books Ltd, 1994).

34. Damian Hannan and Richard Breen, 'School and Gender', *Girls Don't Do Honours*, p. 100.

35. Maeve Beech, *The Copper Beech* (London: Orion Books Ltd, 1991).

36. Maeve Binchy, *There's Something About a Convent School Girl*, ed. Jackie Bennett and Rosemary Forgan (London: Virago, 1991), p. 27.

37. Raymond Williams quoted in 'Cultural Studies: an Introduction', in *Cultural Studies*, p. 5. Alice Taylor's characteristic style can be seen in *The Village* (Dingle: Co. Kerry: Brandon, 1992).

38. See Mary Louise Pratt, 'Linguistic Utopias', in *The Linguistics of Writing: Arguments between Language and Literature*, ed. Nigel Fabb, Derek Attridge, Alan Durant and Colin MacCabe (Methuen: London, 1987), pp. 48–66; and Biddy Martin and Chandra Talpade Mohanty, 'Feminist Politics: What's Home Got to Do With It?', *Feminist Studies/Critical Studies*, ed. Teresa de Lauretis (Bloomington: Indiana University Press, 1986), pp. 191–212.

39. These include those already referred to as well as *Firefly Summer* (London: Century Hutchinson Ltd, 1987), *The Lilac Bus* (1984: London: Arrow Books, 1990), and *The Glass Lake* (London: Orion Books Ltd, 1994.)

40. I borrow this computer terminology as the closest approximation to the stylistic structure of Binchy's and Scanlan's novels and as a suggestion that literary criticism needs to consider the possible effects of computer compo-

sition on the contemporary novel.
41. Quoted in Geraghty, p. 46.
42. Emer Smyth, 'Labour Market Structures and Women's Employment in the Republic of Ireland', *Women and Irish Society*, p. 64.
43. For a discussion of this anti-abortion amendment crusade and William Binchy's role in it see Emily O'Reilly, *Masterminds of the Right* (Dublin: Attic, 1992.)
44. Every one of Maeve Binchy's books opens with an intense dedication to her writer husband, Gordon Snell.

7 Feminist fiction

1. Maeve Kelly, *Resolution* (Belfast: Blackstaff Press, 1986), p. 49.
2. Rita Ann Higgins, *Goddess and Witch* (Galway: Salmon Press, 1988), p. 79.
3. Nicci Gerrard, *Into the Mainstream*, p. 107.
4. Rita Felski, *Beyond Feminist Aesthetics: Feminist Literature and Social Change* (Cambridge: Harvard University Press, 1989), pp. 49–50.
5. Mary Dorcey in interview with Nuala Archer, 'The Spaces Between the Words', *Women's Review of Books*, 8: 3 (Dec., 1990): 21.
6. Maeve Kelly, *Necessary Treasons* (London: Michael Joseph Ltd, 1985). Page references are cited in the text.
7. Iris Murdoch, *The Red and the Green* (1965. London: Penguin, 1967).
8. Cited by Rosalind Coward, 'The True Story of How I Became My Own Person', in *The Feminist Reader: Essays in Gender and the Politics of Literary Criticism*, ed. Catherine Belsey and Jane Moore (London: Macmillan, 1989), p. 35.
9. Rosalind Coward, 'The True Story' and 'This Novel Changes Women's Lives: Are Women's Novels Feminist Novels?' *Feminist Review* 5 (1980). In this earlier article Coward had used the term 'women-centred writing' very loosely, including all novels about women as long as women's experiences were central to the work.
10. I do not discuss in this chapter three important authors whose work is clearly, sometimes self-consciously, marked by feminist thought: Leland Bardwell, Clare Boylan and Julia O'Faolain.
11. This term is used by a character from a Mary Dorcey short story, 'A Sense of Humour', *A Noise from the Woodshed* (London: Onlywomen Press, 1989), p. 43.
12. Linda Anderson, *Cuckoo* (Cooleen, Co. Dingle: Brandon, 1986).
13. Linda Anderson, 'A Lack of Alternatives', in *HU/the Honest Ulsterman* 91 (1991): 92–3.
14. Linda Anderson, *To Stay Alive* (London: The Bodley Head, 1985 and New York: Ticknor and Fields, 1985). American title *We Can't All Be Heroes, You Know.*
15. I am indebted in this definition to Gayle Greene's excellent discussion in *Changing the Story: Feminist Fiction and the Tradition* (Bloomington: Indiana University Press, 1991) as well as to Rita Felski's book (n. 4 above), Rosalind Coward's articles (n. 9 above) and to the helpful comments of Ailbhe Smyth and Christina Strobel in personal correspondence.

16. Meaney, *Sex and Nation*, p. 7.
17. Longley, *From Cathleen to Anorexia*, p. 3.
18. Ailbhe Smyth, 'Introduction', to *Wildish Things*, pp. 8, 12.
19. Janet Madden-Simpson, 'Introduction', to *Woman's Part: an Anthology of Short Fiction By and About Irish Women 1890–1960* (Dublin: Arlen House, 1984), p. 11.
20. Emma Cooke, *A Single Sensation* (Dublin: Poolbeg, 1981), p. 17.
21. Emma Cooke, *Eve's Apple* (Belfast: Blackstaff Press, 1985), p. 6. Other page references are cited in the text.
22. Emma Cooke, Interview with the author, Lillaloe, Co. Clare, 25 July 1991.
23. For an extended discussion of Maeve Binchy's fiction, see Chapter 6.
24. In what is considered a very cautious estimate, depending on the willingness of the woman or the ability of the state to recognize nationality, the *Second Commission on the Status of Women* states that in '1991, 4,152 women from the Republic of Ireland had abortions in England, up from 4,063 in 1990' (p. 335). A similar need to travel to England for abortion prevails in the Protestant North where abortion is not usually available either. See Eileen Evason, *Against the Grain: the Contemporary Women's Movement in Northern Ireland* (Dublin: Attic Press, 1991), p. 53.
25. Maeve Binchy, 'Shepherd's Bush', *Victoria Line/Central Line*, p. 187.
26. Eilís Ní Dhuibhne, *The Inland Ice and other stories* (Belfast: The Blackstaff Press, 1997); *The Bray House* (Dublin: Attic Press, 1990).
27. Eilís Ní Dhuibhne, *Eating Women is Not Recommended* (Dublin: Attic Press, 1991), pp. 133, 140. Other page references are cited in the text.
28. Moya Roddy, *The Long Way Home* (Dublin: Attic Press, 1992), p. 35.
29. bell hooks, 'Feminism: a transformational politic', *Talking Back: Thinking Feminist, Thinking Black* (Toronto: Between the Lines, 1988), p. 21.
30. Maggie Humm, *Border Traffic: Strategies of Contemporary Women Writers* (Manchester: Manchester University Press, 1991), pp. 60–1.
31. Mary Rose Callaghan, *The Awkward Girl* (Dublin: Attic Press, 1990). Page references are cited in the text. For an illuminating discussion of the castrated woman in literature, see the discussion of Margaret Atwood's *Lady Oracle* by Molly Hite, *The Other Side of the Story*, p. 147.
32. Mary Dorcey, 'A Country Dance', in *A Noise from the Woodshed*, pp. 54–5. Other page references are cited in the text.
33. Janet Shepperson, untitled review, *Krino* 15 (Spring, 1994): 103.
34. I am indebted to Maggie Humm for the term 'visionary terrain', which she uses to describe feminist literature. *Border Traffic*, p. 26.
35. Katy Hayes, *Forecourt* (Dublin: Poolbeg, 1995).
36. Evelyn Conley, *My Head is Opening* (Dublin: Attic Press, 1987).
37. Mary Dorcey, 'A Sense of Humour', *A Noise from the Woodshed*, pp. 23–43.
38. Mary O'Donnell, *The Light-Makers* (Dublin: Poolbeg, 1992).
39. Evelyn Conlon, *Stars in the Daytime* (Dublin: Attic Press, 1989). Page references are cited in the text.
40. Patricia Ferreira, 'Ten Years of Attic Press', *Irish Literary Supplement* 12: 1 (Spring, 1993): 14. Attic has been absorbed by Cork University Press.
41. Some of the attacks on the contemporary women's movement come, appropriately enough, from within. One example is Carol Coulter's analysis of Irish feminism whose development she traces not to Ireland's

participation in an international liberation movement, but to an indigenous tradition within the centuries old Irish nationalist struggle. While her own ideological focus on nationalist politics creates too narrow a focus for so complex and diffuse a phenomenon as feminism, she does usefully chronicle the ways some women have been organizing politically in Ireland long before second wave feminism. *The Hidden Tradition: Feminism, Women and Nationalism in Ireland* (Co. Cork: Cork University Press, 1993).

42. Anne Haverty, 'In Novel-land', *Times Literary Supplement* (19 July 1985): 800.
43. Gayle Greene, *Changing the Story*, p. 196.
44. One finds the same story of the Limerick refuge, albeit in the discourse of the public report, in a document written by Maureen Lyons, Helen Ruddle, Joyce O'Connor and Maeve (O'Brien) Kelly: *Seeking a Refuge from Violence: the Adapt Experience* (Dublin: Policy Research Centre, 1992).
45. Mary Dorcey, 'The Spaces Between the Words', p. 22.
46. Angela Bourke, 'Language, Stories, Healing', in *Gender and Sexuality in Modern Ireland*, pp. 305–6.

Bibliography

Primary literary texts

Anderson, Linda. *To Stay Alive*. London: Bodley Head, 1985. (US title: *We Can't All Be Heroes, You Know*. New York: Ticknor and Fields).

Anderson, Linda. *Cuckoo*. Cooleen, Co. Dingle: Brandon, 1988.

Bardwell, Leland. *The Mad Cyclist*. Dublin: New Writers Press, 1970.

Bardwell, Leland. *Girl on a Bicycle*. Dublin: The Irish Writers' Co-operative, 1977.

Bardwell, Leland. *That London Winter*. Dublin: Co-op Books, 1981

Bardwell, Leland. *The House*. Cooleen, Co. Dingle: Brandon, 1984.

Bardwell, Leland. *Different Kinds of Love*. Dublin: Attic Press, 1987.

Bardwell, Leland. *There We Have Been*. Dublin: Attic Press, 1989.

Bardwell, Leland. *Dostoevsky's Grave: New and Selected Poems*. Dublin: The Dedalus Press, 1991.

Barr, Fiona. *The Wall Reader*. Dublin: Arlen House, 1979.

Barr, Fiona, Barbara Haycock Walsh and Stella Mahon, *Sisters*. Belfast: the Blackstaff Press, 1980.

Beckett, Mary. *A Belfast Woman*. Dublin: Poolbeg, 1980.

Beckett, Mary. *Give Them Stones*. New York: William Morrow, 1987.

Beckett, Mary. *A Literary Woman*. London: Bloomsbury, 1990.

Binchy, Maeve. *Light a Penny Candle*. London: Century, 1982.

Binchy, Maeve. *Echoes*. London: Century, 1985.

Binchy, Maeve. *Firefly Summer*. London: Century Hutchinson, 1987.

Binchy, Maeve. *Victoria Line/Central Line*. London: Coronet, 1987.

Binchy, Maeve. *Silver Wedding*. London: Century, 1988.

Binchy, Maeve. *Tara Road*. London: Orion Books Ltd, 1991.

Binchy, Maeve. *The Lilac Bus*. 1984. Reprinted London: Arrow Books, 1990.

Binchy, Maeve. *Circle of Friends*. London: Century Hutchinson, 1991.

Binchy, Maeve. *The Copper Beech*. London: Orion Books Ltd, 1991.

Binchy, Maeve. *The Glass Lake*. London: Orion Books Ltd, 1994.

Binchy, Maeve. *Evening Class*. Boston: Little Brown, 1996.

Blackwood, Caroline. *Great Granny Webster*. Boston: G.K. Hall, 1979.

Boland, Eavan. *In a Time of Violence*. Manchester: Carcanet, 1994.

Bourke, Angela. *By Salt Water*. Dublin: New Island Books, 1996.

Boylan, Clare. *Holy Pictures*. London: Hamish Hamilton, 1983.

Boylan, Clare. *Black Baby*. New York: Doubleday, 1989.

Boylan, Clare. *Home Rule*. London: Hamish Hamilton, 1992.

Burke, Helen Lucy. *A Season for Mothers*. Dublin: Poolbeg, 1980.

Callaghan, Mary Rose. *The Awkward Girl*. Dublin: Attic Press, 1990.

Callaghan, Mary Rose. *Emigrant Dreams*. Dublin: Poolbeg, 1996.

Carr, Ruth. *There is a House*. County Donegal: Summer Palace Press, 1999.

Carr, Ruth and Gráinne Tobin, Sally Wheeler and Ann Zell eds. *Word of Mouth: Poems*. Belfast: the Blackstaff Press, 1996.

Craig, Patricia. *Rattle of the North: an Anthology of Ulster Prose*. Belfast: the Blackstaff Press, 1992.

Casey, Daniel J. and Linda M. Casey, eds. *Stories by Contemporary Irish Women*. Syracuse: Syracuse UP, 1990.

Casey, Juanita. *Horse of Selene*. Portlaoise, Ireland: Dolmen, 1971.

Casey, Maude. *Over The Water*. London: Macmillan, 1987.

Chambers, Anne. *The Geraldine Conspiracy*. Dublin: Marino Books, 1995.

Conlon, Evelyn. *My Head is Opening*. Dublin: Attic Press, 1987.

Conlon, Evelyn. *Stars in the Daytime*. Dublin: Attic Press, 1987.

Cooke, Emma. *A Single Sensation*. Dublin: Poolbeg, 1981.

Cooke, Emma. *Wedlocked*. Dublin: Poolbeg, 1994.

Cooke, Emma. *Eve's Apple*. Belfast: the Blackstaff Press, 1985.

Costello, Mary. *Titanic Town*. London: Methuen, 1992.

Cowman, Roz. *The Goose Herd*. Galway: Salmon, 1989.

Coyle, Kathleen. *A Flock of Birds*. 1930. Reprinted Dublin: Wolfhound, 1995.

Crone, Anne. *Bridie Steen*. London: William Heinemann, 1949.

Daly, Ita. *The Lady with the Red Shoes*. Dublin: Poolbeg, 1980.

Daly, Ita. *Dangerous Fictions*. London: Bloomsbury, 1989.

Daly, Ita. *Unholy Ghosts*. London: Bloomsbury, 1996.

DeSalvo, Louise, Kathleen Walsh, and Katherine Hogan, ed. *Territories of the Voice: Contemporary Stories by Irish Women*. London: Virago, 1990.

Devlin, Anne. *The Way-Paver*. London: Faber and Faber, 1986.

Devlin, Anne. *After Easter*. London: Faber and Faber, 1994.

Devlin, Polly. *Dora or The Shifts of the Heart*. London: Chatto and Windus, 1990.

Dillon, Eilís *Across the Bitter Sea*. London: Hodder and Stoughton, 1973.

Dillon, Eilís. *Blood Relations*. London: Hodder and Stoughton, 1977.

Dolan, Margaret. *Nessa*. Dublin: Poolbeg, 1994.

Donoghue, Emma. 'Going Back.' in *Alternative Loves: Irish Gay and Lesbian Stories,* ed. David Marcus. Dublin: Martello Books, 1994, pp. 208–221.

Donoghue, Emma. *Stir Fry*. London: Hamish Hamilton, 1994.

Donoghue, Emma. *Hood*. London: Hamish Hamilton, 1995.

Donovan, Katie, A. Norman Jeffares and Brendan Kennelly, ed. *Ireland's Women: Writings Past and Present*. Dublin: Gill and Macmillan, 1994.

Dorcey, Mary. *A Noise from the Woodshed*. London: Onlywomen, 1989.

Dorcey, Mary. *Moving into the Space Cleared by Our Mothers*. Galway: Salmon Publishing, 1991.

Dorcey, Mary. *The River That Carries Me*. Galway: Salmon Publishing, 1995.

Dorcey, Mary. *Biography of Desire*. Dublin: Poolbeg, 1997.

Doyle, Rose. *Kimbay*. Dublin: Town House, in association with Macmillan, London: 1994.

Duffaud, Briege. *A Wreath Upon the Dead*. Dublin: Poolbeg, 1993.

Duffaud, Briege. *Nothing Like Beirut*. Dublin: Poolbeg, 1994.

Enright, Anne. *The Wig My Father Wore*. London: Jonathan Cape, 1995.

Farrell, Fiona. *The Skinny Louie Book*. Auckland: Penguin, 1992.

Ferguson, Kathleen. *The Maid's Tale*. Dublin: Torc, 1994.

Foster, Aisling. *Safe in the Kitchen*. London: Hamish Hamilton, 1993.

Higgins, Rita Ann. *Goddess and Witch*. Galway: Salmon, 1988.

Higgins, Rita Ann. *Philomena's Revenge*. Galway: Salmon, 1992.

Hill, Niki. *Death Grows on You*. London: Michael Joseph, 1990.

Hooley, Ruth, ed. *The Female Line: Northern Irish Women Writers*. Belfast: Northern Ireland Women's Rights Movement, 1985.

Hayes, Katy. *Forecourt*. Dublin: Poolbeg, 1995.

Johnston, Denis. 'The Old Lady Says "No!"' ed. Christine St. Peter. Washington, DC: CUA; Gerrards Cross, Bucks: Colin Smythe, 1992.

Johnston, Jennifer. *Shadows on Our Skin*. London: Hamish Hamilton, 1977.

Johnston, Jennifer. *The Old Jest*. London: Hamish Hamilton, 1979.

Johnston, Jennifer. *The Christmas Tree*. London: Hamish Hamilton, 1981.

Johnston, Jennifer. *The Railway Station Man*. London: Hamish Hamilton, 1984.

Johnston, Jennifer. *Fool's Sanctuary*. London: Hamish Hamilton, 1987.

Johnston, Jennifer. *The Nightingale and Not the Lark*. Dublin: Raven Arts, 1988.

Johnston, Jennifer. *The Invisible Worm*. London: Sinclair-Stevenson, 1991.

Kelly, Maeve. *A Life of Her Own*. Dublin: Poolbeg, 1976.

Kelly, Maeve. *Necessary Treasons*. 1985. Reprinted London: Methuen, 1986.

Kelly, Maeve. *Resolution*. Belfast: the Blackstaff Press, 1986.

Kelly, Maeve. *Florrie's Girls*. London: Michael Joseph, 1989.

Kelly, Maeve. *Orange Horses*. London: Michael Joseph, 1990.

Kelly, Rita. *The Whispering Arch and Other Stories*. Dublin: Arlen House, 1986.

Larkin, Mary. *The Wasted Years*. London: Warner Books, 1993.

Leland, Mary. *The Killeen*. London: Hamish Hamilton, 1985.

Leland, Mary. *Approaching Priests*. London: Sinclair-Stevenson, 1991.

Lentin, Ronit. *Night Train to Mother*. Dublin: Attic Press, 1989.

Lentin, Ronit. *Songs on the Death of Children*. Dublin: Poolbeg, 1996.

Lingard, Joan. *The Lord on our Side*. London: Hodder and Stoughton, 1970.

Lingard, Joan. *The Twelfth Day of July*. New York: Thomas Nelson, 1970.

Lingard, Joan. *Sisters by Rite*. New York: St Martin's, 1984.

Madden, Deirdre. *Hidden Symptoms*. New York: Atlantic Monthly, 1986.

Madden, Deirdre. *The Birds of the Innocent Wood*. London: Faber and Faber, 1988.

Madden, Deirdre. *Remembering Light and Stone*. London: Faber and Faber, 1992.

Madden, Deirdre. *Nothing is Black*. London: Faber and Faber, 1994.

Madden, Deirdre. *One by One in the Darkness*. London: Faber and Faber, 1996.

Maguire, Aisling. *Breaking Out*. Belfast: the Blackstaff Press, 1996.

Mahon, Bríd. *Devogilla*. Dublin: Poolbeg, 1994.

Mahon, Stella. 'On the Front Line'. *Sisters*. Belfast: the Blackstaff Press, 1980, pp. 73–84.

Manning, Kitty. *The Between People*. Dublin: Attic Press, 1990.

Marcus, David, ed. *Alternative Loves: Irish Gay and Lesbian Stories*. Dublin: Martello Books, 1994.

McCrory, Moy. *Bleeding Sinners*. London: Methuen, 1988.

McGuckian, Medbh. *Marconi's Cottage*. Loughcrew, Co. Meath: Gallery, 1991.

Meehan, Paula. *The Man Who Was Marked by Winter*. Loughcrew, Co. Meath: Gallery, 1991.

Mills, Lia. *Another Alice*. Dublin: Poolbeg, 1996.

Mitchell, Jane. *Different Lives*. Dublin: Poolbeg, 1996.

Molloy, Frances. *No Mate for the Magpie*. London: Virago, 1985.

Molloy, Frances. *Women Are the Scourge of the Earth*. Belfast: The White Row Press, 1998.

Mulvihill, Margaret. *Low Overheads*. London: Pandora, 1987.

Murdoch, Iris. *The Red and the Green*. 1965. Middlesex: Penguin, 1967.

Murphy, Brenda. 'A Social Call', in *The Hurt World: Short Stories of the Troubles*, ed. Michael Parker. Belfast: the Blackstaff Press, 1995, pp. 270–2.

Nelson, Dorothy. *In Night's City*. Dublin: Wolfhound, 1982.

Nelson, Dorothy. *Tar and Feathers*. Dublin: Wolfhound, 1987.

Ní Chuilleanáin, Eiléan. *The Brazen Serpent*. Loughcrew, Co. Meath: Gallery, 1994.

Ní Dhuibhne, Éilís. 'Midwife to the Fairies', in *Territories of the Voice: Contemporary Stories by Irish Women*, ed. Louise DeSalvo, Kathleen Walsh D'Arcy and Katherine Hogan. London: Virago, 1990: 31–8.

Ní Dhuibhne, Eilís. *The Bray House*. Dublin: Attic Press, 1990.

Ní Dhuibhne, Eilís. *Eating Women Is Not Recommended*. Dublin: Attic Press, 1991.

Ní Dhuibhne, Eilís. *The Inland Ice and Other Stories*. Belfast: the Blackstaff Press, 1997.

O'Brien, Edna. *The Country Girls*. London: Hutchinson, 1960.

O'Brien, Edna. *The Lonely Girl*. London: Jonathan Cape, 1962.

O'Brien, Edna. *Girls in Their Married Bliss*. London: Jonathan Cape, 1964.

O'Brien, Edna. *A Pagan Place*. London: Weidenfeld and Nicolson, 1970.

O'Brien, Edna. *Mother Ireland*. London: Weidenfeld and Nicolson, 1976.

O'Brien, Edna. *The High Road*. London: Weidenfeld and Nicolson, 1988.

O'Brien, Edna. *House of Splendid Isolation*. London: Weidenfeld and Nicolson, 1994.

O'Brien, Edna. *Down By the River*. London: Weidenfeld and Nicolson, 1996.

O'Brien, Kate Cruise, *The Homesick Garden*. Dublin: Poolbeg, 1991.

O'Brien, Kate Cruise. *If Only: Short Stories of Love and Divorce by Irish Women Writers*. Dublin: Poolbeg, 1997.

O'Carroll, Harriet. 'The Day of the Christening.' *Territories of the Voice: Contemporary Stories by Irish Women*, ed. Louise DeSalvo, Kathleen Walsh D'Arcy and Katherine Hogan. London: Virago, 1990, pp. 53–61.

O'Connor, Clairr. *When You Need Them*. Galway: Salmon Publishing, 1989.

O'Connor, Clairr. *Belonging*. Dublin: Attic Press, 1991.

O'Connor, Clairr. *Love in Another Room*. Dublin: Marino Books, 1995.

O'Donnell, Mary. *The Light-Makers*. Dublin: Poolbeg, 1992.

O'Donnell, Mary. *Virgin and the Boy*. Dublin: Poolbeg, 1996.

O'Faolain, Julia. *No Country for Young Men*. London: Allen Lane, 1980.

O'Faolain, Julia. *Women in the Wall*. London: Faber and Faber, 1975. Reprinted London: Virago, 1985.

O'Faolain, Julia. *The Irish Signorina*. New York: Viking, 1984, and London: Alder and Alder, 1986.

O'Faolain, Julia. *The Judas Cloth*. London: Sinclair-Stevenson, 1992.
O'Farrell, Kathleen. *The Fiddler of Kilbroney*. Co. Kerry: Brandon, 1994.
O'Hara, Elizabeth. *Singles*. Dublin: Basement Press, 1994.
O'Malley, Mary. *Where the Rocks Float*. Dublin: Salmon Publishing, 1993.
O'Riordan, Kate. *Involved*. London: Flamingo: London: HarperCollins, 1995.
Parker, Michael, ed. *The Hurt World: Short Stories of the Troubles*. Belfast: the Blackstaff Press, 1995.
Richards, Maura. *Interlude*. Dublin: Ward River Press, 1982.
Ryan, Mary. *Whispers in the Wind*. Dublin: Attic Press, 1990.
Scanlan, Patricia. *City Girl*. Dublin: Poolbeg, 1990.
Scanlan, Patricia. *Apartment 3B*. Dublin: Poolbeg, 1991.
Scanlan, Patricia. *Finishing Touches*. Dublin: Poolbeg, 1992.
Scanlan, Patricia. *Foreign Affairs*. Dublin: Poolbeg, 1994.
Scanlan, Patricia. *Promises*. Dublin: Poolbeg, 1996.
Scanlan, Patricia. *Mirror, Mirror*. Dublin: Poolbeg, 1997.
Slade, Jo. *The Vigilant One*. Galway: Salmon Poetry, 1994.
Smyth, Ailbhe, ed. *Wildish Things: an Anthology of New Irish Women's Writing*. Dublin: Attic, 1989.
Strong, Eithne, *Flesh, the Greatest Sin* (1980). Reprinted Dublin: Attic Press, 1993.
Strong, Eithne. *Patterns*. Dublin: Poolbeg, 1981.
Strong, Eithne. *Spatial Nosing: New and Selected Poems*. Dublin: Salmon Poetry, 1993.
Strong, Eithne. *The Love Riddle*. Dublin: Attic Press, 1993.
Swift, Todd and Martin Mooney, ed. *Map-Makers' Colours: New Poets of Northern Ireland*. Montreal: Nu-Age Editions, 1988.
Urquhart, Jane. *Away*. Toronto: McClelland and Stewart, 1993.
Walshe, Dolores. *Where the Trees Weep*. Dublin: Wolfhound, 1992.
Walshe, Dolores. *Moon Mad*. Dublin: Wolfhound, 1993.
Wells, Helen. *Cherry Ames, Student Nurse*. 1943. London: World, 1956.
Women's Work VIII: an Eighth Anthology of Poems by Women. Wexford: the Works, 1997.
Woods, Una. *The Dark Hole Days*. Belfast: Blackstaff, 1984.
Woolf, Virginia. *A Room of One's Own*. 1929. New York: Harcourt, Brace and World, 1957.
Zell, Ann. 'Nature Programme' in *Word of Mouth*, ed. Ruth Carr *et al*. Belfast: the Blackstaff Press, 1996.

Selected critical bibliography

Altman, Rick, ed. *Genre: The Musical: a Reader*. London: Routledge and Kegan Paul, 1981.
Anderson, Linda. 'A Lack of Alternatives'. *HU/the Honest Ulsterman* 91 (1991): 92–3.
Aretxaga, Begoña. *Shattering Silence: Women, Nationalism, and Political Subjectivity in Northern Ireland*. Princeton, NJ: Princeton UP, 1997.
Ashcroft, Bill, Gareth Griffiths and Helen Tiffin, ed. *The Post-Colonial Studies Reader*. London: Routledge, 1995.

Atwood, Margaret. *Second Words: Selected Critical Prose*. Boston: Beacon, 1982.
Bal, Mieke. *Narratology: Introduction to the Theory of Narrative*. Toronto: U of Toronto P, 1985.
Bardwell, Leland. Personal interviews with the author, 2 July 1992 and 20 November 1993.
Barry, Ursula. *Lifting the Lid: Handbook of Facts and Information on Ireland*. Dublin: Attic Press, 1986.
Barry, Ursula. 'Women In Ireland. *Women's Studies International Forum* 11:4 (1987): 317–19.
Bartky, Sandra Lee. *Femininity and Domination: Studies in the Phenomenology of Oppression*. London: Routledge, 1990.
Beale, Jenny. *Women In Ireland: Voices of Change*. Dublin: Gill and Macmillan, 1986.
Beckett, Mary. Personal interview with the author, 1 July 1992.
Belsey, Catherine and Jane Moore, ed. *The Feminist Reader: Essays in Gender and the Politics of Literary Criticism*. London: Macmillan, 1989.
Bennett, Jackie and Rosemary Forgan, ed. *There's Something About a Convent School Girl*. London: Virago, 1991.
Bew, Paul and Gordon Gillespie. *Northern Ireland: a Chronology of the Troubles 1968–1993*. Dublin: Gill and Macmillan, 1993.
Bhabha, Homi K. *Nation and Narration*. London: Routledge, 1990.
Bhreathnach-Lynch, Sighle. 'Landscape, Space, and Gender: Their Role in the Construction of Female Identity in Newly-Independent Ireland', *Canadian Woman Studies/cf* 17: 3 (1997): 26–30.
Binchy, Maeve. Personal interview with the author, 4 October 1992.
Boland, Eavan. 'An Interview with Eavan Boland, with Jody Allen Randolph. *Irish University Review* 23:1 (Spring/Summer 1993): 117–30.
Boland, Eavan. *A Kind of Scar: the Woman Poet in a National Tradition*. Dublin: Attic Press, 1989.
Boland, Eavan. Lecture. International Association of Anglo-Irish Studies Conference. Dublin, 13 July 1992.
Boland, Eavan. *Outside History*. Manchester: Carcanet, 1990.
Boland, Eavan. *Object Lessons: the Life of the Woman and the Poet in Our Time*. 1995. Manchester: Carcanet, 1996.
Bourke, Angela. 'Language, Healing, Stories', in *Gender and Sexuality in Modern Ireland*, ed. Anthony Bradley and Maryann Gialanella Valiulis. Amherst: University of Massachusetts Press, 1997, pp. 299–314.
Bradley, Anthony and Maryann Gialanella Valiulis, ed. *Gender and Sexuality in Modern Ireland*. Amherst: University of Massachusetts Press, 1997.
Brown, Terence. *Ireland: a Social and Cultural History 1922–1985*. London: Fontana, 1981.
Buck, Claire, ed. *Bloomsbury Guide to Women's Literature*. London: Bloomsbury, 1992.
Butler, Judith and Joan W. Scott, eds *Feminists Theorize the Political*. London: Routledge, 1992.
Byrne, Anne and Madeleine Leonard, eds *Women and Irish Society: a Sociological Reader*. Dublin: Beyond the Pale, 1997.
Cahalan, James M. *Great Hatred, Little Room: the Irish Historical Novel*. Syracuse, NY: Syracuse University Press, 1971.

Cahalan, James M. 'Forging a Tradition: Emily Lawless and the Irish Literary Canon. *Colby Quarterly* 27:1 (March 1991): 27–49.

Cairns, David and Shaun Richards. *Writing Ireland: Colonialism, Nationalism and Culture.* Manchester: Manchester University Press, 1988.

Carlson, Julia, ed. *Banned in Ireland.* Athens: University of Georgia Press, 1990.

Chow, Rey. *Writing Diaspora: Tactics of Intervention in Contemporary Cultural Studies.* Bloomington, Ind.: Indiana University Press, 1993.

Clifford, James and George E. Marcus. *Writing Culture: the Poetics and Politics of Ethnography.* Berkeley: University of California Press, 1986.

Colman, Ann Ulry. *A Dictionary of Nineteenth Century Irish Women Poets.* Galway: Kennys Bookshop, 1996.

Conlon, Evelyn. 'Millions Like Us.' *Graph* 5 (1988): 4.

Conway, Sheelagh. *The Faraway Hills Are Green: Voices of Irish Women in Canada.* Toronto: Women's Press, 1992.

Cooke, Emma. Personal interview with the author, 25 July 1991.

Coulter, Carol. *The Hidden Tradition: Feminism, Women and Nationalism in Ireland.* Co. Cork: Cork UP, 1993.

Coward, Rosalind. 'The True Story of How I Became My Own Person'. *The Feminist Reader: Essays in Gender and the Politics of Literary Criticism,* ed. Catherine Belsey and Jane Moore. London: Macmillan, 1989, pp. 35–47.

Coward, Rosalind. 'This Novel Changes Women's Lives: Are Women's Novels Feminist Novels?' *Feminist Review* 5 (1980): 53–65.

Crowley, Ethel. 'Making a Difference? Female Employment and Multinationals in the Republic of Ireland', in *Women and Irish Society: a Sociological Reader,* ed. Anne Byrne and Madeleine Leonard. Belfast: Beyond the Pale, 1997, pp. 81–96.

Crowley, Ethel and Jim Mac Laughlin eds. *Under the Belly of the Tiger: Class, Race, Identity and Culture in the Global Ireland.* Dublin: Irish Reporter Publications, 1997.

Cullen, Mary, ed. *Girls Don't Do Honours.* Dublin: Women's Education Bureau, 1987.

Cullen, Mary. 'Towards a New Ireland: Women, Feminism and the Peace Process', in *Women and Irish History,* ed. Maryann Gialanella Valiulis and Mary O'Dowd. Dublin: Wolfhound Press, 1997, pp 260–77.

Cunningham, Francine. 'Maeve in Full Flow in Dalkey'. *Irish Times* 4 October 1990: 8.

Curtin, Chris, Pauline Jackson and Barbara O'Connor, eds. *Gender in Irish Society.* Galway: Officina Typographica, 1987.

Curtis, Liz. *Ireland: the Propaganda War: the British Media and the Battle for Hearts and Minds.* London: Pluto Press, 1984.

Dalsimer, Adele M., ed. *Visualizing Ireland: National Identity and the Pictorial Tradition.* Boston: Faber and Faber, 1993.

Daly, Mary E. 'Women in the Irish Free State, 1929–39: the Interaction between Economics and Ideology.' *Journal of Women's History.* 6: 4/7: 1 (Winter/ Spring 1995): 99–116.

Daly, Mary. *Women and Poverty.* Dublin: Attic Press, 1989.

Daly, Mary E. *Women and Work in Ireland.* Dublin: The Economic and Social History Society of Ireland, 1997.

Davies, Celia and Eithne McLaughlin. *Women, Employment and Social Policy in Northern Ireland: a Problem Postponed?* Belfast: Policy Research Institute, 1991.
De Lauretis, Teresa, ed. *Feminist Studies/Critical Studies*. Bloomington: Indiana UP, 1986.
De Plessis, Rachel Blau. *Writing Beyond the Ending*. Bloomington: Indiana UP, 1985.
Devlin, Bernadette. *The Price of My Soul*. New York: Knopf, 1969.
Devlin, Polly. *All of Us There*. Belfast: the Blackstaff Press, 1983.
DiCenzo, Maria R. 'Charabanc Theatre Company: Placing Women Center-Stage in Northern Ireland.' *Theatre Journal* 45 (1993): 175–84.
Diner, Hasia R. *Erin's Daughters in America: Irish Immigrant Women in the Nineteenth Century*. Baltimore: Johns Hopkins University Press, 1983.
Donoghue, Emma. 'Noises from the Woodshed: Tales of Irish Lesbians 1886–1989', in *Lesbian and Gay Visions of Ireland*, ed. Ide O'Carroll and Eoin Collins. London: Cassell, 1995, pp. 158–70.
Donovan, Katie. *Irish Women Writers: Marginalized by Whom?* Dublin: Raven Arts, 1988.
Dorcey, Mary. 'The Spaces Between the Words'. Interview with Nuala Archer. *Women's Review of Books* 8:3 (December 1990): 21–2.
Dublin Lesbian and Gay Men's Collectives. *Out for Ourselves: the Lives of Irish Lesbians and Gay Men*. Dublin Lesbian and Gay Men's Collectives and Women's Community Press, 1986.
Duffaud, Briege. Personal interview with the author, 19 July 1994.
Dunne, John. 'Canon Fodder'. *Books Ireland* 96 (Sept. 1985): 142.
Dyer, Richard. 'Entertainment and Utopia', *Movie* 24 (Spring 1977): 175–89.
Enzensberger, Hans Magnus. *The Consciousness Industry: On Literature, Politics and the Media*. New York: Seabury, 1974.
Evason, Eileen. *Against the Grain: the Contemporary Women's Movement in Northern Ireland*. Dublin: Attic Press, 1991.
Eyler, Audrey S. and Robert F. Garrett, eds. *The Uses of the Past: Essays on Irish Culture*. Newark: University of Delaware Press, 1988.
Fabb, Nigel, Derek Attridge, Alan Durant and Colin MacCabe, ed. *The Linguistics of Writing: Arguments between Language and Literature*. Methuen: London, 1987.
Fairweather, Eileen, Roisín McDonough and Melanie McFadyean. *Only the Rivers Run Free: Northern Ireland: The Women's War*. London: Pluto, 1984.
Feeney, Aoife. 'Wallowing in Overwriting', *Irish Literary Supplement* 4: 2 (Fall 1985): 50.
Felski, Rita. *Beyond Feminist Aesthetics: Feminist Literature and Social Change*. Cambridge: Harvard University Press, 1989.
Feminist Review (Special Irish Issue) 50 (1995).
Ferreira, Patricia. 'Ten Years of Attic', *Irish Literary Supplement* 12:1 (Spring 1993): 14.
Ferris, Mary, Anna McGonigle, Patricia McKeown, Theresa Moriarty and Marie Mulholland (National Union of Public Employees Women's Committee, Northern Ireland). *Women's Voices: an Oral History of Northern Women's Health (1900–1990)*. Dublin: Attic Press,1992.
Finch, Mark. 'Sex and Address in *Dynasty*', *Screen* 27: 6 (Nov/Dec.1986): 33.
Fleishman, Avrom. *The Historical Novel: Walter Scott to Virginia Woolf.*

Baltimore: Johns Hopkins University Press, 1971.

Foley, Timothy P. and Lionel Pilkington, Sean Ryder and Elizabeth Tilley. *Gender and Colonialism*. Galway: Galway University Press, 1995.

Foster, John Wilson, ed. 'The *HU* Critical Forum', *HU/The Honest Ulsterman* 83 (Summer 1987): 39–70.

Foster, John Wilson, ed. *Colonial Consequences: Essays in Irish Literature and Culture*. Dublin: Lilliput, 1991.

Foster, John Wilson. 'Irish Fiction 1965–90', *The Field Day Anthology of Irish Writing*, VIII, ed. Seamus Deane. Derry: Field Day Publications, 1991, pp. 937–43.

Foster, R.F. *Modern Ireland: 1600–1972*. New York: Viking, 1988.

Franklin, Sarah, Celia Lury and Jackie Stacey, eds. *Off-Centre: Feminism and Cultural Studies*. London: Harper Collins Academic, 1991.

Gallagher, S.F. *Woman in Irish Legend, Life and Literature*. Gerrards Cross, Bucks: Colin Smyth, 1983 and Totowa, New Jersey: Barnes and Noble Books, 1983.

Gerrard, Nicci. *Into the Mainstream: How Feminism Has Changed Women's Writing*. London: Pandora, 1989.

Geraghty, Christine. *Women and Soap Opera: a Study of Prime Time Soaps*. Cambridge: Polity, 1991.

Gilbert, Sandra M. and Susan Gubar. *The Madwoman in the Attic*. New Haven: Yale University Press, 1979.

Goffman, Erving. *Stigma: Notes on the Management of Spoiled Identity*. Englewood Cliffs, NJ: Prentice-Hall, 1963.

Greene, Gayle. *Changing the Story: Feminist Fiction and the Tradition*. Bloomington: Indiana University Press, 1991.

Gregory, Philippa. 'Historical Present'. *Sunday Times*, 3 October 1993: 6, 12.

Grossberg, Lawrence, Cary Nelson and Paula A. Treichler, ed. *Cultural Studies*. New York: Routledge, 1992.

Haberstroh, Patria Boyle. *Women Creating Women: Contemporary Irish Women Poets*. Syracuse, NY: Syracuse University Press; Dublin: Attic, 1996.

Hall, Stuart. 'Cultural Identity and Diaspora', in *Colonial Discourse and Post-Colonial Theory*, ed. Patrick Williams and Laura Chrisman. London: Harvester Wheatsheaf, 1993, pp. 392–403.

Hannan, Damian and Richard Breen. 'School and Gender', in *Girls Don't Do Honours*, ed. Mary Cullen. Dublin: Women's Education Bureau, 1987, pp. 100–15.

Harris, Mary N. 'Beleaguered But Determined: Irish Women Writers in Irish', *Feminist Review* 51 (Autumn 1995): 26–40.

Harte, Liam and Michael Parker, ed. *Contemporary Irish Fictions: Themes, Tropes, Theories*. London: Macmillan, 1999.

Hartigan, Anne Le Marquand. *Clearing the Space: a Why of Writing*. Knockeven, Co. Clare: Salmon, 1996.

Haverty, Anne. 'In Novel-land'. *Times Literary Supplement* 19 July 1985: 800.

Hearne, Dana. 'The *Irish Citizen* 1914–1916: Nationalism, Feminism, and Militarism', *Canadian Journal of Irish Studies* 18:1 (July 1992): 1–14.

Heilbrun, Carolyn G. *Writing a Woman's Life*. New York: Norton, 1988.

Herr, Cheryl. 'The Erotics of Irishness', *Critical Inquiry* 17:1 (Spring, 1990): 1–34.

Hirsch, Marianne. *The Mother-Daughter Plot: Narrative, Psychoanalysis, Feminism*.

Bloomington: Indiana University Press, 1989.

Hite, Molly. *The Other Side of the Story.* Ithaca: Cornell University Press, 1989.

hooks, bell. 'Feminism: a Transformational Politic', in *Talking Back: Thinking Feminist, Thinking Black.* Toronto: Between the Lines, 1988, pp. 19–27.

Hooley, Ruth, ed. *The Female Line: Northern Irish Women Writers.* Belfast: Northern Ireland Women's Rights Movement, 1985.

Hoy, Suellen and Margaret MacCurtain. *From Dublin to New Orleans: the Journey of Nora and Alice.* Dublin: Attic Press, 1994.

Hoy, Suellen. 'The Journey Out: the Recruitment and Emigration of Irish Religious Women to the United States, 1812–1914', *Journal of Women's History* 6: 4/7: 1 (Winter/Spring 1995): 64–98.

Humm, Maggie. *Border Traffic: Strategies of Contemporary Women Writers.* Manchester: University of Manchester Press, 1991.

Hussey, Gemma. *Ireland Today: Anatomy of a Changing State.* London: Penguin, 1995.

Hutcheon, Linda. 'Circling the Downspout of Empire: Post-colonialism and Postmodernism', in *The Post-Colonial Studies Reader*, ed. Bill Ashcroft, Gareth Griffiths and Helen Tiffin. London: Routledge, 1995: 130–35.

Ignatiev, Noel. *How the Irish Became White.* London: Routledge, 1995.

Ingoldby, G.D. 'Wiping a Waxed Floor with Men.' *Fortnight* (Belfast) 191 (Feb. 1983): 20.

Ireland. National and Social Council. *The Economic and Social Implications of Emigration.* No. 90. Dublin: Stationery Office, 1991.

Irigarary, Luce. 'And the One Doesn't Stir Without the Other', *Signs* 7:1 (Winter 1981): 60–7.

Irigarary, Luce. *Speculum of the Other Woman.* Ithaca: Cornell UP, 1985.

Irigaray, Luce. 'Power of Discourse', in *This Sex Which Is Not One*, trans. Catherine Porter. Ithaca: Cornell University Press, 1985.

Jacobus, Mary, ed. *Women Writing and Writing About Women.* New York: Barnes and Noble Books, 1979.

Johnson, Toni O'Brien and David Cairns, ed. *Gender in Irish Writing.* Buckingham: Open University Press, 1991.

Johnston, Jennifer. 'Q. and A. with Jennifer Johnston', with Michael Kenneally. *Irish Literary Supplement* 3:2 (Fall 1984): 25–7.

Johnston, Rory. *Orders and Desecrations: the Life of Denis Johnston.* Dublin: Lilliput, 1992.

Jump, Harriet Devine, ed. *Diverse Voices: Essays on Twentieth-Century Women Writers in English.* London: Harvester Wheatsheaf, 1991.

Kearney, Richard, ed. *The Irish Mind.* Dublin: Wolfhound, 1985.

Kearney, Richard, ed. *Across the Frontiers.* Dublin: Wolfhound, 1988.

Kearney, Richard. *Transitions: Narratives in Modern Irish Culture.* Manchester: Manchester UP, 1988.

Kellman, Steven G. 'The Fiction of Self-Begetting', *Modern Language Notes* 91 (December 1976): 1243–56.

Kelly, A.A., ed. *Pillars of the House: an Anthology of Verse by Irish Women from 1690 to the Present.* Dublin: Wolfhound, 1988.

Kelly, Maeve. 'Making a Space.' Unpublished speech. Women Writers Circle, Fourth International Interdisciplinary Congress on Women. Hunter College, New York, 1990.

Kelly, Maeve. Personal interview with the author, 3 July 1992.

Kenneally, Michael, ed. *Cultural Contexts and Literary Idioms in Contemporary Irish Literature*. Gerards Cross: Colin Smythe, 1988.

Kiberd, Declan. 'The War Against the Past', in *The Uses of the Past: Essays on Irish Culture*, ed. Audrey S. Eyler and Robert F. Garrett. Newark: University of Delaware Press, 1988, pp. 24–53.

Kroker, Arthur and Marilouise, ed. *The Hysterical Male: New Feminist Theory*. Montreal: New World Perspectives, 1991.

Kuhn, Annette. *Women's Pictures: Feminism and Cinema*. London: Routledge and Kegan Paul, 1982.

Leland, Mary. Personal interview with the author, 24 November 1994.

Lendennie, Jessie. 'The Female Metaphor', *Books Ireland* 121 (March 1988): 37.

Lennon, Mary, and Marie McAdam. *Across the Water: Irish Women's Lives in Britain*. London: Virago, 1988.

Leonard, Madeleine. 'The Politics of Everyday Living in Belfast', *Canadian Journal of Irish Studies* 18:1 (July 1992): 83–94.

Levenson, Leah and Jerry H. Natterstad. *Hanna Sheehy-Skeffington: Irish Feminist*. Syracuse, NY: Syracuse UP, 1986.

Levine, June and Lyn Madden. *Lyn: a Story of Prostitution*. Dublin: Attic Press, 1987.

Lingard, Joan. Personal interview with the author, 17 July 1993.

Lloyd, David. *Anomalous States: Irish Writing and the Postcolonial Movement*. Durham, NC: Duke UP, 1993.

Lloyd, David. 'Nationalism Against the State: Towards a Critique of the Anti-Nationalist Prejudice', *Gender and Colonialism*, ed. Timothy P. Foley *et al*. Galway: Galway University Press, 1995, pp. 256–81.

Longley, Edna. 'Women, Criticism and Ireland', *Krino* 15 (Spring 1994): 1–12.

Longley, Edna. *From Cathleen to Anorexia: the Breakdown of Irelands*. Dublin: Attic Press, 1990.

Longley, Edna. *The Living Stream: Literature and Revisionism in Ireland*. Newcastle-upon-Tyne: Bloodaxe, 1994.

Luddy, Maria and Cliona Murphy, ed. *Women Surviving: Studies in Irish Women's History in the 19th and 20th Centuries*. Dublin: Poolbeg, 1990.

Luftig, Victor. '"Something Will Happen To You Who Read": Adrienne Rich, Eavan Boland', *Irish University Review* 23:1 (Spring/Summer, 1993): 57–66.

Luftig, Victor. 'Frances Molloy: In Memoriam', *Irish Literary Supplement* (Fall 1993): 39.

Lukács, George. *The Historical Novel*. London: Merlin, 1962.

Lyons, Maureen, Helen Ruddle, Joyce O'Connor and Maeve (O'Brien) Kelly. *Seeking a Refuge from Violence: the Adapt Experience*. Dublin: Policy Research Centre, 1992.

Madden-Simpson, Janet, ed. *Woman's Part: an Anthology of Short Fiction By and About Irish Women 1890–1960*. Dublin: Arlen House, 1984.

Martin, Biddy and Chandra Talpade Mohanty. 'Feminist Politics: What's Home Got to Do With It?' in *Feminist Studies/Critical Studies*, ed. Teresa de Lauretis. Bloomington: Indiana UP, 1986, pp. 191–212.

Martin, Carol. 'Charabanc Theatre Company: "Quare" Women "Sleggin" and "Geggin" the Standards of Northern Ireland by "Tappin" the People', *Drama Review* 31: 2 (Summer 1987): 88–99.

McCafferty, Nell. *The Armagh Women*. Dublin: Co-op Books, 1981.

McCafferty, Nell. *A Woman to Blame: the Kerry Babies Case*. Dublin: Attic Press, 1985.

McCafferty, Nell. *Peggy Deery: a Derry Family at War*. Dublin: Attic Press, 1988.

McCafferty, Nell. 'A Women's Party Outwits the System in Northern Ireland', Reprinted 1996. *Ms. Magazine Candian Woman Studies/Les cahiers des femmes, 17:3 (Summer/Fall 1997)*: 64–8.

McElroy, James. 'The Contemporary Fe/Male Poet: a Preliminary Reading', in *New Irish Writing: Essays in Memory of Raymond J. Porter*, ed. James D. Brophy and Eamon Grennan. Boston: Twayne-G.K. Hall, 1989, pp. 189–202.

McGuckian, Medbh. 'Birds and Their Masters', *Irish University Review* 23:1 (Spring/Summer 1993): 29–30.

McIlroy, Brian. *World Cinema 4: Ireland*. Trowbridge, Wiltshire: Flick Books, 1988.

McIlroy, Brian. 'When the Ulster Protestant and Unionist Looks: Spectatorship in (Northern) Irish Cinema.' *Irish University Review* 26:1 (Spring/Summer 1996): 143–54.

McKay, Susan. 'A Literature of Our Own: Recent Fiction by Irish Women', *Linen Hall Review* 1.1 (Spring, 1984): 12–14.

McLaughlin, Eithne and Celia Davies. *Women, Employment and Social Policy in Northern Ireland*. Belfast: U of Ulster P, Policy Research Institute, 1991.

McMinn, Joseph. 'Contemporary Novels on the Troubles', *Etudes Irlandaises* 5 (1980): 113–21.

Meaney, Gerardine. *Sex and Nation: Women in Irish Culture and Politics*. Dublin: Attic Press, 1991.

Midland Review: a Journal of Contemporary Literature, Literary Criticism and Art 3 (Winter, 1986).

Miles, Angela. 'Confessions of a Harlequin Reader: Romance and the Myth of Male Mothers.' *The Hysterical Male: New Feminist Theory*, ed. Arthur and Marilouise Kroker. Montreal: New World Perspectives, 1991, pp. 93–131.

Miller, Nancy. 'Arachnologies: the Women, the Text and the Critic', in *The Poetics of Gender*. Ed. Nancy Miller. New York: Columbia University Press, 1986, pp. 270–95.

Moane, Geraldine. 'Lesbian Politics and Community', in *Women and Irish Society: a Sociological Reader*, ed. Anne Byrne and Madeleine Leonard. Belfast: Beyond the Pale Publications, 1997, pp. 431–46.

Modleski, Tania. *Loving with a Vengeance: Mass-Produced Fantasies for Women*. Hamden, CT: Archon, 1982.

Modleski, Tania, ed. *Studies in Entertainment: Critical Approaches to Mass Culture*. Bloomington: Indiana UP, 1986.

Moi, Toril. 'Feminist, Female, Feminine', in *The Feminist Reader: Essays in Gender and the Politics of Literary Criticism*, ed. Catherine Belsey and Jane Moore London: Macmillan, 1989, pp. 117–32.

Murphy, Cliona. *The Women's Suffrage Movement and Irish Society in the Early Twentieth Century*. Brighton: Harvester Wheatsheaf, 1989.

Murphy, Maureen. 'The Fionnuala Factor: Irish Sibling Emigration at the Turn of the Century', in *Gender and Sexuality in Modern Ireland*, ed. Anthony Bradley and Maryann Gialanella Valiulis. Amherst: University of Massachusetts Press, 1997, pp. 85–101.

Nash, Catherine. 'Remapping and Renaming: New Cartographies of Identity, Gender and Landscape in Ireland'. *Feminist Review* 44 (Summer 1993): 39–57.

Neville, Grace. '"She Never Then After That Forgot Him": Irishwomen and Emigration to the United States in Irish Folklore', in *Mid-America: an Historical Review* 74: 3 (October 1992): 271–89.

Ní Chuilleanáin, Eiléan. 'Woman as Writer: the Social Matrix', in *Crane Bag* 4: 1 (1980): 101–5

Ní Chuilleanáin, Eiléan, ed. *Irish Women: Image and Achievement*. Dublin: Arlen House, 1985.

Ní Dhuibhne, Eilís, ed. *Voices on the Wind: Women Poets of the Celtic Twilight*. Dublin: New Island Books, 1995.

O'Carroll, Ide. *Models for Movers: Irish Women's Emigration to America*. Dublin: Attic Press, 1988.

O'Carroll, Ide. 'A Lesbian Vision of Ireland.' Speech. American Conference of Irish Studies/Canadian Association of Irish Studies. Belfast, July 1995.

O'Carroll, Ide and Eoin Collins, ed. *Lesbian and Gay Visions of Ireland*. London: Cassell, 1995.

O'Connor, Theresa. *The Comic Tradition in Irish Women Writers*. Gainsville, FL: U of Florida P, 1996.

O'Connor, Pat. *Emerging Voices: Women in Contemporary Irish Society*. Dublin: Institute of Public Administration, 1998.

O'Donnell, Mary. '*In Her Own Image* – an Assertion that Myths are Made by Men, by the Poet in Transition', *Irish University Review* 23:1 (Spring/Summer 1993): 40–4.

O'Donohue, Jo. Letter to the author, 16 November 1992.

O'Faolain, Nuala. 'Irish Women and Writing in Modern Ireland', *Irish Women: Image and Achievement*, ed. Eiléan Ní Chuilleanáin. Dublin: Arlen House: 1985, pp. 127–35.

O'Faolain, Nuala. *Are You Somebody? The Life and Times of Nuala O'Faolain*. Dublin: New Island, 1996.

O'Flynn, Gráinne. 'Our Age of Innocence', in *Girls Don't Do Honours*, ed. Mary Cullen. Dublin: Women's Education Bureau, 1987, pp. 77–99.

O'Reilly, Emily. *Masterminds of the Right*. Dublin: Attic Press, 1992.

Owen, Mairead. 'Reinventing Romance: Reading Popular Romantic Fiction', *Women's Studies International Forum* 20:4 (Fall 1997): 537–46.

Owens, Rosemary Cullen. *Smashing Times: a History of the Irish Suffrage Movement*. Dublin: Attic Press, 1984.

Parker, Andrew and Mary Russo, Doris Sommer and Patricia Yaeger eds. *Nationalism and Sexualities*. London: Routledge, 1992.

Patten, Eve. 'Women and Fiction: 1985–1990', *Krino* 8–9 (1990): 1–7.

Perry, Ben Edwin. *The Ancient Romances: a Literary-Historical Account of Their Origins*. Berkeley: U of California P, 1967.

Pratt, Mary Louise. 'Linguistic Utopias', in *The Linguistics of Writing: Arguments between Language and Literature*, ed. Nigel Fabb, Derek Attridge, Alan Durant and Colin MacCabe. Methuen: London, 1987. Pp. 48–66.

Quinn, John, ed. *A Portrait of the Artist as a Young Girl*. London: Methuen, in association with Radio Telefís Éireann, 1986.

Radway, Janice. 'Mail-Order Culture and its Critics: the Book-of-the-Month Club, Commodification and Consumption, and the Problem of Cultural

Authority', in *Cultural Studies*, ed. Lawrence Grossberg, Cary Nelson and Paula Treichler. London: Routledge, 1992, pp. 512–30.

Radway, Janice. 'Women Read the Romance: the Interaction of Text and Context', *FS/Feminist Studies* 9:1 (Spring 1983): 52–78.

Radway, Janice. *Reading the Romance: Women, Patriarchy and Popular Literature.* Chapel Hill, NC: University of North Carolina Press, 1984.

Rich, Adrienne. *Of Woman Born: Motherhood as Experience and Institution.* Tenth anniversary edition. New York: Norton, 1986.

Robinson, Lillian S. *Sex, Class and Culture.* Bloomington: Indiana University Press, 1978.

Robinson, Mary. 'Women in the Law in Ireland', in *Irish Women's Studies Reader*, ed. Ailbhe Smyth. Dublin: Attic Press, 1993, pp. 100–6.

Roche, Anthony. 'The Ante-Room as Drama', in *Ordinary People Dancing: Essays on Kate O'Brien*, ed. Eibhear Walshe. Co. Cork: Cork UP, 1993, pp. 85–100.

Roddy, Moya. 'Writing as an Irish Woman in England', in *In Other Words: Writing as a Feminist*, ed. Gail Chester and Sigrid Nielsen. London: Hutchinson, 1987.

Rose, Kieran. *Diverse Communities: the Evolution of Lesbian and Gay Politics in Ireland.* Cork: Cork UP, 1994.

Rossiter, Ann. 'Bringing the Margins into the Centre: a Review of Aspects of Irish Women's Emigration from a British Perspective', in *Irish Women's Studies Reader*, ed. Ailbhe Smyth. Dublin: Attic Press, 1993, pp. 177–202.

Said, Edward W. *Culture and Imperialism.* New York: Alfred A. Knopf, Inc., 1993.

St. Peter, Christine. 'Jennifer Johnston's Irish Troubles', in *Gender in Irish Writing*, ed. Toni O'Brien Johnson and David Cairns. Milton Keynes: Open University Press, 1991, pp. 112–27.

St. Peter, Christine. 'Reconstituting the Irish Nationalist Family Romance: *No Country for Young Men*', in *Historicité et Métafiction dans les îles britanniques.* Textes réunis par Max Duperry. Aix-en-Provence: Publications de l'université de Provence, 1994, pp. 151–66.

St. Peter, Christine. '*Black Baby* Takes Us Back: Dreaming the Postcolonial Mother', *Canadian Woman Studies/cf*, 17: 3 (Summer/Fall 1997): 36–40.

St. Peter, Christine. 'Petrifying Time: Incest Narratives by Irish Women', in *Contemporary Irish Fictions*: Themes, Tropes, Theories, ed. Liam Harte and Michael Parker. London: Macmillan, 1999.

St. Peter, Christine and Ron Marken, eds. *Women and Irish Politics: Special Issue, Canadian Journal of Irish Studies* 18:1 (July 1992).

Sales, Rosemary. *Women Divided: Gender, Religion and Politics in Northern Ireland.* London: Routledge,1997.

Schweickart, Patrocinio P. and Elizabeth A. Flynn, eds. *Gender and Reading: Essays on Readers, Texts and Contexts.* Baltimore: The Johns Hopkins University Press, 1986.

Scott, Bonnie Kime. 'Feminist Theory and Women in Irish Writing', *The Uses of the Past: Essays on Irish Culture*, ed. Audrey S. Eyler and Robert F. Garratt. Newark: University of Delaware Press, 1988, pp. 55–63.

Second Commission on the Status of Women: Report to Government. Dublin: Government of Ireland, 1993.

Seidel, David. *Exile and the Narrative Imagination.* New Haven: Yale University , 1986.

Shepperson, Janet. 'Revtew of "A Country Dance"', in M. Dorcey, *A Noise from the Woodshed, Krino* 15 (Spring 1994): 103.

Smyth, Ailbhe. *Women's Rights In Ireland*. Dublin: Irish Council for Civil Liberties, Ward River, 1983.

Smyth, Ailbhe. 'Ireland', *Bloomsbury Guide to Women's Literature*, ed. Claire Buck. London: Bloomsbury, 1992, pp. 36–41.

Smyth, Ailbhe. 'States of Change'. *Feminist Review* 50 (Summer 1995): 25–43.

Smyth, Ailbhe, ed. *Wildish Things: an Anthology of New Irish Women's Writing*. Dublin: Attic Press, 1989.

Smyth, Ailbhe, ed. *The Abortion Papers: Ireland*. Dublin: Attic Press, 1992.

Smyth, Ailbhe, ed. *Irish Women's Studies Reader*. Dublin: Attic Press, 1993.

Smyth, Ailbhe, ed. 'Irish Supplement', *Writing Women* 11: 3/12: 1, 1995.

Smyth, Emer. 'Labour Market Structures and Women's Employment in the Republic of Ireland', in *Women and Irish Society: a Sociological Reader*, ed. Anne Byrne and Madeleine Leonard. Dublin: Beyond the Pale, 1997, pp. 63–80.

Steedman, Carolyn. 'Culture, Cultural Studies, and Historians', in *Cultural Studies*, ed. Lawrence Grossberg, Cary Nelson and Paula A. Treichler. New York: Routledge, 1992, pp. 613–22.

Steiner-Scott, Liz, ed. *Personally Speaking: Women's Thoughts on Women's Issues*. Dublin: Attic Press, 1985.

Strong, Eithne. 'An Interview with Eithne Strong.' With Nancy Wright Means and Dennis Hannan. *Irish Literary Supplement* (Spring 1994):13.

Taylor, Alice. *The Village*. Cooleen, Co. Dingle: Brandon, 1992.

Tóibín, Colm. *Bad Blood: A Walk Along the Irish Border*. 1987. Reprinted London: Vintage, 1994.

Valiulis, Maryann Gialanella. 'Defining Their Role in the New State: Irishwomen's Protest Against the Juries Act of 1927', *Canadian Journal of Irish Studies* 18:1 (July 1992): 43–60.

Valiulis, Maryann Gialanella. 'Power, Gender, and Identity in the Irish Free State', *Journal of Women's History* 6: 4/7: 1 (Winter/Spring 1995): 117–136.

Walsh, Caroline, ed. *Virgins and Hyacinths: an Attic Book of Fiction*. Dublin: Attic Press, 1993.

Walsh, Caroline. 'Happy to Be Back from Killinarden.' *Irish Times* 2 November 1984: 13.

Walshe, Eibhear. 'Women in the Annex: Women Writers talk to Eibhear Walshe about the Field Day Anthology, *Irish Studies Review* 2 (Winter, 1992): 13–14.

Walshe, Eibhear, ed. *Ordinary People Dancing: Essays on Kate O'Brien*. Co. Cork: Cork University Press, 1993.

Ward, Catherine. 'Land and Landscape in Novels by McLaverty, Kiely and Leland.' *Eire-Ireland* 23:3 (Fall 1988): 77–8.

Ward, Margaret and Marie-Thérèse McGivern. 'Images of Women in Northern Ireland', *Crane Bag* 4:1 (1980): 66–72.

Ward, Margaret. *Unmanageable Revolutionaries: Women and Irish Nationalism*. London: Pluto, 1983.

Ward, Margaret. *The Missing Sex: Putting Women into Irish History*. Dublin: Attic Press, 1991.

Ward, Margaret. '"Suffrage First – Above All Else!" An Account of the Irish Suffrage Movement', in *Irish Women's Studies Reader*, ed. Ailbhe Smyth. Dublin: Attic Press, 1993, pp. 20–44.

Ward, Margaret. *Hannah Sheehy Skeffington: a Life*. Dublin: Attic Press, 1997.

Watson, Leah. *Taking Back History: Irish Women's Fiction 1928–1988*. Dissertation. University of Saskatchewan, 1991.

Weekes, Ann Owen. 'Diarmuid and Gráinne Again: Julia O'Faolain's *No Country for Young Men*', *Éire-Ireland* 21:1 (Spring 1986): 89–102.

Weekes, Ann Owen. *Irish Women Writers: an Uncharted Tradition*. Lexington, KY: University of Kentucky Press, 1990.

Weekes, Ann Owen. *Unveiling Treasures: the Attic Guide to the Published Works of Irish Women Literary Writers of Drama, Fiction and Poetry*. Dublin: Attic Press, 1993.

Williams, Patrick and Laura Chrisman, eds. *Colonial Discourse and Post-Colonial Theory*. London: Harvester Wheatsheaf, 1993.

Williamson, Judith. 'Woman as an Island: Femininity and Colonization', in *Studies in Entertainment: Critical Approaches to Mass Culture*, ed. Tania Modleski. Bloomington: Indiana University Press, 1986, pp. 99–118.

Index